"Christine Jeske's book beautifully examines the necessary multiplicities contained in any quest for justice. Simultaneously deeply personal and deeply researched, meditative and analytic, sobering and hopeful, this book lovingly and productively agitates its readers to do better."

Hahrie Han, professor and director of the SNF Agora Institute at Johns Hopkins University

"This book is both a much-needed mirror and window into the patterns of White Christianity. Offering keen, research-driven insights within a Christian frame, this book will force you to reflect on things that people often want to avoid and learn why people want to avoid them. Drawing from rigorous research, Christine Jeske outlines phenomena that will be familiar to those who have navigated White Christian spaces and offers a constructive path forward. As you read, you realize why people get stuck and what it takes to engage with racial justice for the long haul."

Raymond Chang, president of the Asian American Christian Collaborative and executive director of the TENx10 Collaboration at Fuller Seminary

RACIAL JUSTICE
FOR THE LONG HAUL

HOW WHITE CHRISTIAN ADVOCATES PERSEVERE (& WHY)

Christine Jeske

An imprint of InterVarsity Press
Downers Grove, Illinois

InterVarsity Press
P.O. Box 1400 | Downers Grove, IL 60515-1426
ivpress.com | email@ivpress.com

©2026 by Christine Jeske

All rights reserved. No part of this book may be reproduced in any form without written permission from InterVarsity Press.

InterVarsity Press® is the publishing division of InterVarsity Christian Fellowship/USA®. For more information, visit intervarsity.org.

All Scripture quotations, unless otherwise indicated, are taken from The Holy Bible, New International Version®, NIV®. Copyright © 1973, 1978, 1984, 2011 by Biblica, Inc.™ Used by permission of Zondervan. All rights reserved worldwide. www.zondervan.com. The "NIV" and "New International Version" are trademarks registered in the United States Patent and Trademark Office by Biblica, Inc.™

The author donates all proceeds from sales of this book to organizations committed to racial justice.

While any stories in this book are true, some names and identifying information may have been changed to protect the privacy of individuals.

The publisher cannot verify the accuracy or functionality of website URLs used in this book beyond the date of publication.

Cover design: Faceout Studio, Tim Green
Interior design: Daniel van Loon

ISBN 978-1-5140-1103-4 (print) | ISBN 978-1-5140-1104-1 (digital)

Printed in the United States of America ∞

Library of Congress Cataloging-in-Publication Data
Names: Jeske, Christine author
Title: Racial justice for the long haul : how White Christian advocates persevere (and why) / Christine Jeske.
Description: Downers Grove, IL : IVP Academic, [2026] | Includes appendices. | Includes bibliographical references and index.
Identifiers: LCCN 2025028135 (print) | LCCN 2025028136 (ebook) | ISBN 9781514011034 paperback | ISBN 9781514011041 ebook
Subjects: LCSH: Anti-racism–Religious aspects–Christianity | Race relations–Religious aspects–Christianity | White people–Race identity–United States | Christians, White–United States
Classification: LCC BT734.2 .J47 2025 (print) | LCC BT734.2 (ebook)
LC record available at https://lccn.loc.gov/2025028135
LC ebook record available at https://lccn.loc.gov/2025028136

There are so many individuals I could name whose lives bear witness to the power of anti-racist White people. . . . It would take pages and pages to share their stories. These pages should be written. Everyone should hear their testimony.

bell hooks, *Teaching Community*

For bell hooks and everyone else

who asked for these pages.

Contents

Author's Note — ix

PART 1 Is Perseverance Possible?
1. The Gaze — 3
2. Why White Christians? — 23

PART 2 Dare We Hope?
3. What Hope? — 35
4. Delusional Hope — 47

PART 3 Collisions
5. White Imagination Meets Reality — 69
6. Colliding with Ranking and Invisibility — 88
7. Colliding with Injustice and Culpability — 105

PART 4 Asking a Lot of Why
8. Big Problems — 121
9. Pitfalls to Perseverance — 141

PART 5 Responding to Grace
10. What to Do with Guilt — 163
11. Where Grace Meets Race — 182

PART 6 Abiding Hope
12. Why Hope — 209
13. What to Hope For — 228
14. What to Do with Hope — 252

Afterword: Kindred — 271
Acknowledgments — 283
Appendix A: People Studying People — 285
Appendix B: Questions for Reflection and Discussion — 293
Index — 299

Author's Note

THE EVENTS AND EXPERIENCES in this book are all true according to the memory of the storytellers. This is a work of ethnography—an analysis of a cultural phenomenon based on many hours of interviews and participant observation. All quotes from individuals are written word-for-word with light editing for clarity, from recorded interviews or from field notes taken during or immediately after those events. Unless otherwise noted, names and a few identifying details have been changed or omitted to protect the confidentiality of individuals and organizations, and to allow those involved to tell, or not to tell, their own stories elsewhere as they so choose.

PART 1

Is Perseverance Possible?

ONE

The Gaze

WHERE SHALL WE BEGIN?

Let's begin with a gaze.

A Black man faces a White woman across a dinner table. He breathes in. Breathes out. Searches for words. Considers how to respond to the story he has just heard. Let's call him Mark, her Hannah.[1] Let's listen to the story Hannah has just told Mark as a casual contribution to a dinner conversation among family and friends.[2]

Years earlier, Hannah decided to dress for a Halloween party as one of her heroes. This was in the early 1990s, and across America people were celebrating the world records and Olympic victories of runner Florence Griffith Joyner, known widely as Flo-Jo. As a track runner herself, Hannah decided to dress as that hero. She studied pictures of Griffith Joyner's Olympic races to copy her clothing, her pinny number, and her colorful nail polish. Then Hannah went to the store and bought makeup to match her light skin to Griffith Joyner's dark tone.

Hannah did not know the history of blackface—how in the nineteenth and early twentieth century White people coated their faces in dark pigment to ridicule Black people in minstrel shows, how imitating

---

[1] Unless otherwise noted, names of research participants are pseudonyms. Some identifying details have been omitted or changed to protect confidentiality.

[2] When stories in this book involve multiple people, whenever possible I have sought out the accounts of multiple people involved. I was unable to contact Mark, however, so this story is an account as told to me by Hannah according to her memory and interpretation of events.

someone else's body in a Halloween costume can insult their dignity and history. She grew up attending a private school with only a few Black classmates, all of them upper and middle class. When she visited a Black schoolmate's home as a child, she saw the mom and thought, *Gorgeous model*, saw the dad and thought, *Impossibly cool*. She learned bits about American slavery but didn't know how racism continued after the Emancipation Proclamation, didn't know that the average White household during her lifetime held ten times the wealth of African American households.[3] Blackness, in her mind, was "dazzling." When she put on the Halloween costume for a college party, she did not know about the symbolic violence of wearing blackface, nor did she know anyone who could tell her. No one told her to stop. It was the 1990s at the University of Wisconsin–Madison, where 93 percent of students were White.[4]

"I remember as I was doing it," she reflected later, "there was something inside of me as I was making the choice, like, *I don't know, should I be doing this?* I thought about it for a while and I was slightly uncomfortable, but I'd never been taught about minstrel shows or any of that. I didn't know any of that. And so ultimately, I decided to do it because I thought, *I'll bet you if I go ahead and do it and it's not the right thing to do, I'm going to learn something from it*. And boy, did I ever."

So she went to a store and bought the cake of brown makeup. She stood before a mirror and wiped it on her face, her arms, her chest.

And then, years after that Halloween, she sat at this dinner table across from this Black man Mark, a professor and longtime family friend. And she casually told him about that Halloween costume.

Then silence. And this gaze.

---

[3] Neil Bhutta et al., "Disparities in Wealth by Race and Ethnicity in the 2019 Survey of Consumer Finances," Federal Reserve, September 28, 2020, www.federalreserve.gov/econres/notes/feds-notes/disparities-in-wealth-by-race-and-ethnicity-in-the-2019-survey-of-consumer-finances-20200928.html.
[4] Devi Shastri, "UW–Madison's Black Student Enrollment Has Never Exceeded 3%," *Milwaukee Journal Sentinel*, February 6, 2022, www.jsonline.com/story/news/education/2022/06/02/university-wisconsin-madison-struggles-recruit-Black-students/7171091001/.

"That moment is probably the most charged moment of my whole life," she said as she discussed it with me later. Her voice began to crack. When she regained her voice, she told me that then, too, in the eyes of Mark's gaze, she had begun to cry. "Oh, no, you don't," she would recall Mark saying when he saw her tears. "You don't get to do that." This was years before the phrase "White tears" would spread across social media to name the ways White people deflect confrontation about racism by focusing attention on their own emotions instead of the experiences of racial minorities. She didn't know the term, and perhaps Mark didn't either, but he was not about to let her drop out of the conversation to protect her emotional vulnerability. He held the gaze.

"It wasn't like the revulsion look," she said, describing his expression, "but it was—his face looked different than I'd ever seen it. And I know he loves me deeply. Right? And he shifted into this other expression that I have seen on Black people since then, whenever they're talking about racism. It's fascinating. It's super focused and it's like they're trying to communicate something with you. And it's probably—you know what I think it is? I think there's a little part of them that has hope, you know? That this stupid White girl might learn something, like she might just learn something. But then—" Here she paused before speaking with emphasis. "I'm sure they've been disappointed so many times. Like, *do you dare even hope for that?*"

||||||||

This gaze moment, which we'll return to in later chapters, portrays not just an interaction between two individuals but a freeze-frame of three deeper questions: Can people change for the better when so many forces keep us moving as we always have been? Can humans repair the seemingly irreparable harms between each other? And how should we dare hope for such things?

As a researcher, I heard many stories similar to that of Hannah and Mark, sometimes recounted by a White person in the story, sometimes by a person of color, and sometimes one after another. An Indigenous woman described a day when her White coworker used a clip from a war movie in an attempt to motivate their team to action. She would recall hearing a White commander in the video telling White soldiers: "This is your land. You can do whatever you want with it. Build your house and have your family here because this is your land." Until this moment in the meeting, she had been taking notes, listening intently and hopefully. Now she put down her pen and sat, her face a motionless gaze while her thoughts raced and emotions swirled through her body. "I was sitting there just trying to hold myself together," she said. "Historically that was not the truth of what happened. Indigenous people were there, and there was genocide. They were killed off, and they were displaced, and they were moved, and they were assimilated. They were terminated. All these things." She walked away, back to her hotel room, unable to stop shaking. She found a friend who listened as they unpeeled layers of pain. Later, with her friend's support, she wrote to the man about the video clip. He said he was sorry it caused pain, but he didn't understand why. She wrote again. He replied saying he was still confused. Eventually she gave up the conversation. "I don't want to be cast the burden of having to be responsible for his learning," she said. He was not ready to hear the explanation behind her gaze. "Multiply that story times at least once a week, something like that happens," she told me. "It gets really wearisome."

Something profound is contained in that gaze. It's a gaze that searches to see something in another person even more clearly than that person sees it in themselves. It sees both crime and context. It chooses to stay, at least for this moment. It exercises a powerful freedom, refusing to decide according to someone else's demands whether to berate, walk away, or hold steady. The Marks at the table know that the Hannahs might not learn something and might not change. They know that if they get this wrong, or even if they get it right, someone will probably get hurt again. Probably it will be someone on their side of the table. If Mark opens himself to hoping that Hannah will change, he carries that risk. Hope is costly and dangerous.

This is a book about what happens in the quivering possibilities of that gaze—whether people can love after irreversible harm, how people become agents of change toward racial justice, and how we even dare hope for that. I believe that the ways we answer these questions matter for all humanity.

These questions have haunted me since youth, and often I have felt alone in my search for answers.[5] Over the decades, I discovered many others who wrestled with the same questions, and eventually I spent several years carefully studying their journeys. Because I wanted to study a smaller group than the whole of America, I started by choosing a subgroup among White people—White Christians. One reason for this choice was that White Christians tend to think a lot about hope. For another reason, as we'll see in the coming chapters, they make for an important test case of how to hope for racial justice because they are especially disengaged from struggles against racism. In a recent survey asking how motivated people were to address racism, White Christians were half as likely as the wider White population to be highly motivated, and only one-fifth as likely as Black Christians.[6]

How does one go about studying the ways people hope and the myriad factors that cause people to orient their lives toward one value or another?

About fifteen years ago, after I had tried out more jobs, homes, and countries than could fit on a résumé, I happened to be in the right time and place for someone to ask me to teach a class called Anthropology and Intercultural Communication. I had taken a graduate-level class called Intercultural Communication, but I didn't quite know what anthropology was. They had a textbook, so I gave it a try.

---

[5]To read how my own life story led me to write this book, see the afterword.
[6]Christina Barland Edmondson and Chad Brennan, *Faithful Anti-Racism: Moving Past Talk to Systemic Change* (InterVarsity Press, 2022), 17.

That class changed my life. I was teaching at a seminary in South Africa where students came from across the continent. We had conversations comparing how Malawians and Zambians hug, why missionaries translated "God" as "Big-big" in isiZulu, and how Chinese companies build roads across Burundi. I learned that anthropology doesn't just teach people *about* each other; it teaches people *how* to learn *from* each other and *with* each other. I discovered that anthropologists had explored questions my previous degrees hadn't answered, such as how humans decide what makes a good life, how people imagine reality, how much control individuals have over their own lives, and how our answers to these questions contribute to suffering and flourishing. Anthropology aims to study not just what people do in a controlled experiment in a lab, but in everyday life. It's like very slow journalism, with lots of interviews and lots of time spent in the middle of everyday life happenings. Anthropologists observe, not just to catch the latest big event but to analyze ordinary humanity. Eventually I went on to get a PhD at the University of Wisconsin–Madison in this thing called anthropology. Then I found a job teaching it so I could keep exploring questions like these.

So when I tackle questions such as what leads White people to care about racism, I start by listening to people and hanging out with people. But which people?

As I was beginning to consider this research, I mentioned my plans during a podcast interview. A few weeks later, I received an email from a White man in my city. He said my plan to study White people pursuing racial justice caught his attention, and he thought, "That sounds like me." So he offered, "I know it's a bit bold to offer myself for this, but if it's helpful, know that I'd be a willing participant."

I had met this man before, but I didn't know him well. His email brought into focus a concern I'd had from the start of the research: What criteria should I use to choose participants? People who volunteered for the study? People who met certain characteristics signaling their commitment to racial justice? If so, what characteristics? Should they check boxes on a list of belief statements, or pass a test of their knowledge? Or would they best be selected not for what they knew and believed but for what they did? Should they work in certain jobs, live in certain neighborhoods, or volunteer in certain ways?[7] Does a White person committed to racial justice contact their legislators, volunteer in a school, attend talks by leaders of color, or regularly find themselves the only White person in the room? What counts as a White person committed to racial justice?

Clearly any of these criteria might exclude and include different sets of people. But was I even the one to decide? I was not. That much I knew. The criteria for choosing White people who demonstrated a commitment to racial justice had to come not from me or any other White person but as directly as possible from people of color. They are the most affected, and over their lifetimes they weigh the consequences of the complex overlapping patterns of White people's choices. In this study, I wanted to center their perspectives.[8]

People of color are not monolithic. Scholars of color hold differing positions in ongoing conversations about what racial justice means and

---

[7]The methodologies of two of the most similar books to this one selected organizations working to address racism and then chose participants from among the White volunteers and staff of those organizations. See Eileen O'Brien, *Whites Confront Racism: Antiracists and Their Paths to Action* (Rowman & Littlefield, 2001); Mark R. Warren, *Fire in the Heart: How White Activists Embrace Racial Justice* (Oxford University Press, 2010). Others have drawn largely on renowned historical figures or on the author's own personal experiences and acquaintances. See Drick Boyd, *Disrupting Whiteness: Talking with White People About Racism* (Arch Street, 2021); Karen Johnson, *Ordinary Heroes: How Studying the Past Can Help Us Move Past Racial Divides* (InterVarsity Press, 2025); Clifford Williams, *The Uneasy Conscience of a White Christian: Making Racial Equity a Priority* (Wipf & Stock, 2021). Others focus on narrowly controlled parameters such as the extent of individuals' social ties. See Mary R. Jackman and Marie Crane, "'Some of My Best Friends Are Black . . .': Interracial Friendship and Whites' Racial Attitudes," *The Public Opinion Quarterly* 50, no. 4 (1986): 459-86; Doug McAdam and Ronnelle Paulsen, "Specifying the Relationship Between Social Ties and Activism," *American Journal of Sociology* 99, no. 3 (1993): 640-67. In one study, researchers interviewed people of color about White allies, but the study did not extend to those White people described. Cassandra L. Hinger et al., "Defining Racial Allies: A Qualitative Investigation of White Allyship from the Perspective of People of Color," *Journal of Counseling Psychology* 70, no. 6 (2023): 631-44.

[8]In considering how to accomplish this, I was inspired in part by the ways in which W. E. B. Du Bois centered the activism and perspectives of Black people even within his biography of White abolitionist John Brown. W. E. B. Du Bois, *John Brown* (Oxford University Press, 2007).

how to accomplish it. I wanted to allow space for participants in the research to define that nebulous concept. People's own understandings of the term *racial justice* would change across their journeys, and the study was meant to uncover those changes. I also wanted to hear not only from academics but from people across a range of class and educational backgrounds. I planned to pay particular attention to perspectives of Christians of color, given the focus on Christians in this study, but even that subset would include a wide range of experiences and views.

And so this study had three phases. In 2022, I began phase one by meeting with thirty people of color who led churches or organizations focused on addressing racism.[9] I chose them by beginning with leaders I was familiar with and then following their recommendations to meet others. I listened as they described what racial justice meant to them—what happens when it goes well and when it goes poorly. I asked them to describe what they hoped for and also the ways they hoped. They told stories of interactions with White people and what people of all races can do to pursue justice together.

At the end of each interview with a person of color, I asked for their recommendations of White people to interview. I asked, "If you knew a White Christian who was new to this journey and who was looking for a White Christian mentor, who would you recommend? Or who do you know who has been at this for something like a decade or more, who's still committed and seems like they will be long term?" I wrote down names they listed and asked them to explain why they chose these individuals. Sometimes they paused, thought for a bit, and admitted they could not think of anyone to recommend. These moments of hesitation led to insightful conversations as well. Some people gave names but emphasized that no one had this process down to perfection. The White people I interviewed often stressed the same thing: They were not experts, exemplars, or heroes. They were just the best option somebody in

---

[9] I also conducted a few interviews between 2019 and 2022 to refine my research questions and methods.

their life could think of. They'd done something well, but never everything. Often, when describing why they chose these individuals, people of color would name the mistakes they had made as well as their successes—it wasn't just getting things right that qualified them; it was how they responded when they got things wrong.[10]

In phase two, I interviewed forty of the White Christians who'd been recommended by those faith leaders of color. Interviews usually lasted at least two hours, much of which was spent describing their life histories. Other questions explored their definitions of racial justice, practices and challenges they experienced in pursuit of racial justice, and their hopes.

This methodology had the benefit of allowing me to hear some of the same stories recounted from multiple perspectives. When possible, I asked White individuals about details mentioned by their acquaintances of color, and vice versa. I knew of no other studies that had taken this approach of studying White transformative journeys through the lenses of their own perspectives and of people of color around them, and I read accounts by at least two authors wishing they had.[11] No individual goes through life making changes by their own efforts alone—transformation always happens in a social context—and I wanted a methodology that would uncover at least some of those interactions from multiple perspectives.

To catch those interactions across a social network, I also committed to conducting most of the research within one geographic and social space—the city of Madison, Wisconsin. Madison is my home and has been for nearly twenty years. My longtime familiarity with the city allowed me to catch references and ask questions an outsider might not consider. When I asked people in the study to describe Madison, I commonly heard a sentiment expressed in this quote by a Black Christian leader: "I think people *think* it's progressive. It's a very educated, tolerant area that hasn't done really well of including people of color into the

---

[10]For more details about the research sites and methodology, see appendix A.
[11]O'Brien, *Whites Confront Racism*; Warren, *Fire in the Heart*.

fabric." He said a typical attitude he encounters from White people is, "We'll tolerate you as long as you assimilate or play the game." As one White man put it, Madison has "lots of liberals with conviction but lacking experience." Compared to many cities of its size, Madison's 280,000 people are quite White: 73 percent White, 7 percent Black, 8 percent Asian, 9 percent Hispanic or Latino, 9 percent two or more races, and less than 1 percent Indigenous.[12]

Focusing most of the research in one city allowed me to analyze interlocking networks, events, and institutions that shaped this social space. But because Madison, like any place, has its own idiosyncrasies, I also selected three other locations with contrasting characteristics. I spent several days in each, conducting interviews and observations with people of color and White people. I leave out information identifying the locations of most events in this book as a way to protect the confidentiality of those involved, but you'll read examples from each research site. One location was a predominantly Black urban neighborhood on the East Coast. Another site was a rural town in a formerly Confederate Southern state. Additionally, in order to compare a very different historical and cultural setting with a predominantly Black population, I returned to an area where I had lived for five years in South Africa. By comparing accounts across four regions and subcultures, I was able to confirm consistencies across all locations and also observe how these trends play out differently across different kinds of communities. To read more about these research settings, see appendix A.

As an anthropologist, I also value another important element of research in addition to interviews: participant observation. What people say about their lives is always shaped by their own self-awareness and choices about how they present themselves to others. One way to supplement what they say is to watch what they do. Anthropologists

---

[12]These percentages do not total 100 percent because Hispanic overlaps with other categories. "Quick Facts: Madison City, Wisconsin," US Census Bureau, 2024, www.census.gov/quickfacts/fact/table/madisoncitywisconsin/PST045224#PST045224.

attentively spend time alongside people, joining meetings, workplaces, and online communication networks to watch and even share experiences. To this end, I joined spaces where White people learn about racial justice—conferences, events, and community-based trainings. I visited eleven churches with a wide range of demographics and denominations. In between visiting other churches, I spent time with the predominantly White church of which I am a member and with a predominantly Black church that I have attended monthly for several years. I had begun attending both of these churches before beginning this study, and my involvement there was a personal choice rather than a research choice, but I was inevitably attuned to research questions even on ordinary Sunday mornings. In the same way, I inevitably also drew on my ten years of experience teaching about racism at Wheaton College, a predominantly White Christian liberal arts college.

As I conducted the research, I worked alongside a research assistant, Princess Vaulx, a Black Christian woman who had recently graduated from the University of Wisconsin–Madison. I recorded each interview, and Princess and I read transcriptions and relistened to every interview while we coded—a process of listing and sorting every answer to every question asked. We met weekly to talk through what we noticed, and she contributed valuable insights that shaped this book.

All that interviewing and observing produces a mountain of data—thousands of words based on hundreds of hours of note taking. For a while, managing all those notes feels like wandering through a forest in an unfamiliar ecosystem. It's hard to imagine you will make sense of all the organic textures and seeming randomness that surrounds you, much less ever find your way out. But eventually, you start to notice repetitions and find pathways. This practice is similar to the ways mathematicians solve complex problems. You gather as much data as you can, sort it into an organized system, and then look for ways to describe it elegantly enough to communicate something. For me it involved a lot of lying face-down on my bed and walking up and down my road, shifting ideas around like Sherlock Holmes in his mind palace. Qualitative data usually can be sorted into not one but many patterns. There are probably as many books that could be written from this data as there are humans willing to pay attention and set their fingers to a keyboard. A writer must choose one pattern and begin. This one is mine.

But it also isn't just mine. There was one more important phase to this research. Once I had begun sketching a draft outline of this book, I revisited many people in the study, especially people of color, and asked whether my analysis seemed to be on the right track. I gave talks and invited everyone involved in the research to listen and give feedback. I shared drafts with other scholars and trusted experts, many of whose names appear in the acknowledgments of this book. All of this is a way of testing for internal validity—that results make sense not just to outsiders but to those who experienced the phenomenon firsthand. It's also a way to test for this elusive thing that qualitative researchers call saturation—a point when new data mostly just reveal a repetition of what's already been learned. In reality there is no such thing as perfect saturation—the joy and curse of interviewing is that every conversation always, always offers something new to learn. I do not claim to have found everything, nor could I fit it all in one book. Another test of validity will come from you—how does this challenge, overturn, or make sense of your own ways of being in the world? I hope it will do all of those and more.

Every interview and interaction for the purpose of research is a gift. No one was paid for their time in this study except my research assistant through the generosity of a research grant.[13] Everyone invited to participate had the freedom to say no, and in the few cases when people did, I am grateful that they prioritized the many other important ways they make a difference in their community. I don't take lightly the extraordinary generosity of every person and group that contributed to this

---

[13]I am grateful for two John Stott Faculty Grants in Human Needs and Global Resources that supported this research.

book. They gave gifts of grace to me and to you. There's joy in receiving such gifts, and also responsibility. I hope that this book joins you and me together with one long string of gifts received and passed along, forward and forward.

|||||||||

Here's what I do not have for you in this book. I do not have another how-to manual of ten neat steps to make yourself and your organization into a bastion of antiracism. I don't have a case for how Christian theology does or doesn't line up with antiracism, or how to preach that to a congregation.

I also don't have an analysis of how White Christians became entangled with racism, both blatantly and in subtle forms such as colorblindness. I am able to write this book because many others have written those books already.[14] I'm not here to invite the White Christians who are not in this book to defend themselves, nor to raise anybody's hackles about them. Let them be for a minute—let's turn our attention elsewhere.

Neither am I offering my own personal story of discovering some beautiful path you can follow straight to success. I cannot promise political victories, church transformation, or structural change. I know that's not great news, but I think you don't expect great news anymore, and you can handle it.

Here's what I do have for you: evidence that, if you care even just a little bit about both of these crazy bedfellows of Christianity and racial justice, you are not alone. Your people are out there. They have been for a very long time, and from what I can tell, they are not going away.[15]

---

[14] One of the most recent and direct examples of such research is Anthea Butler's *White Evangelical Racism: The Politics of Morality in America* (University of North Carolina Press, 2021).

[15] Historians who have documented their existence include Drick Boyd, who offers a similar reason for his work: "I hope that Whites and People of Color reading this book can see that, despite the horrific history of White racism over the past five hundred years, there is also a legacy of opposition by White antiracist allies from whom we can learn and in whose steps we can follow." Boyd, *Disrupting Whiteness*, 10; see also Johnson, *Ordinary Heroes*.

You exist, and others like you exist, and the questions and experiences you have cradled matter.

And when I say "they exist," I mean not just people who signed up for a book club last fall because they saw something in the news that made them feel sad or guilty, or people who watched one YouTube video after another until they could feel emotionally alive again, or people who jumped on a bus to go to a protest last summer because their friends were going and it was all very fun. I'm talking about people who weave racial justice into the very fabric of their communities, their work, their families. It's the normal of their lives. They're the ones who know how to get stuff done. You probably know many people who have tried out fair-weather fandom of racial justice. I want to make sure you know folks who are lifers.

Most of all, I'm excited to tell you about a pattern that showed up across all seventy interviews and thousands of pages of notes and observations that went into this research. That pattern tells us something about how people come to pursue racial justice in the long term and how they hope. I'll walk you through each piece of that pattern in the coming chapters, but here's the short version.

Among those White Christians invited in this study, I found three interlocking elements in common across nearly every journey. These elements didn't always happen in the same order, and they often repeated in deepening cycles, but they were nearly always all present. If one piece was missing, people of color around them often noticed the gap.

Efforts aimed at training White people to address racial injustice often focus on just one aspect of the person or problem. Those who see racism as a shortage of good intentions focus on what we might refer to as the *heart*—emotions and passions. Others focus on racism as a shortage of information—a fix for what we might call the *mind*. Another approach concentrates on spiritual issues such as sin, forgiveness, and vindication—concerns of the *soul*. Still others want to move directly into action, addressing the material and economic effects of racism—concerns of *strength*.

But humans cannot be neatly divided into segments like that.[16] These categories blend and intertwine, and each is necessary. The primary call given to Christians—the commandment that Jesus himself referred to as most important—is to love God with one's entire heart, soul, mind, and strength (Mark 12:30; Deuteronomy 6:5). Likewise racism cannot be undone through a discrete package of actions that address one portion of human life or another. The three elements I found across people's life stories offer a holistic picture of racial justice that engages heart, mind, soul, and strength.

The first element we'll look at is what I call a *collision*—an encounter in which the reality of racial justice hits home in a conscious and often emotionally salient way. Collisions contribute toward engaging the *heart*. People look back at collision moments to remember why they care.

The second element is that they had spent extended time engaged in what I call *asking a lot of why*. They had learned from people from a wide variety of walks of life how the idea of race came to be, how racism shaped their nation and local setting, and how racism persists through the centuries. They could name ways that institutions and systems such as education, incarceration, housing, hiring, and law create and perpetuate inequalities across racial groups. Asking why engages the *mind*. This kind of learning gives people a deep understanding of the scope of the problem and what solutions might work.

These two elements are where a lot of training about racism focuses, and many other researchers have corroborated that these steps matter both for individual and societal change, whether people are Christians

---

[16] I noticed the parallel to *heart*, *mind*, *soul*, and *strength* after I had already written most of the book, so they did not shape my analytical decisions. I offer these only as what could be a useful mnemonic, not as discrete categories. Psychological research has shown, for example, that even decisions that we perceive to be most rationally driven by the "mind" are shaped by the sorts of emotions, biases, and reactionary responses that we associate with "heart." Jonathan Haidt, *The Righteous Mind: Why Good People Are Divided by Politics and Religion* (Pantheon Books, 2012); Daniel Kahneman, *Thinking, Fast and Slow* (Farrar, Straus & Giroux, 2011).

or not. But here's the problem I discovered—when White people have only these two elements, they often crash into brick walls of hopelessness. These two elements are very good at stripping away naive hopes. In that hopelessness, White people can too easily walk away. Unlike people of color, White people in the United States usually have the option of not thinking about racism, and when all they can see of racism is that it's big, nasty, and persistent, it's just so much easier to look elsewhere.

But there's a third element in these journeys that took me by surprise, and I think it might surprise you too. It's something Hannah mentioned when she told the story about Mark, and often it happened at the point in people's life stories where their voices choked up or tears began. This element engages the *soul*. It's a shift in how a person spiritually and physically interacts with the world that I call *responding to grace*.

Whereas the first two elements tend to strip away delusional hopes and expose people to despair, this third element, responding to grace, plays a crucial role in converting despair into hope. It's a kind of linchpin that brings together these two questions—how White Christians become advocates for racial justice and how tough hope is forged. Once we've seen how people combine these three elements, we'll turn our attention to the ways they engaged their *strength*—the postures and practices that characterize an abiding and active kind of hope.

As we take a close look at that persevering way of hoping, you'll see the postures and active practices that characterize people who pursue racial justice long term. We'll examine the bedrock foundation for this hope, the feeling of walking in it, and the goals toward which it aims. We'll see how advocates for the long haul engage their *whole selves*.

This is no one-size-fits-all action plan. As one Asian American man told me, "Solving racism can't be reduced to another checklist item." But with some creativity, you'll find practices described here that you can adapt to the shape of your own life and the asymmetrical relationships you find yourself in. At the end of this book you'll find questions for reflection and discussion, and I hope you'll take the time to chew on these on your own and with a community. We'll be focusing on the question of how to address racial injustice, but much of what you'll read here can also inform struggles against other social injustices such as sexism, ableism, and poverty. My intention is that you too will find a hope that is weathered and wild. A hope that grows in the composted remains of suffering and produces the nourishing fruit of love.

I know that for a lot of us, hope itself is hard to even hope for. If you feel yourself hanging on by only a thread of hope—hope either for racial justice, or for the church, or for this thin sliver of overlap between the two—I wrote this book with you in mind.

Maybe this is the very first book you've read with *race* in the title, or with *Christians* in the title, and you've got a lot of questions. Maybe you're a person who can't say the word *antiracism* without rolling your eyes a little, or maybe instead you're a person who rolls your eyes at *those* people. Maybe just holding this book feels like a risk. I'm glad you're here. Welcome.

Maybe you're a person of color, and despite having to go through every day figuring out White people's ways, you're still curious or fed up enough to read some more research on White people. Maybe you've tried to "be a bridge" in diverse spaces, a bridge that stretches so wide it creaks and groans. You've seen White people come like tourists into your spaces, wafting the stench of colonialism, and you've done your own work to figure out how White people think, and you want to know why White people can't get on with it and do the same.

Maybe you've spent time around Christians and thought that responding to racial injustice should be a pretty low bar to ask of Christians, who are supposed to be all about love and reconciliation and faith against the odds and tapping into the power of the Creator of the universe. You ask yourself, *If the church can't get this right, is it time to admit that this is not just accidental, but some intrinsic flaw in the very fiber and structure of the religion itself?*

To all readers, I hope that when you encounter something unsettling or troubling, you will listen a little longer, hold your judgments a little looser, stretch a little further, breathe a little deeper. Whoever you are, this book is for you if you share just one thing: Deep down you feel a kind of vibrating uncertainty about what can be done about injustice and the future of this country and this world. You just don't know anymore. There may have been a time when you could believe things would get better. Some days you still can. But there's a darkness you have faced, and when you look into that darkness, it's hard to be so sure. There's a weariness in your body and your soul that comes over you so heavily sometimes that you cannot shake it off. Permeating through whatever shields of sarcasm or bitterness or hardheaded perseverance you use, there comes a scarier emotion—a sadness, and a fear, and a fear of more sadness.

In this book, you and I and all the people you'll meet here come together, seeing each other with something like the gaze between Hannah and Mark. I ask you to pause in the discomfort of that gaze. Let your body be still. Linger longer than is polite. Ignore the awkwardness of not knowing what another human thinks or what you should do next. Tune out all the distractions tugging you to look away. Quiet the voices guessing what you'll find on the next page, predetermining whether you'll like it. You might find yourself hoping that Mark will say, "Heck no, I'm done with trying to explain my life and pain to another White person." Or you might be hoping they'll find a way to make it right somehow. You might imagine that it shouldn't be so hard. Or you might think that it most certainly will be hard. Maybe you find yourself hoping for nothing at all, sitting exhausted beside an empty well of hope, unable to muster the energy to care anymore. Whether you feel yourself on Hannah's side of the table, or Mark's, or in a complicated mixed experience of both, there's something for you here. In that gaze we waver in the precarious liminality between love and hate, hope and despair.

I wouldn't ask this of you lightly. If you are anything like me, this journey comes with a lot of tears, some cursing, and throwing a book or two across the room. It can be lonely and tedious. It very well may break your heart. But let me say again what I want you to know: You are not alone. You are going to meet a certain kind of unusual people in this book. Together we're going to scoop out the litter that has clogged up our wellspring of hope, scrub it out, and see whether we find something shimmering.

I wrote this book to contribute to what we collectively know about how to repair racism, but I also wrote it for another reason: It's personal. I too am a White person on a journey of learning to pursue racial justice. I too identify as Christian. Whether you prefer to read it now or later, in the afterword to this book you'll find my own story of coming to take racism seriously. I've experienced both healing and hurt in the church. Like many people interviewed in this research, I resonate with Tony Campolo's paraphrase of Augustine of Hippo's words from the fifth century: "The church is a whore, but she's my mother."[17]

And I've seen my own ways of hoping splinter and crack. This book took me decades to be ready to write. Researching has opened windows into memories of my own encounters with desperation, my own collisions and learning and years spent wanting someone to please just tell me how to hope. I have felt in the very writing of this book that my own hopes were being tested. Writing is an act of mind—learning and clarifying and organizing—but also of heart and strength. Sometimes when I'm writing I feel the need to walk into the sunlight and stretch my arms as wide as they will reach. Other times writing makes me want to curl up in a ball and make myself small. I think something in me knows that if anything will break through the cracks of darkness with a shard of light, it will be both strong and small. It will also require me to hold a pen, curve fingers over a keyboard, lengthen my spine—the body must

---

[17]Anthony Campolo, *Letters to a Young Evangelical* (Basic Books, 2006), 68.

commit as well as the mind. But most of all writing is an act of soul. Soul is all that can carry the other two onward long enough. Writing this book, I often felt like a midwife holding out my hands asking for some incarnation of some kind of God to be born into these up-turned palms. It is absurd. But it is what I have—to keep outstretching arms, waiting, hoping for something undeserved and raucous.

TWO

Why White Christians?

WHEN I WROTE TO NAOMI, an Asian American leader in a multiethnic church, asking whether she would like to meet to discuss my research, she wrote back with a list of questions.¹ "Am I understanding correctly that the target audience for your research is White Christians and that you are interviewing BIPOC folks to gather information that can inform White Christians? What books are you drawing upon? What do you plan to do with the research?"² I wrote back as honestly and thoroughly as I could. It didn't surprise me that she would have questions about the research. After all, my introductory email told her that I'd heard her name from a White Christian man whom she'd called out

---

¹In this book I use the general term *Asian American* rather than more specific descriptions of people's ethnic and national backgrounds only because doing so protected people's confidentiality. I recognize that the term is not ideal, as it glosses over vast differences in national, cultural, and ethnic backgrounds, including both recent and distant immigration experiences. Similarly, for the sake of confidentiality, I have used the terms *Indigenous, Latin American, Latino*, and *Latina* to encompass a wide variety of experiences. Participants referred to as Black in this study included descendants of enslaved African Americans as well as more recent immigrants from African nations. Likewise, I use *White* to describe people who identified as White, which included many ethnic backgrounds and degrees of identification with those ethnicities. For participants of mixed ethnic or racial backgrounds, for the sake of confidentiality I made the difficult choice to name only one, usually the first they mentioned in the interview or one they related to an included quote. Such is the nature of race—it is a system of categorizations that ignores other ways in which people meaningfully identify themselves, such as ethnicity or family traditions. I provide more details in appendix A about the diversity of ethnic and national backgrounds represented among research participants.

²BIPOC stands for Black, Indigenous, and People of Color. The term is often used to acknowledge both the shared experiences of people of color and that Black and Indigenous people often experience more severe forms of racism.

directly for hurting people of color. Like anyone participating in this research, she had reasons to be hesitant.

Naomi did agree to meet, and she did not mince words. We sat in soft chairs with our feet resting on a coffee table, holding cups of tea as she recounted story after story of working among White Christians. As one of the only leaders of color in her denomination, she was often asked to join panels and committees focused on diversity. "Everyone likes the optics of it," she said. "So I get asked to do everything." For years she led events and conversations bringing together various churches to address racism. When people of color in other ministries needed to have a difficult conversation with White coworkers, they had asked Naomi to accompany them. When Christian organizations wanted to teach their White constituents about race, they had called her.

But as the years passed, she began wondering why these events seemed to circle around the same entry-level questions. She diagnosed the problem as a snag at the very core of White Christians' theology: "Many White Christians do theology without any awareness or acknowledgment that there's a specificity to it—that theology arises from specific bodies. They cannot, for the life of them, acknowledge that their theology is specifically for White bodies."

To explain what she meant, she told a story. An unarmed Black man was fatally shot by police in her city. She arrived at a prayer meeting the following day emotionally weary. "I remember showing up at that meeting really upset." Her voice replayed her tone of urgency as she recalled, "I was like, 'What are we going to *do*?'" But listening to the White Christians at the meeting, she found them to be in a very different place. In a dreamy tone, she recounted the kinds of things they were saying. "I've never thought about this! I never knew. How could this happen?" She had arrived ready to mourn. To hold a prayer vigil. To set up a plan to confront racial bias among police officers and change systems. They were simply baffled. They weren't sure there was even a problem to address. "I did so much work with race and faith, and it was all centering

White people," she told me. "I am tired of trying. Why should I beg people to listen? It's a waste of my time." Piece by piece, disappointing interactions chipped away her energy to work for racial justice with White Christians.

When I asked Naomi to describe White Christians she knew who were committed to racial justice, the first words out of her mouth were, "I don't have any." She paused and took a breath before choosing words carefully. "I know that sounds bad. And in some ways, I know they care and value this. But are they actively doing that work?" She raised an eyebrow and peered into my face, then answered her own rhetorical question. "Honestly, the most gracious thing I could say is, 'I think they care.' But for the most part, I've never heard any of them say anything that actually feels daring or risky. Ever. And my very existence is a risk every day. So—" She shrugged and trailed off.

Naomi's sharp critiques of White Christians reminded me of words written five decades earlier in one of the most famous letters of American history. On April 12, 1963, law officers in Birmingham, Alabama, arrested Martin Luther King Jr. for violating a ban on protests passed just two days earlier. The day of his arrest happened to fall on Good Friday, the day when Christians commemorate the crucifixion of Jesus. That same day, White clergy leaders published an open letter to King in the local newspaper. "We recognize the natural impatience of people who feel that their hopes are slow in being realized," the pastors and rabbis wrote. "But we are convinced that these demonstrations are unwise and untimely." Urging King and all of the city to withdraw from demonstrations, they wielded their own way of hoping as reason: "We do not believe that these days of new hope are days when extreme measures are justified."[3]

From his jail cell, King began scrawling his response, filling scraps of notepaper and margins of newspapers. He too had much to say about

---

[3]"White Clergymen Urge Local Negroes to Withdraw from Demonstrations," *Birmingham News*, April 13, 1963, https://bplonline.contentdm.oclc.org/digital/collection/p4017coll2/id/746/.

hope. His was not a justification for waiting quietly in the glow of hope. Instead, he openly wondered whether he had held the wrong sort of hope. "Maybe I was too optimistic. Maybe I expected too much. I guess I should have realized that few members of a race that has oppressed another race can understand or appreciate the deep groans and passionate yearnings of those that have been oppressed, and still fewer have the vision to see that injustice must be rooted out by strong, persistent and determined action." A few pages later King repeated, "Maybe again, I have been too optimistic."[4]

King singled out one group with whom he was particularly dismayed: White *Christians*. "I have been so greatly disappointed with the White church and its leadership," he wrote. "I say it as a minister of the gospel, who loves the church; who was nurtured in its bosom; who has been sustained by its spiritual blessings and who will remain true to it as long as the cord of life shall lengthen." With palpable emotion, he continues, "Yes, I see the church as the body of Christ. But, oh! How we have blemished and scarred that body through social neglect and fear of being nonconformists."[5]

When I decided to study what it takes for White people to build long-term commitments to racial justice, I realized that if there was one group struggling to make that change, the choice was clear—not just any White people but White *Christians*. This group presented a real challenge, a test of what transformation requires and to what extent it's possible. And it was a group I knew well—one that had nurtured and sustained me, and to which I, however hesitantly, belonged.

|||||||||

It is no secret that White Christians have played central roles in designing and defending the institutions and ideologies that have upheld racism

---

[4]Martin Luther King Jr., "Letter from a Birmingham Jail," African Studies Center—University of Pennsylvania, April 16, 1963, 13, 16, www.africa.upenn.edu/Articles_Gen/Letter_Birmingham.html.

[5]King, "Letter from a Birmingham Jail."

from inception to the present. Because Christianity was the dominant European religion at the time when Europeans were inventing the schema of hierarchically ranked human categories that became the Western racial framework of today, they drew on Christian concepts to justify that system and Christian institutions to implement it. Christian leaders wrote documents labeling non-Europeans as less than human. Missionaries taught a story line that painted White people as saviors and Black and Brown people as degraded and childlike, while at times ignoring or outright supporting colonial exploitation. Christians preached a distorted Bible story to claim dark-skinned people were forever-cursed children of Noah's son Ham. In the post–Civil War era, they made lynchings into church picnics and spoke long prayers over Klan events. They preached against desegregation and interracial marriage, and when *Brown v. Board of Education* and *Loving v. Virginia* made these illegal, they formed their own "desegregation academy" alternative schools and went on banning interracial couples in their colleges. More recently, White Christian approaches to racism have often favored a colorblind approach—treating the "race problem" as a matter of getting people of color to assimilate into a few prominent positions in predominantly White congregations without any disruptive talk of racial inequities.[6]

Like many Christians concerned about racial injustice, Naomi referenced the statistic that over 80 percent of White evangelicals voted

---

[6]Among the many historians, sociologists, and other scholars to document the history of Christian racism, see Anthea Butler, *White Evangelical Racism: The Politics of Morality in America* (University of North Carolina Press, 2021); Mark Charles and Soong-Chan Rah, *Unsettling Truths: The Ongoing, Dehumanizing Legacy of the Doctrine of Discovery* (InterVarsity Press, 2019); Angela Denker, *Red State Christians: Understanding the Voters Who Elected Donald Trump* (Fortress, 2019); Darren Dochuk, *From Bible Belt to Sunbelt: Plain-Folk Religion, Grassroots Politics, and the Rise of Evangelical Conservatism* (Norton, 2011); Michael O. Emerson and Christian Smith, *Divided by Faith: Evangelical Religion and the Problem of Race in America* (Oxford University Press, 2001); Robert P. Jones, *White Too Long: The Legacy of White Supremacy in American Christianity* (Simon & Schuster, 2020); William E. Pannell, *My Friend, the Enemy* (Word Books, 1968); Tom Skinner, *Black and Free* (Zondervan, 1970); Andrea Smith, *Unreconciled: From Racial Reconciliation to Racial Justice in Christian Evangelicalism* (Duke University Press, 2019); Jemar Tisby and Lecrae Moore, *The Color of Compromise: The Truth About the American Church's Complicity in Racism* (Zondervan, 2019); Isabel Wilkerson, *Caste: The Origins of Our Discontents* (Random House, 2020).

for Donald Trump, a candidate whose words and actions regularly diminished and harmed people of color.[7] For many, that number represented the ongoing rejection of racial justice efforts by White Christians, especially those identifying as evangelical. While one statistic alone disguises complexities in the decisions Christians made at the polls, Naomi knew that deprioritizing racial justice wasn't new for White Christians in 2016.

Yes, there have also been notable exceptions to White Christians' racism throughout history. Some White Christians were among influential activists in movements for abolition, anti-apartheid, civil rights, labor rights, and more. Some Christians—including White Christians—have pushed back against racism since its inception. White Christians have worked alongside Black, Latino, Asian, Indigenous, Jewish, Arab, and other leaders in abolition movements, liberation movements, and cultural revitalization movements throughout history.[8] Those consistent and committed exceptions are the reason I wrote this book—I wanted to know how they come to be. But we cannot miss the context of their stories: Actively pursuing racial justice is not typical among White people, and even less typical among White Christians.

Christian complicity in racism continues today, to a degree many Christians themselves are unaware of. When I ask Christian college

---

[7]This percentage held in 2016, 2020, and 2024 elections, according to Pew Research Center surveys and AP VoteCast exit polls. Justin Nortey, "Most White Americans Who Regularly Attend Worship Services Voted for Trump in 2020," Pew Research Center, August 30, 2021, www.pewresearch.org/short-reads/2021/08/30/most-white-americans-who-regularly-attend-worship-services-voted-for-trump-in-2020/; Peter Smith, "White Evangelical Voters Show Steadfast Support for Donald Trump's Presidency," *AP News*, November 7, 2024, https://apnews.com/article/white-evangelical-voters-support-donald-trump-president-dbfd2b4fe5b2ea27968876f19ee20c84.

[8]Alfred A. Cave, "The Delaware Prophet Neolin: A Reappraisal," *Ethnohistory* 46, no. 2 (1999): 265-90; Drick Boyd, *Disrupting Whiteness: Talking with White People About Racism* (Arch Street, 2021); W. E. B. Du Bois, *John Brown* (Oxford University Press, 2007); Robin D. G. Kelley, *Freedom Dreams: The Black Radical Imagination* (Beacon, 2003); Karen Johnson, *Ordinary Heroes of Racial Justice: A History of Christians in Action* (InterVarsity Press, 2025); David R. Swartz, *Moral Minority: The Evangelical Left in an Age of Conservatism* (University of Pennsylvania Press, 2012); Mark R. Warren, *Fire in the Heart: How White Activists Embrace Racial Justice* (Oxford University Press, 2010).

students whether they think Christians are better or worse than the general population at addressing racism, most answer "better." The data say otherwise. A survey in mid-2020 found that only 9 percent of White Christians self-identified as "very motivated to address racial injustice."[9] Let me repeat—*9 percent*. For comparison, in the same survey, twice as many White non-Christians identified as very motivated to address racial injustice. And five times as many Black Christians. In other words, it wasn't Whiteness alone or Christianity alone that drove people away from addressing racial injustice, but the combination of the two.

White Christians aren't just demotivated regarding racism, they are skeptical. In a survey asking whether "Black people are generally treated less fairly than White people in regard to hiring, pay, and promotions," only 28 percent of White evangelicals answered yes.[10] Nonevangelical White Christians are more likely to answer yes, but they are still fifteen percentage points less likely than White non-Christians.[11]

The tendrils intertwining Christianity with racism are long and tangled. We cannot wish these truths away, or pray them away, or smile them away with a handful of acts of kindness. To address racism requires contending with Christians—their beliefs, their institutions, their powerful influences across society. Their numbers are fewer than they once

---

[9]Christina Barland Edmondson and Chad Brennan, *Faithful Anti-Racism: Moving Past Talk to Systemic Change* (InterVarsity Press, 2022), 17.

[10]In this book I chose not to differentiate evangelical from nonevangelical Christians except when citing others' research. Individuals participating in the research often moved in and out of churches and networks that would or would not be considered evangelical, and most preferred to avoid labeling themselves or others according to that category. Across history the term has incorporated a shifting range of church denominations and theological positions. Some scholars attempt to uphold its association to specific doctrinal positions and historical trajectories that focus on beliefs about the importance of the church's outward-facing orientation. In popular usage, *evangelical* has increasingly come to imply "politically conservative and White," making it a complicated category for participants in this research. On the politics of evangelical Christians, see Anand Edward Sokhey and Paul A. Djupe, eds., *Trump, White Evangelical Christians, and American Politics: Change and Continuity* (University of Pennsylvania Press, 2024); Timothy Larsen and Daniel J. Treier, eds., *The Cambridge Companion to Evangelical Theology* (Cambridge University Press, 2007).

[11]Racial Justice Unity Center, "Race, Religion, and Justice Project Survey," 2019; Edmondson and Brennan, *Faithful Anti-Racism*, 20, 16.

were in this country, but they are not disappearing—more than 60 percent of Americans identify as Christian.[12]

Some Christians are oblivious to—or even grateful for—the trend of Christian disinterest in racism, but others are painfully aware of their fellow Christians' racism. For increasing numbers, that has become reason enough to leave the religion behind. In 1964, King wrote, "I am meeting young people every day whose disappointment with the church has risen to outright disgust."[13] You can meet them every day today, too. One White man I interviewed said he'd left gatherings of White Christians "wanting to throw up in my mouth. In White spaces, Christianity gets conflated with nationalism. With specific political issues. With retention of power. I mean, it's just, I see so many of my friends leaving the church, and I feel like, totally, I would leave that too." One White woman who grew up in a Christian family said she left Christianity largely because White Christians seemed to respond to racism only with bureaucratic loops, distrust of leaders of color, and simplistic hope in the power of love without willingness to address systemic issues. Naomi was not the only person of color who struggled to think of a single White Christian to recommend as an active advocate for racial justice. When another Asian American man drew a blank in answer to my request for recommendations, he commented, "That's telling in itself, isn't it?"

These individuals' observations are not just anecdotal. The rate of people leaving Christianity for agnosticism, atheism, or other practices accelerated from the 1990s through the early 2000s.[14] Their reasons are diverse, but for many, the association between Christianity, politics, and racism is at the top of the list. In an interview, Black Christian rapper and

---

[12]Gregory A. Smith et al., "Decline of Christianity in the U.S. Has Slowed, May Have Leveled Off: Findings from the 2023–24 Religious Landscape Study," Pew Research Center, February 26, 2025, www.pewresearch.org/religion/2025/02/26/decline-of-christianity-in-the-us-has-slowed-may-have-leveled-off/.

[13]King, "Letter from a Birmingham Jail."

[14]"How U.S. Religious Composition Has Changed in Recent Decades," Pew Research Center, September 13, 2022, www.pewresearch.org/religion/2022/09/13/how-u-s-religious-composition-has-changed-in-recent-decades/.

music producer Lecrae admitted he nearly became one of those data points. "My faith was pretty critically damaged by just hearing a Western predominantly White Euro-centric perspective of Christianity especially at a time when there was a lot of hostility between races in America . . . and I wasn't hearing a lot of my White brothers and sisters give any answers or any thoughts on what was going on. I felt hurt, and for me I just assumed that this was how the whole faith was."[15]

When *New York Times* writer Jessica Grose asked readers about declining religious observance in America, she received nearly seventy-five hundred responses in twenty-four hours. She summarized these responses in an article titled "Christianity Has a Branding Problem," quoting readers such as Cynthia Jackson, who left her church in Minnesota because it felt too politically conservative, saying she still believes "in redemption," but she feels like she is "in exile."[16] "Unchurched believers" like Cynthia, who identify as not religiously affiliated while believing many of the basic tenets of Christianity, rose from 4 to 11 percent of Americans between 1988 to 2012. During that time the percentage of non–religiously affiliated adults rose by eighteen percentage points among liberals while only rising by three percentage points among conservatives.[17] While the choice of political liberalism or conservatism is not a complete proxy for attitudes and actions regarding racism, many believers interested in racial justice are finding Christianity untenable.

By those numbers alone, White Christians would seem to be a futile group on which to pin any hopes of change in the direction of addressing racial injustice.

After naming all the reasons for his disappointment in White people and especially Christians, King shifts his attention to the rare individuals

---

[15] *Unspoken* (DLC Media Group, 2022), www.unspokenmovie.com/.
[16] Jessica Grose, "Christianity's Got a Branding Problem," *New York Times*, May 10, 2023, www.nytimes.com/2023/05/10/opinion/christian-religion-brand-nones.html.
[17] Michael Hout and Claude S. Fischer, "Explaining Why More Americans Have No Religious Preference: Political Backlash and Generational Succession, 1987–2012," *Sociological Science* 1 (2014): 423-47.

who defied that trend: The few "noble souls from the ranks of organized religion have broken loose from the paralyzing chains of conformity and joined us as active partners in the struggle for freedom." They are "still all too small in quantity, but they are big in quality." They are witnesses, he says, of "the true meaning of the Gospel in these troubled times." King managed to hold two truths in tension that you and I will hold in tension throughout this book: White Christian perpetrators of racial injustice are many, but White Christians who advocate for racial justice do also exist. King said of those few, "They have carved a tunnel of hope through the mountain of disappointment."[18]

Christians ushered the way into racism, but in this book we'll see how they also participate in finding ways out. I base this not on some vague inkling but on evidence. The question is not whether Christians can be a part of dismantling racism; it is what it takes for the White Christians among them to join and keep going.

So here's the thing—if we want to understand hope by studying some case of a social problem that looks pretty hopeless, racism offers a clear place to start. And more specifically, we can narrow in on racism perpetuated not just by any White people but White Christians specifically. Not a lot of them keep on pursuing racial justice with any serious level of commitment for very long.

And yet some do.[19] They are the rare ones. If some White Christians today are still tunneling hope through mountains of despair, we do well to find out what keeps them digging. When the hands of everyone they work alongside are blistered and bleeding, when the tunnel walls are shaking and the canary has died, what keeps them from tossing down the shovel and walking out?

To find out, we're going to tunnel alongside them in the chapters ahead. It's going to get colder down there. It's time to talk about how we hope.

---

[18]King, "Letter from a Birmingham Jail."
[19]For additional research on this subset of "other" White evangelicals, see Wes Markofski, *Good News for Common Goods: Multicultural Evangelicalism and Ethical Democracy in America*, Oxford Scholarship Online (Oxford University Press, 2023); Brian Steensland, *The New Evangelical Social Engagement* (Oxford University Press, 2013); Swartz, *Moral Minority*.

PART 2

Dare We Hope?

THREE

What Hope?

I WAS STILL TRYING TO NARROW in on a question and methodology for this research when I visited a White couple named Amy and Patrick.[1] At the time, I was feeling restless. My previous book—an account of the ways racism affects workplaces in South Africa and the ways people pursue good lives even so—was done and released, but something felt unfinished. I had spent my PhD and the years since reading reams testifying that racism exists. I knew how to trace the history of racism and how it continues to shape lives from generation to generation. I had a tenure-track job as a professor, and nearly every class I taught included lessons on how to recognize and address racism.

But something was gnawing at me. I wasn't entirely convinced that these worked.

Could White people—especially the ones raised in communities where racism wasn't even recognized as a problem—really change enough to become a part of the solution? Was there reason to hope for a solution? And what was the solution supposed to be, anyway? We knew to be *anti*, against this thing called racial *injustice*, but would we know racial *justice* if we found it? What were we all supposed to be hoping for?[2]

---

[1]Some portions of this chapter appeared earlier in my article "Introduction: Hopes of and for Whiteness," *Journal for the Anthropology of North America* 25, no. 2 (2022): 54-73.
[2]Researcher Mark Warren also highlights the need for more research on the question of what racial justice advocates hope for, writing, "Scholars of social movements have typically concentrated on what people are for in the very immediate sense of movement demands; surprisingly

Amy and Patrick were longtime friends, and I knew enough about their lives to think they could have some good advice. Besides, they were fun to be around. I could count on Patrick for cut-to-the-heart honesty and Amy for table-pounding enthusiasm. They did not fail to deliver on both accounts.

Patrick and Amy traced their initial interests in racial justice to a summer when they were in college. Together they attended a six-week summer urban immersion program run by a Christian student organization. It profoundly changed the course of their lives. That summer, a series of shootings occurred in their neighborhood, and the church they partnered with responded readily. "We got to be there watching them respond in multiple different ways. They're like, in the news, and I'm learning how to pray, and what is worship, what is ministry, and how are people investing their lives in this place. It was foundational." They returned the next year, and the next. Eventually Patrick joined the church staff. When they married, they moved near the church in a predominantly non-White neighborhood.

A few years later, the leaders of that church and a nearby White church decided to merge congregations. It was, according to Amy, "a classic, epic fail," like a marriage followed one year later by a divorce. "The White people fled." Patrick and Amy had been a part of the Black church prior to the merger, so they watched White people fleeing with a perspective they would not have otherwise had. "It was almost like a metaphor," Amy said. "Our Black friends—the people closest to us—asked us, 'Are you going to leave, too?'" She became emotional as she recalled what she heard from Black friends. "You can leave and never think about race again. We can't. We could leave this church, but we will *always* think about this. Do you realize that we can't leave? This is our life. There is no enclave where we can just be Black. I'm the only Black person at work. My kids are the only Black people in school. I have to be fluent in your culture."

---

little research has been conducted on activists' broader visions." Warren, *Fire in the Heart: How White Activists Embrace Racial Justice* (Oxford University Press, 2010), 21.

As Patrick and Amy realized that choosing whether to engage with racism was a choice their Black friends did not have, they faced a problem: if they were going to keep their feet planted alongside people of color, they were going to need more resilient hope. Patrick said they began noticing that their Black friends had a different kind of hope. In conversations about seemingly positive changes in the neighborhoods, a Black friend might say, "All right. We're getting somewhere. This *could* change this community." Then the friend would follow that with, "Well, we'll see how long this lasts." Patrick explained, "Because there's just too much history of being disappointed. That's what it's like being Black in America. It's being able to hold those two things in balance—we can be gracious and welcoming and hopeful and all those things, and yet be aware of the history and ready to be disappointed tomorrow."

Amy continued. "What I've learned about hope is this interesting thing." She paused to find words, then stated it this way: "I was sold a bill of goods that's wrong."

I asked what she meant. Her energy picked up with each sentence. "As a White person, I was sold a bill of goods that's inaccurate. I was told to hope in your circumstances, hope in the strength that you can change something, hope in optimism." Like a purchase she'd been told to buy that came out worthless, she'd been handed hopes that would not last. As an example, she mentioned the popular Christian book of the early 2000s *The Prayer of Jabez*, based on the obscure verse from 1 Chronicles: "Oh, that you would bless me and enlarge my territory!" (1 Chronicles 4:10). She reflected, "It's fascinating that we would zoom in on that one scripture that's about"—she dropped into a deep booming voice, "*more. I can just expand my tent.*"

Amy saw something entirely different in the hopes at her Black church. "It's like, they put their faith and hope in something, but it's not contingent. Your hope is in *God*. Even when more family members die of Covid in our church this last year than probably five White churches together because of the disparity of medical stuff—" She trailed off and began another example. "Or even when there's movement around George Floyd and Black Lives Matter and then White people get scared and they're like, 'No, no, no, we don't really mean change.'" She shifted into a whimpering voice, mimicking the voices of White people, "Oh, are you saying it's my fault?" Despite all this, she said, Black people respond "with a graciousness towards White people who want to engage in the conversation, but they're also like, 'Please, for the love of God, just get a backbone! And stand! And open your eyes!'" She dropped to a low, pleading voice. "How do you not get super cynical? It's a different definition of hope. How do you lead systemic change when racism is *embedded* in the very foundation of the country, and nobody wants to let go of that power? How do you have hope in the face of that?"

She crushed her hands into her face and made a gasping sound. "You could just be like, 'Oh, good God!' It's *so* bad.' And yet—" Suddenly she pounded her fist on the table. "And yet how is it that these Black Christians don't just crumble? Their hope is in something different! It's a different kind of hope. It's nothing that I was told. I was told"—she shifted into a sweet, high voice—"'Oh, if you work hard enough, you can get whatever you want.' Blah, blah, blah!" Now she was pounding her fist with every sentence. "How do you make it in the face of all of the systemic ways that everything is and yet still stand? And not just cave? That's a whole different reservoir of something that I just want to be close to. I just want to draw from that!"

Amy's fist resounded with the question ringing through all the history of the fight for racial justice. *How do you hope?*

||||||||

When I began the research that led to this book, I did not plan to write about hope. I planned to look for patterns across the lives of White Christians who had come to spend years of their life intentionally pursuing racial justice and to write about how to replicate that process. But when I asked White people how they changed along that journey, they talked about hope. And when I asked people of color to compare the White people they knew whose interest in racial justice flamed out quickly versus those with a persevering commitment, they also talked about hope.

Early in my research I sat talking with Luis, a Latino pastor, in a sunny meeting room at his church. As we were finishing the questions I had prepared for the interview, Luis got talking about the kind of hope he witnesses among Latino and Latina Christians. He said in his church, more than in White churches he has seen, congregants want opportunities to tell testimonies—stories about what God has done in their life. He said often these stories start out sounding like tragedies. He listed stories he heard about a daughter nearly being raped, a family losing their home in a flood, someone going days without food, someone crossing the border hidden in the back of a semi filled with cattle and manure. "And I'm listening thinking, *Where is God in that?*" he said. "But here's the thing. Their testimony is that in the midst of a storm, God was there, and I'm so happy." He summed up what he notices in these testimonies: "A lot of White people just focus on the resurrection. But people who have this suffering as a part of life, because of poverty or race or whatever, they live on the cross."

And this, he suggested, is something White people intuitively know is missing from their Christian practice. "You know," Luis went on, "one of the reasons why many churches here, especially White churches, do mission trips to Mexico and Central America is because they're going to experience something with God over there that they're not experiencing here. And this is what it is: There's a lot of hope in those that have nothing. There's not a lot of hope in those that have it all. When something good happens in the White community, it's like, 'Oh, thank you, God.' But really, you weren't even trusting God. You knew your dad was going to come through. You knew the bank was going to come through. You knew you were going to get that job. But for us, the hope is in the Lord because the Lord is really the only one that has been able to help. The government hasn't helped. The rich community hasn't helped. My race hasn't helped. The doctors haven't helped. And so is this strong hope versus just having this flaky hope."

From conversations like these, I realized I needed to know more about hope—how the hopes of one group of people came to differ from hopes among other groups, and what this word *hope* even means. I checked out a stack of library books about hope and set them on my nightstand to get to when I had time.

And then my research—and the whole world—was interrupted by one of the greatest assaults on hope in living memory.

▌▌▌▌▌▌▌▌

The Covid-19 pandemic drew back a curtain of collective denial in the United States, revealing that health, trust, and safe work are not—and have not been—evenly distributed in this country. The great tectonic plates of political parties rumbled and crashed, breaking families and opening new chasms across our communities. And just as we were starting to use phrases like "the new normal," a police officer in Minneapolis pressed his knee into the neck of a Black man named George Floyd in broad daylight and held him there as he pleaded for breath. Until his breath was gone.

For many, an already floundering hope breathed its last along with George Floyd. For others, a different kind of hope sprang to life. In the days that followed, millions took to the streets to demonstrate, posted on social media, and spoke with anyone who would listen about how we might collectively stop causing the premature deaths of so many Black people. A few days later, podcaster Ezra Klein interviewed Ta-Nehisi Coates, author of several books about "the beautiful struggle" of navigating American life as a Black man.[3] When Klein asked what Coates

---

[3]Ta-Nehisi Coates, *The Beautiful Struggle: A Father, Two Sons, and an Unlikely Road to Manhood* (One World, 2008).

saw across the country in that moment, Coates replied, "I can't believe I'm gonna say this, but I see hope."[4]

Do you even dare hope for that? Apparently, Coates did.[5] And many other people wanted to hope. Through what became known as the double pandemic of Covid-19 and racism, the word *hope* cropped up everywhere. People flew banners above immigration detention centers to encourage those held within, *Soy nube de esperanza*, "I am a cloud of hope."[6] Artists painted a giant colorful mural with the words "Hold on to hope" on an Asian food store near my home.[7] A Christian organization in my city organized a conference on hope, and we sat in our homes watching the little boxes of each other's faces on the screen telling each other how to hope. A massive mobilization was kicked into action to figure out how to produce a vaccine for this disease, and so too were millions of people intent on figuring out how to multiply this thing called hope for the sake of our collective survival. But hope, like vaccinations, turns out to be more complicated and controversial than you'd think.

Social media posts, institutional statements, articles, podcasts, book clubs, projects, and workshops deploring racism poured out in a flood. Many began with the words, "Since George Floyd's death, we've been . . ."

---

[4]Ezra Klein, "Why Ta-Nehisi Coates Is Hopeful," The Ezra Klein Show, n.d., www.vox.com/2020/6/5/21279530/ta-nehisi-coates-ezra-klein-show-george-floyd-police-brutality-trump-biden.

[5]As another example of a Black scholar expressing a tentative hope around that time, Anthea Butler closes her 2021 book, *White Evangelical Racism*, using the word *hope* seven times in one page. "I watched with trepidations and a sliver of hope as evangelicals marched on a Sunday in Washington, D.C., in support of Black Lives Matter, with Senator Mitt Romney joining the group. . . . The sentiments are welcome. But there must be more. . . . Can you step away from the headiness of being in the position of power to see the brokenness of your neighbors and the nation? . . . If you feel one ounce of conviction, then there is hope for you. There may even be hope for our nation. I hope these words find root in you. I hope they trouble you. I hope they sear your soul. I hope they make you change. There is only a little time left, but there is time. The time is now." Butler, *White Evangelical Racism: The Politics of Morality in America* (University of North Carolina Press, 2021), 147-48.

[6]The team, led by artist Beatriz Cortez, flew banners above eighty locations. Mandelit Del Barco, "With Fleets of Planes, Artists Take to Skies Nationwide to Protest Mass Detention," *NPR*, July 4, 2020, www.npr.org/2020/07/04/887129552/with-fleets-of-planes-artists-take-to-skies-nationwide-to-protest-mass-detention.

[7]Brian Kehoe and Ray Mawst of Oh-Ya studio created the mural. "Hold On to Hope," Oh-Ya Studio, www.ohyastudio.com/exterior-murals/hold-on-to-hope.

They rode the crest of a giant wave of public interest, and many reaped a harvest of clicks, likes, and viral posts. But already in that moment, and now all the more looking back, one might ask, What happens in the shallow trough before the next news hype? Were there people doing anything about racism before George Floyd's death? And if that single tragic, viral news story was the primary motivator to so much behavioral change, would any of that change last?

Not long after we had begun leaving our homes without face masks again, I attended a concert in which singer-songwriter Peter Mulvey performed with SistaStrings, the artists Chauntee and Monique Ross. Near the end of the concert, they performed a song by Mulvey titled "A Song for Michael Brown." The song, written in 2014 after Michael Brown was shot by police in Ferguson, Missouri, takes the form of a plea to listeners. "I'm asking you, to have some compassion, for young, dead Michael Brown." The sentence continues, radiating outward to the many others affected by the death. "And for his family, and for his city, and for the man who shot him down . . . for the marchers . . . for the angry White man on TV . . . for the mothers, and the hopeful, and the fearful, and the hateful, and the righteous, and you and me." The kicker comes at the close of the verse: "And most especially, for the next child, for the next child, we know will fall." Hearing the song seven years after it was written, in the wake of a continuing list of Black individuals killed by police, the line hit me like a punch. People struggling for racial justice over the long haul know we're going to need compassion and hope not just for the previous tragic death but for the next. Because there will be a next.

In the years that followed, I began noticing the word *hope* in conversations about racism everywhere. In 2023, Angela Denker, author of the book *Red State Christians*, wrote a Substack post titled, "Am I Hopeful?" She began, "In recent weeks, I find myself being asked about hope and talking about hope more than anything else." She admitted to readers, sometimes it's easier to be "hard-bitten and cynical and angry and frustrated and funny" than it is to be hopeful. "But dangit. I'm hopeful. . . . I

What Hope?

just can't shake it."[8] Around the same time, another popular White Christian blogger, Sarah Bessey, wrote a post titled "For the Days When You're Feeling a Bit Hopeless."

> These years have been an unveiling, a revealing or revelation, an uncovering. Everything that was hidden has been dragged—sometimes kicking and screaming—into the open. We are exposed. The lights are on and we're blinking helplessly into the honest mirror of our culture, our selfishness, our racism, our rampant individualism, our lack of neighborliness, injustice, all of it. And under it all: hopelessness.[9]

Others were asking what to hope for. "There's something that just feels unsettling about training folks to be in a stance of opposition toward something without being very clear about what we are a proponent for," psychologist Dr. Krystal Hays said in a 2024 interview about her co-authored book *Healing Conversations on Race*. "That's the piece that feels like something is missing." As a clinical psychologist, Hays said she would never ask someone to be "anti-drug-user."[10] You can't just name what you're avoiding. You have to know what you desire. What vision draws you forward? In the early 2020s, just as people were relearning how to live without masks, they were relearning how to hope.

As I finished editing this book in early 2025, the surrounding political events made it abundantly clear that though the circumstances and machinations of racism may change, racism has not gone away. Our need is as great as ever for an answer to the question, *How do you dare hope?*

∥∣∣∣∣∣∣∣

---

[8] Angela Denker, "Am I Hopeful?," *I'm Listening* (blog), November 1, 2022, https://angeladenker.substack.com/p/am-i-hopeful.

[9] Sarah Bessey, "For the Days When You're Feeling a Bit Hopeless," *Field Notes* (blog), June 21, 2022, https://sarahbessey.substack.com/p/hope-tree.

[10] "Krystal Hays and Veola Vazquez: Healing Conversations on Race," *Women Scholars and Professionals Podcast*, February 20, 2024, https://allshallbewell.podbean.com/e/krystal-hays-and-veola-vazquez-healing-conversations-on-race/.

When the pandemic forced libraries to close across the country, the pile of library books frozen on my nightstand included painfully appropriate titles such as *The Paradox of Hope* and *Embracing Hopelessness*.[11] When my energy was no longer fully occupied with learning to be human on Zoom and breathing through a mask or just breathing at all, I began working my way through that stack.

Before I got far, I realized that even defining this thing we call *hope* would be trickier than you might expect. One literature review identified twenty-six different theories and fifty-four definitions of hope.[12] Eventually I pieced together words to land on a definition I'll use for this book: *Hope is a way of orienting oneself toward an unknown future that anticipates good.*

Notice three key concepts: orienting, unknown, and good. Hope is first a way of orienting or aiming oneself. It is tied to thoughts and emotions but is not just a mental exercise. Hope manifests in actions. It is a way of placing ourselves into stories we tell about how the world works and what gives that world meaning.

Second, hope becomes operative when we face an *unknown future*. If we know the future with certainty, we are not hoping. We are knowing, expecting, predicting, or just ignoring altogether. I orient my life around the expectation that the earth will turn another rotation in the next twenty-four hours. There may be a sliver of uncertainty in that future, but it's too slight to consider. I am not hoping that the world will turn; I'm expecting. Hope, in contrast, bridges a gap between the known and unknowable.

Finally, hope orients toward an unknown future while anticipating good rather than bad. If I'm anticipating bad, I might cope with it using cynicism or pessimism, or I might experience dread—a feeling of being utterly unprotected from that bad. Hope, in contrast, *anticipates good*.

---

[11]Cheryl Mattingly, *The Paradox of Hope* (University of California Press, 2010); Miguel A. De La Torre, *Embracing Hopelessness* (Fortress, 2017).

[12]Shane J. Lopez et al., *Positive Psychological Assessment: A Handbook of Models and Measures* (American Psychological Association, 2003), 91-106.

In the 1940s, psychologist Viktor Frankl spent three years imprisoned in concentration camps under Nazi Germany. Surrounded by death and despair, he began wondering what accounted for the differences between those who succumbed to sickness and starvation versus those—including himself—who did not. His answer was hope. Inspired by this idea that hope could prolong or save lives, a wave of researchers in decades that followed documented the effects of hope on health.[13] Scholars created one-dimensional scales to measure individuals' hopes from less to more, treating hope as a quantifiable measurement like blood pressure or cholesterol level.

But they soon ran into a problem. Hope is not a uniform entity that we can simply accumulate or prescribe in lesser or greater quantities. Hope comes in so many flavors. There are hopes for the world to stay as it is and hopes for a world remade. Some hopes tell you to rest and be still, while other hopes tell you to lift your feet and trudge, walk, or run. There are hopes founded on a belief that luck favors the prepared, or time heals all wounds, or we're all prisoners of fate. People have based their hopes on the market's invisible hand, the scientific method bringing the next great technology, democracy dishing out liberty, or children bringing a new and innocent beginning. Historians point out that across the nineteenth and twentieth centuries in the United States, the dominant warrants for hope shifted from God, to science, to nation, and then to the self.[14] There are hopes that focus on a concrete goal, such as the new trumpet my son prayed for every night as a toddler, and hopes with amorphous goals, such as the prayer my young daughter prayed during that season: "God, help people who are sick or sad or poor or lonely."[15]

---

[13] Jaklin A. Eliott, "What Have We Done with Hope? A Brief History," in *Interdisciplinary Perspectives on Hope*, ed. Jaklin A. Eliott (Nova, 2004), 3-45; Viktor E. Frankl, *Man's Search for Meaning*, 4th ed. (Beacon, 2000); E. Kübler-Ross, "Chapter 8: Hope," in *On Death and Dying* (Tavistock, 1970); Karl Menninger, "The Academic Lecture: Hope," *The American Journal of Psychiatry* 116 (1959): 481-91.

[14] Andrew Delbanco, *The Real American Dream: A Meditation on Hope* (Harvard University Press, 2000); Eliott, "What Have We Done."

[15] We never got him a trumpet, and none of us regrets it.

There are hopes grounded in unexamined conviction that life always goes pretty well, so why shouldn't it continue as such, and there are hopes that squeeze from your soul with hot tears when everything has already gone wrong, so, dang it, you're going to press on anyway. Each of these forms of hope points to different approaches to racial justice.

If we want to understand our hopes, we need to ask a lot of questions. Why do we hope? What do we hope for? What do we think we should do with our hope? And it would also serve us well to ask where we learned our hopes. We don't just muster up our hopes from within; we learn them from our social world. As one scholar writes, "Different individuals and social classes, at different historical junctures, embedded in different social relations, enjoying different opportunities and facing different constraints, will experience hope in different ways."[16] As an anthropologist, I'm interested not only in the ways our hopes wax and wane individually but also in how we cocreate ways of hoping through social and cultural interactions. Whereas theologians might be best suited to winnow out one true way of hoping that matches scriptural interpretation, anthropologists acknowledge that humans find a wide variety of ways to hope, and those differing hopes have differing effects on all of us.

If we want to pursue racial justice for the long haul, what matters is not just how *much* we hope but what *sort* of hope it is. This is what people like Amy and Patrick were discovering. They wanted not just more hope but a "whole different reservoir," as Amy put it. Too often across the history of racism, reservoirs of hope have done more poisoning than quenching of thirst. Sermons and inspirational coffee-table books overflow with exhortations to have more hope, but when we're operating with the wrong kind of hope, multiplying it can do more harm than good. Before we turn to the ways people find those new reservoirs of hope, we need to consider how hope goes wrong.

---

[16]Darren Webb, "Pedagogies of Hope," *Studies in Philosophy and Education* 32, no. 4 (2013): 398.

FOUR

Delusional Hope

HEARING PEOPLE SUCH AS AMY, Patrick, and Luis talk about the need for a deeper reservoir of hope for racial justice, I decided to include questions about hope in every interview. Near the end of the interview, as a prompt to ask about hope, I would ask people to complete the following sentences: "In regard to racial justice, I used to hope _____. Now I hope _____." Often people seemed grateful and a little surprised to be asked about hope. Some responded initially with expressions of befuddlement. "I've never thought about that." "Good question." "What *is* the goal?" "I'm not sure." Long pauses. Usually their first response was to fill in things they hoped *for*—goals that characterized racial justice, such as *for unity*, *enough*, or *freedom*. Once they explained those, I also asked people to fill in the sentence again with adverbs and adjectives to describe their *ways* of hoping. They chose and explained words such as *blindly*, *optimistically*, or *small*.

My own life also traces a journey toward new ways of hoping. As a social scientist, I am keenly aware that my own life circumstances shape the questions, perspectives, and interpretations that find their way into my research. And so before returning to the lessons I learned through this study, it seems appropriate to tell you how I came to be writing a book about hope. If I could trace the seed of this book to one moment, it might begin with this scene.

In a small upstairs classroom, some forty to fifty people are seated, pressed tightly in a circle around the room. Some raise their hands with their eyes closed; others bend forward and back in a rhythm like reeds in wind. Their voices overlap in layers of sound, some musical and some monotone, some soft and some loud, in a dozen languages from across the continent of Africa. Their voices beat out a pounding waterfall of prayer. The sound flows through the open windows, across the courtyard of a seminary founded nearly a century earlier by White missionaries full of optimism. Today that seminary is bankrupt.

But first, to back up. You can find more of my story in the afterword, but to summarize here, I was a White person who didn't know much about race or injustice until college. Then a number of collisions and learning opportunities expanded my understanding of racial and colonial systems. When I graduated, I wanted to do something about social inequalities. I got married right after I graduated, and my husband and I started looking for a way to live and work in an underresourced community. Through a series of introductions, we spent a year in a Nicaraguan village doing whatever was asked of us, then two years in China teaching English while we completed master's degrees in international economic development. Then we moved to South Africa to work for a microfinance organization, followed by this seminary.

Those years brought enough failures to fill another book. In Nicaragua, I attempted to create a demonstration vegetable garden using my thimbleful of training from one subtropical agriculture college class. Roaming pigs rooted out all my first seedlings, and when I built a meager fence and tried again, chickens scratched out the next batch. I managed to harvest one handful of potatoes weighing less than the original seed potatoes—a strange feat of harvesting less than I'd planted. I nurtured one lone squash plant from a seed I'd accidentally tossed behind a building, until a drunk man tumbled over and crushed it.

In our first two years in South Africa, we fared just about as badly. Within two years we had shut down the microfinance organization that hired us to come to the country. The American founder—who had spent less than six months in South Africa—dreamed the project would multiply across the continent, but she vastly underestimated the challenges that Black South Africans faced in founding and expanding businesses. From our first day on the job, signs were rampant that the organization's aims were unfeasible in the rural community she had chosen, much less at the massive scale she had envisioned. Meanwhile, the church we attended was reeling with the discovery that the pastor had sexually abused several children at an orphanage, and the news reached us that two separate churches we had previously attended back in the United States were also closing. When the microfinance organization closed, we packed up and moved a few hours down the highway to teach at this South African seminary.

We lived in seminary housing alongside students and staff from across the African continent. In our first weekend there, thieves broke into our car and stole a ten-dollar radio, costing us fifty dollars in repairs. The next weekend thieves stole all the tires off another car in the parking lot. The following weekend another car lost its tires, and a few weekends later thieves held an axe to the car window of a fellow professor as he pulled into the apartment driveway, threatening to kill him if he didn't crawl away on the ground. He did, losing the car but saving his life. At night, I would lie in bed in our first-floor apartment looking at the big picture window. Unlike most windows in the city, we had no burglar bars. I would plot what I might do if a thief smashed through the window. As the most fluent isiZulu speaker in our family, would I negotiate? Like a movie scene, could I perhaps heroically stun a thief into mercy with some act of kindness? Or should I run to lock our children's bedroom door? Or dive under the bed?

All this might have been unbearable were it not for all the neighbors just beyond that picture window. Those neighbors—seminary students and staff—modeled each day how to go on living there. There was the family from Rwanda who had narrowly escaped genocide, and three families from Burundi who fled similar violence. Many families came as refugees from war, and at least one man had spent jail time in his home country for refusing to participate in a corrupt military. From Zambia, Zimbabwe, Mozambique, Nigeria, and the Democratic Republic of Congo came individuals who would not see their families for years at a time. Each had somehow saved thousands of dollars to be here, often through decades of church offerings that yielded only a few dollars per week. There was the Congolese family next door, who could afford to send only one child to school at a time, and the Nigerian family with five teenagers living in a two-bedroom apartment, and the Burundian family who cared for so many orphaned children I lost track of who was family.

In addition to learning what it's like to lie awake anticipating the next burglary, we learned in our first weeks at the seminary that the institution was in a catastrophic budget crisis. The seminary had just selected its first-ever Black president, a gentle and steady-voiced man who invited us to dinner the week we arrived. Some members of the board had protested the decision, saying that choosing this Black candidate over a White candidate was "reverse racism," a biased act of affirmative action for an unqualified figurehead who would surely sink the institution. They created a self-fulfilling end to that prediction by slandering the new president among the seminary's White financial supporters.

Money disappeared. Funders withdrew hundreds of thousands of dollars. This coincided with the 2008 financial crisis in the United States, which spread like a tsunami of canceled donations and funding cuts across the world. Bills went unpaid. A leaky roof went unrepaired. Salaries were cut. We raised our own support to cover our salary, but most of our colleagues could raise only a fraction of their salaries from their African connections. One day the administrators made the dreaded announcement that financial aid promised to current students would be discontinued. Students who had saved for years to arrive here, buoyed by scholarships, now faced the likely possibility of dropping out before completing their degrees.

My husband shifted all his working hours to contacting funders and coaching students and colleagues to do the same. Almost daily I heard neighbors say, "God will provide." They talked about donations of ten and twenty dollars miraculously appearing in their accounts, but I kept wondering about the tens of thousands still lacking. Their gratitude and faith felt to me like denial before impending doom.

And so it was that one day some students called this meeting to pray for the seminary budget. We gathered in a bare room and pulled chairs from nearby classrooms into a circle, packing shoulder to shoulder. As was customary, everyone prayed at once. Most began quietly naming characteristics of God, then slowly rose in volume, pleading earnestly until the sound must have covered the entire campus. I closed my eyes and began dutifully doing my part, asking God to somehow solve this funding crisis.

But the more I tried to pray, the more I faced something I'd been avoiding. The truth was, I did not have any hope left. I did not expect God to solve this problem, and didn't even know how to imagine God could. I saw the tendrils of this problem stretching across the continent, across nations, across time. How do you pray in the face of a global financial crisis caused by the greed of Wall Street moguls, and the power-laden trade agreements that shut Africa out of global trade for centuries, and the colonizers who stole this land and forced African people to work for their profit, and the mismanagement of government funds, and the racism that dismantled our college leadership? How do you pray for anything good when the trajectory of centuries seems so targeted at bad?

I had nothing left to ask, no belief in something good to come, no hope. Slowly my mouth stopped. I went silent.

And I listened.

My right shoulder was pressed against the fleshy outstretched arm of a woman who had fled war with three small children. From her mouth came a steady torrent of words in a language I could not understand. To my left, a man who had survived terminal illness without health care pounded his fist into his hand and shouted declarations of God's goodness. Tears streamed down faces. Everywhere around the circle, I saw people whose lives from womb to the present teemed with disappointment, and they kept on hoping. Their hope was like circular breathing, taking in more air through the nose even as the mouth pressed out unceasing music.

Their prayers did not result in the money the seminary needed. Scholarships ended. Faculty and staff went without pay. Seminary leaders began acknowledging that the seminary would close its doors. My husband and I began reluctantly making plans to move back to the United States. Before we left, a group of Americans came to visit an organization down the road from us. They listened to local leaders explain South African history. They bought crafts from local artisans, painted walls, and carried lumber. Their organization had a name that was something like "Bringing New Hope." With the symphony of that prayer meeting still in my ears, I thought, *How? How can you call yourselves bringers of hope to people whose hope operates on a whole different realm?* Such absurdity, for White college kids to think they had some charitable offering of hope when here were people scraping up hope from the dust of the soil with bleeding fingers. These kids brought hope like a fake plastic knickknack. It was a facsimile that might lodge in a person's mind and block all remembrance of what real hope means. It all seemed so naive. So ignorant. Offensive, even. I wasn't sure at the time what persevering hope was, but I knew it was not what these White Americans brought to Africa. What they carried was more delusion than hope.

It bothered me, I see now, mostly because I could see myself reflected in them.

To persevere in the long-term work of racial justice, people need something more than a delusional hope. They need an abiding, rugged, radical hope. In the chapters ahead, we'll see how White people learn that persevering hope. They don't learn it in a vacuum: They learn by struggling for justice alongside people who have endured injustice, drought, funding shortages, political chaos, diseases, poverty, and more. We'll meet White people whose ways of hoping have been stripped down, retooled, and duct-taped back together. But before we get there, we need to understand what they're starting with. What are the pervasive, dominant, normalized ways of hoping that White Christians absorb through their everyday lives?

In this chapter we'll look at three characteristics of a way of hoping that I'll refer to as *delusional hope*. Delusional hope is optimistic, conventional, and damaging. By learning to recognize this type of hope as the intruder that it is, we'll be on our way toward finding a hope with the enduring strength to compel people toward justice.

|||||||||

Delusional hope is first of all optimistic. One way to define *optimism* would be to say it is a practice of *psychologically distancing oneself from negative outcomes*.[1] Optimism distances itself from both materially and psychologically negative outcomes. It pushes the bad to a distance, ignoring or denying it. Optimism is an unstable basis for hope. Faced with a glimpse of the bad, optimistic hope feels threatened. Optimists must always keep accumulating realms where they cannot look, think, or tread, and techniques to keep denying realities.

In answer to the question of what to hope for, optimistic hope focuses on happy endings. One White woman told me that she found herself challenged in a class about racism because "We're used to happy endings in fairy tales. We don't have a good way to long for resolution without expecting that it will come." With delusional hope, the road to happy endings shall also be happy, with only brief moments of sadness flitting past.

For White people, optimism can take the form delusional self-conceptions of oneself as a "good" White person. To distance themselves from the psychological "bad" involves blocking out the possibility that

---

[1]From a summary of Martin E. P. Seligman, *Learned Optimism* (Knopf, 1991), in C. R. Snyder, "Hope Theory: Rainbows in the Mind," *Psychological Inquiry* 13, no. 4 (2002): 256.

they might be culpable for racism or that they might not be a part of the solution. One way White individuals protect themselves is through what a student in my class once referred to as "tiptoeing." The student said that often when White people learn about race, the message they absorb is that the best approach to racism is tiptoeing. They observe other White people getting shamed for cultural appropriation, insensitive word choices, or microaggressions, and they fear being singled out like that. And so they decide that the best way to deal with racism will be to dodge the topic. But dodging the topic also means dodging people of color, because by their very being, people of color become a reminder to White people that there could be an unresolved or unresolvable problem.[2]

During a visit to one predominantly White church, I sat on a bench in the atrium drinking coffee before the service. A gray-haired man stood beside me as his wife used the restroom. I asked what he liked about the church, and he said they started coming there because their previous church had "too much drama." My first thought was that their previous church had dramatic performances, but I soon realized that by *drama*, he meant *conflict*. He said he liked that this church gave a lot of money and volunteer hours for the poor, but he hadn't volunteered yet because "sometimes when you try to help the poor it comes around and bites you in the back." At this point his wife returned, and she shushed him, "Don't tell her about that!" I steered the conversation back to what they liked about the church, and she reiterated what he'd said. "Here there's never been drama. I honestly don't know how our pastors vote, and I like it that way. This church is not political." For this couple, the ideal church would be sanitized and drama-free, walled off from the messy world of poverty or politics.

At other churches, I met people of color who described the silence around race that preserves a drama-free façade. One Black man said, "When I'm in this place, I've got to watch my temperament. I can't yell or

---

[2]See Du Bois's reflections on the question that this delusional White hope thrusts on people of color, "How does it feel to be a problem?" W. E. B. Du Bois, *The Souls of Black Folk* (Dover, 2016).

get angry or upset. I have to come in here and just be bland." He felt the effects of White people socialized to distance themselves from conversations about race, from people of color, and from fear itself.

Optimistic White hope distances people not only from psychological spaces but also from the physical spaces that they image to be "bad." A White couple who had raised their children in a diverse neighborhood described how easily their White children absorbed racist conceptions of their neighborhood despite their parenting efforts. One year at Christmas, they visited relatives who lived in an affluent, predominantly White suburb. The husband described the setting. "Everyone there talks a certain way. Everyone has power. They have enormous stacks of boxes outside on the curb the day after Christmas." When they drove home, their son seemed to see his own neighborhood differently. "Our little boy looks around, looks at the McDonald's, looks down the street, looks at the 7-Eleven. And he says, 'Daddy, are there robbers here?'" Somewhere he picked up the idea that this place, being less wealthy and less White, was dangerous. This moment rendered visible the dominant White hopes that attach safety to Whiteness and danger to Blackness. Such fears lead White people to physically withdraw from spaces that they do not associate with Whiteness, making them even less likely to question their fears.

Theologian Walter Brueggemann makes a compelling case that the connection between optimism, religion, and oppression is not accidental. In his 1978 book *Prophetic Imagination*, Brueggemann compares two forms of imagination and hope. Each corresponds to a set of religious beliefs and to a social system. The first is a God-centered and resilient form of hope tied to social flourishing, which we'll return to in later chapters. The second is an optimistic hope tied to oppression. He points out that optimistic hope is founded on control—over society, God, and the future. It chooses to remain blind and numb to oppression and does not dare imagine real change. In doing so, it strips away any real possibility of hope, settling instead for "hopeless despair and a grim endurance of the way things now are." He says that oppression is maintained through an "official religion of optimism . . . [that] believes God has no business other than to maintain our standard of living."[3]

We do well to ask, Is optimism the official religion of White Christianity today?

▌▐▌▐▌▐▌▐

Delusional hope is also conventional. That is, it assumes that a better future is just a few small tweaks away, and that future will resemble the present. Conventional hope wants something like the present, only more of it. It's a hope built on addition and multiplication, not subtraction or division. Keep the big structure as is. Macro-level changes should focus on scaling up the already good structures to reach new places and realms. If significant changes must be made, limit those to the personal level.

As I was gathering research for this book, I attended an event in which a panel of influential Christian leaders reflected on the ways the church in the United States deals with social injustice. To close the event, the moderator asked a question typical at such events: What gives you hope these days? One by one, each speaker listed something positive happening in their immediate surroundings. They had interpreted the question "what gives you hope" to mean "what's going well right now." The unspoken warrant for their hope was an assumption that one can draw a straight line from a few data points in present circumstances and extend that line into the future as a trajectory for what will come.

In a nation where White people have maintained dominance over wealth, land, and political power for centuries, it's not hard to see how conventional hope becomes the default for White people. They benefit in keeping, honing, or multiplying the current social structures. Tearing down or redesigning structures feels like loss, not gain. That's not to say that White delusional hopes have no interest in change; it's just to say that the changes hoped for will be for an incremental expansion of what

---

[3]Walter Brueggemann, *The Prophetic Imagination*, 2nd ed. (Fortress, 2001), 64, 43.

already is, or for a return to a mythical White-safe past, or for a pie-in-the-sky heaven so distant as to have no connection to the present. In 1963, when Martin Luther King Jr. was preaching of his dream that Black, White, and all God's children could join hands to sing together "Free at last," Billy Graham instead exemplified a gradualist, conventional hope for racism, preaching, "Only when Christ comes again will little White children of Alabama walk hand in hand with little Black children."[4]

A word often used to describe the conventional approach to racism is *incrementalism*. Incrementalism argues that the only steps that will work are gradual ones, arising directly from what came before with minimal disruption.[5] Incrementalists thought they were speaking for the good of Black Americans when they argued against emancipation, Black enfranchisement, and affirmative action, saying each of these should not come too suddenly. As one White woman observed after the death of George Floyd, "There's this movement around Black Lives Matter and then—" She made a sound and hand gesture of an airplane plummeting. "Yeeeeeonk. People get scared and they're like, 'No, no, no, we don't really mean change the police. We'll just make it a Juneteenth holiday. We'll just do a book club.'"

A Black woman who taught classes on racism spoke of the common tendency among White people to want to purchase a training, finish it, and move on. "We're such a microwave kind of community that we miss just being in an experience and building an everyday practice." Conventional hope orients people toward staging events rather than designing processes. Events can give White people the sense that they have made progress without having to measure whether progress will continue.

---

[4]Quoted in Anthea Butler, *White Evangelical Racism: The Politics of Morality in America* (University of North Carolina Press, 2021), 34.
[5]It's worth noting that in reality, all endeavors are to some degree incremental, in that they come from that which was before. Nobody builds culture from scratch—we use the ideas and imaginations we learned from everything that came before. Even a complete rebuilding of a system draws on the imagination of what came before. But as we'll see in future chapters, there is an alternative to incrementalism that values rather than fears interruption and newness.

Conventional hope lacks resilience. In a multi-year study of evangelical, middle-class, mainly White Christian social activists in Atlanta, anthropologist Omri Elisha found that despite talking a lot about hope, their hopes often ran dry. "Hope is the motivational linchpin of evangelical outreach mobilization," he observes, noting that they attempted to "plant 'seeds of hope' in the lives of those who may be so deprived." These Christians often noted their own limitations in hope. They spoke of being stymied by what they called "compassion fatigue"—a paralysis of social activism that strikes when gaps grow too wide between their moral ambitions and social realities that "threaten to undermine them at every turn." He points to a chronic dilemma among White Christians: Their faith tradition teaches much about hope, but the further they dig into social activism at the heart of their faith tradition—loving neighbors and caring for "the least of these"—the more they see reasons to give up hoping.[6]

Written into that conventional hope are two related assumptions: that Whiteness is better than Blackness and that Whiteness therefore should remain in control. Those assumptions lead White people to implicitly pressure people of color to adapt their habits and culture to match those of White people. As one Black man put it, Whiteness says, "We'll tolerate you as long as you assimilate or play the game."[7] On the flip side, when White people perceive that people of color are gaining power, they can experience what's called *dominant group status threat*, a fear that people perceived to be inferior are doing so well as to threaten the dominant group's status.[8] White status surfaces, for example, when White people

---

[6]Omri Elisha, "Moral Ambitions of Grace: The Paradox of Compassion and Accountability in Evangelical Faith-Based Activism," *Cultural Anthropology*, no. 23 (2008): 179, 178, 155.

[7]In the 1990s, Andrew Hacker, a political science professor, famously stumbled on a quantified value for the value that White people place on Whiteness over Blackness. He asked White undergraduates he was teaching at Queens College in New York how much they would need to be paid to live the next fifty years as a Black person. They settled on $1 million per year, $50 million total. These White students expressed their underlying belief that a White life was easier or more desirable than a Black life. Hacker, *Two Nations: Black and White, Separate, Hostile, Unequal* (Scribner's, 1992), 42.

[8]Diana C. Mutz, "Status Threat, Not Economic Hardship, Explains the 2016 Presidential Vote," *Proceedings of the National Academy of Sciences—PNAS* 115, no. 19 (2018): E4330-39.

express concerns around the Census Bureau prediction that by the year 2042 people of color will outnumber White people in the United States, or evidence that Asian American people are becoming the majority ethnic group in many high-cost suburbs.[9]

People with a conventional hope want the future to follow its present trajectory, but that doesn't mean they will sit by idly when their status is threatened. One example of White people dedicating great effort toward maintaining their supreme status was the series of events that birthed the phrase "great White hope."[10] In the first decade of the twentieth century, a boxer named Jack Johnson had been winning every championship in the segregated heavyweight boxing championships for Black competitors. In 1908, he was allowed to fight against White boxers for the title of world heavyweight champion. He won, and White viewers labeled his victory dubious and offensive. In 1910, the press and other influential figures coaxed a previous world heavyweight champion, a White boxer named James Jeffries, to return from retirement to face up against Johnson in a Fourth of July fight billed as "the fight of the century." Seizing the opportunity to appeal to the racial hatred of the Jim Crow era, the press referred to Jeffries as "The Great White Hope." An editorial in *The New York Times* summed up the conventional hopes of White people: "If the Black man wins, thousands and thousands of his ignorant brothers will misinterpret his victory as justifying claims to much more than mere physical equality with their White neighbors."[11] The fight wasn't even close. Jack Johnson won, knocking Jeffries down twice. Black people across the country celebrated, while White people exploded in

---

[9] Sam Roberts, "Minorities in U.S. Set to Become Majority by 2042," *New York Times*, August 14, 2008, www.nytimes.com/2008/08/14/world/americas/14iht-census.1.15284537.html; Willow S. Lung-Amam, *Trespassers? Asian Americans and the Battle for Suburbia* (University of California Press, 2017).

[10] A movie by that title tells the story, as does Isabel Wilkerson in her book *Caste*. As Wilkerson writes, "The message [of the race riots] was that, even in an arena into which the lowest caste had been permitted, they were to know and remain in their place." Wilkerson, *Caste: The Origins of Our Discontents* (Random House, 2020).

[11] Jeff Nilsson, "A Black Champion's Biggest Fight," *Saturday Evening Post*, July 2, 2020, www.saturdayeveningpost.com/2020/07/a-Black-champions-biggest-fight/.

race riots and attempted lynchings across the country.[12] Conventional White hope was in full effect, and if a boxing match couldn't uphold the conventional racial hierarchy, violence would.

Conventional White hope is founded on a belief that history has been good—at least for White people. It believes that the path from present to hoped-for future will be, for the most part, good, pleasant, and much like today. It has little capacity to cope with the unwelcome or unexpected. It deals with threats to the established racial hierarchy—even a threat so subtle as the mere revealing of that hierarchy's existence—through escapism, denial, or suppression. It has no experience waiting patiently for a better outcome, because good is imagined to be always close at hand. It does not have to stretch to imagine a radically different future. Its imagination grows flabby.

Conventional hope has no interest in God intervening in the race system, nor does it believe in a God who would do such a thing. Theologically, conventional hope imagines a tame God—one who lets time unspool of its own accord. This God is a plasterer who smears spackling here rather than breaking down and rebuilding the existing edifice. This God doesn't interrupt, doesn't smash, doesn't shock. Some would argue that such a god is not God at all, and this hope is not hope at all.[13]

⸻

One word to describe delusional hopes would be *naive*—a mild, innocent word that implies an absence of something, a blank slate, a lack of knowing. There is certainly a lack of knowing to this hope. But it's not just a blank slate. It's a slate that also includes mis-knowing. Delusional hope imagines Whiteness as normal, better, and superior, and projects a

---

[12] Wilkerson, *Caste*, 137-38.
[13] See chapter 13, as well as Jürgen Moltmann, *The Spirit of Hope: Theology for a World in Peril* (Westminster John Knox, 2019); Josef Pieper, *On Hope*, trans. Mary Frances McCarthy (Ignatius, 1986); Miroslav Volf, "Hope Pt. 1, The Thing with Feathers," Yale Center for Faith & Culture, May 9, 2020, https://faith.yale.edu/media/hope-pt-1-the-thing-with-feathers.

future with more of that Whiteness to come, rolling in like a river from beginning to end of time. It discourages people from trying to solve social problems by promising that social problems will swiftly dissolve away of their own accord, and if that doesn't work, by denying that such problems exist at all.

That kind of hope is not benignly delusional. It is acutely damaging. And it deserves a stronger adjective than *naive*. Another fitting description would be *white supremacist*.

If for you the phrase "white supremacist" conjures up a certain kind of hideous bigot doing unspeakable and unimaginable deeds, let me clarify something. Like other social scientists, I use the phrase "white supremacist" to refer to beliefs, practices, or systems that aim to retain the privilege—the supreme place—of White people. White-supremacist behaviors include not just intentional or hate-driven acts but also subtle and unexamined ways people participate in maintaining a racial hierarchy. And that's what delusional hope often does. It aims to keep Whiteness supreme, and often succeeds at that.

White Americans have based their tacit optimistic and conventional hopes on the basis that life has seemed to go well enough for them.[14] This way of hoping ignores the people for whom life has not gone well enough, and the many contributing factors that enrich White people at great cost to other groups: enslavement, indentured servitude, colonization, land theft, military dominance, inheritance laws, and more. White hopes were protected by legal and economic systems that protected their dreams at the expense of other people's hopes. European people didn't just arrive on the land that Indigenous people called Turtle Island armed with guns; they came armed with a narrative of hope. When full-bellied people use that narrative as a bedtime story to pacify those who are hungry, hope can be a dangerous sedative.

---

[14]For additional reflection on the differences between White and Black people's narratives of hope in America, see Angel Adams Parham, "A Tale of Two Stories: Meditations on the American Dream," *Hedgehog Review* 24, no. 1 (2022): 78-83.

People of color have been warning against the dangers of white-supremacist hope for centuries. In 1855, formerly enslaved abolitionist Frederick Douglass wrote that slavery not only imprisons the body; it imprisons the soul by denying the right to hope. "I longed for a future too, with hope in it," Douglass wrote.[15]

Other activists pointed out that White people do more than steal the right to hope; they inflict their own way of hope on people of color like another handout for people who haven't asked for it. One highly effective way to keep people from trying to change a system is to convince them that the system isn't so bad after all, that things will get better if we all patiently carry on with a steady hope. To inflict White American ways of hoping into these situations is like importing a tractor in a rainforest—at best, it simply won't run. At worst, ecological and social destruction will follow. As a Black protagonist discovers in Ralph Ellison's book *The Invisible Man*, Black people are surrounded by people trying to "Hope them to death and keep them running."[16]

Martin Luther King Jr. knew that the struggle over how to hope was central to the struggle against racism. King was no stranger to the causes of despair, and his speeches and sermons are filled with careful explications of a way of hope that is anything but optimistic and conventional. "We must come to see that human progress never rolls in on wheels of inevitability. It comes through the tireless efforts and persistent work of men willing to be co-workers with God, and without this hard work time itself becomes an ally of the forces of social stagnation."[17] He was not just disappointed that White people didn't show up to support Black justice; he was disappointed that they hoped for it with a dangerous passivity.

In the years since, though, King's own words have often been manipulated into a justification for conventional hope. One of his most quoted

---

[15]Frederick Douglass, *My Bondage and My Freedom* (Miller, Orton & Mulligan, 2000), 273, https://docsouth.unc.edu/neh/douglass55/douglass55.html.

[16]Ralph Ellison, *Invisible Man* (Vintage, 1995), 194.

[17]Martin Luther King Jr., "Letter from a Birmingham Jail," African Studies Center—University of Pennsylvania, April 16, 1963, 13, 16, www.africa.upenn.edu/Articles_Gen/Letter_Birmingham.html.

lines is, "We shall overcome because the arc of the moral universe is long, but it bends toward justice," a sentence he adopted from nineteenth-century abolitionist clergyman Theodore Parker.[18] King included the quote in several speeches, and it is engraved on his Washington, DC, memorial. In my interviews, I heard several people quote the phrase. Some used it, as King did, to call for action. But others used it to say that people should sit tight and wait. King went to great effort to fend off that very interpretation.

Barack Obama chose King's "moral arc of the universe" sentence to have embroidered around the edge of a rug in the Oval Office, and he didn't mean it as a justification for passivity. Obama's campaign to become America's first Black president was based largely on the one-word slogan "Hope." Fueled also by his book *The Audacity of Hope*, Obama became a living symbol of a certain way of hoping.[19] Like Martin Luther King Jr., Obama knew that hope was an essential tool to keep chipping away at White supremacy. Like King, Obama also knew that when hope shifts into blind optimism, it can become a weapon wielded for White supremacy. In the preface to his 2020 book *A Promised Land*, written during the first years of Donald Trump's presidency, Obama candidly reflected on hope and racism, questioning whether he had hoped too much, too optimistically, or on the wrong grounding. He mused that perhaps he was "too tempered in speaking the truth as I saw it, . . . convinced as I was that by appealing to what Lincoln called the better angels of our nature I stood a greater chance of leading us in the direction of America as we've been promised. I don't know."[20]

Latino professor of social ethics Miguel De La Torre, in his book *Embracing Hopelessness*, leans still further into concerns about hope.

---

[18]Martin Luther King Jr., "Remaining Awake Through a Great Revolution," sermon, National Cathedral, March 31, 1968, www.youtube.com/watch?v=uFmP3YA3i9g; Theodore Parker, "Justice and the Conscience," in *Ten Sermons of Religion*, 1852, www.fusw.org/uploads/1/3/0/4/13041662/of-justice-and-the-conscience.pdf.
[19]Barack Obama, *The Audacity of Hope: Thoughts on Reclaiming the American Dream* (Crown, 2006).
[20]Barack Obama, *A Promised Land* (Crown, 2020), xv.

Hope that the world will somehow naturally evolve or progress into a safer and more hospitable place for the world's most marginalized, he suggests, may be the most dangerous weapon against them.[21] After reviewing the history of White people using hope to harm people of color, he concludes that Christian hope itself is so tainted by its role in maintaining White supremacy as to become repulsive. "I want nothing to do with Christian hope, the protagonist of too many atrocities conducted in its name," he concludes. "In the midst of unfathomable suffering, the earth's marginalized no longer need pious pontifications about rewards in some hereafter. Nor do they need their oppressors providing the answers for their salvation." According to De La Torre, what is needed is disruption of normalized ways of hoping. Hope, he says, must be learned from the people who have nothing left to lose, for whom work does not set free, for whom there is no such thing as playing it safe.[22] He sides with philosopher Friedrich Nietzsche, who considered hope "the greatest of evils for it lengthens the ordeal of man."[23]

De La Torre makes a compelling case that something needs to change in the white-supremacist patterns of hope, but is hopelessness the only alternative?[24] De La Torre's hopelessness leaves us with the same problem that delusional White hope leaves: Neither presents a valid solution to the problem of evil. What can humans do about the irreparable harms that have been and will continue to be done in the wake of racism? Who could heal such a thing? Optimistic, conventional hope says ignore the

---

[21]Darren Webb similarly recognizes that hope can be put to opposing uses both for resisting and for reinforcing White supremacy in a paper whose title, "Pedagogies of Hope," nods to Paulo Freire's book *Pedagogy of the Oppressed*. See Paulo Freire, *Pedagogy of the Oppressed*, 50th anniversary ed. (Bloomsbury Academic, 2018); Darren Webb, "Pedagogies of Hope," *Studies in Philosophy and Education* 32, no. 4 (2013): 397-414.

[22]Miguel A. De La Torre, *Embracing Hopelessness* (Fortress, 2017), 96-97.

[23]Friedrich Wilhelm Nietzsche, *Human, All Too Human: A Book for Free Spirits*, trans. Alexander Harvey (1878), 102, Project Gutenberg EBook, www.gutenberg.org/files/38145/38145-h/38145-h.htm.

[24]For additional scholarship on Christian hope and racism, see also Matt R. Jantzen, "Neither Ally, nor Accomplice: James Cone and the Theological Ethics of White Conversion," *Journal of the Society of Christian Ethics* 40, no. 2 (2020): 273-90; Vincent Lloyd, "For What Are Whites to Hope?," *Political Theology* 17, no. 2 (2016): 168-81.

harm. Hopelessness says the harm is unmendable. Neither inspires an active pursuit of justice.

In the wake of that lapse, another kind of poisonous hope is different from White delusional hope but equally dangerous. I sat in the living room of Benjamin, a mixed-race Latino and Indigenous man, listening to jazz spinning from his record player as he got up to wash the bottle he had finished giving his infant son. I pressed the soft belly of the eight-pound newborn into my shoulder, waiting for the burp, as we talked about a kind of hopelessness that he'd seen spreading like a virus.

Benjamin had recently attended a breakout session for people of color within a scholarly conference. He sat in the audience listening with a vague sense that something was off in the way the collective energy in the room was heading, when a person of color in the audience posed a question to the presenter: "In this day and age, should I speak out against my relative who is planning to marry a White person? Aren't they denying their own race in that?" Benjamin said in that moment everyone in the room seemed to hold their breath.

As a Brown man of mixed lineage married to a White woman, this question was personal to Benjamin. He and his wife both had careers directly addressing racism. He tried to imagine what would happen if the presenter responded in the way the questioner seemed to expect—yes, you should stop an interracial marriage. That answer would concede that so much harm is being done to Black and Brown people that for a person of color to marry a White person would be detrimental to their own self or their racial group. Benjamin's mind rolled back to all the people through history denied, defamed, or struggling for the right to interracial relationships, and to those who celebrated when the 1967 court case *Loving v. Virginia* guaranteed that right. He thought of his wife, staying at home during that conference to care for this mixed-race child now held in my arms. How had we arrived at a moment when a room full of activist scholars was sincerely questioning whether love was possible between differently racialized people?

Benjamin said he saw people in the room caught in an unmediated spiral of pain. As each told stories of racial pain and acknowledged their sharing of that pain, the pain was multiplying without release. He wondered whether, since George Floyd's death, there had been a speeding up of something that always existed among Black and Brown people—something of a hopelessness that arises when no feasible answers remain. He worried that in the absence of hope and in the presence of a pervasive emotional, spiritual, and psychological unhealth, pain could become a destination and an identity of its own. In that pain, people could forget how to love the other. "If that happens," he said, "we will be fully lost."

The speakers in the breakout room that day responded to the question without condemning interracial relationships. But the question itself left Benjamin unsettled. "I worry about it a lot."

Meanwhile the infant burped, winced, drooped his head into my shoulder, and settled back into sleep.

The people you'll hear from in this book also have a keen sense that something goes wrong with hope, but they're not resorting to hopelessness. They're not giving up on justice, and they're not giving up on love. In the chapters ahead, we'll see what happens when their delusional hopes run dry and how they discover whole new reservoirs of abiding hope.

PART 3

Collisions

FIVE

White Imagination Meets Reality

THE MIDCENTURY RANCHES and split-levels must have been somebody's dream homes when the first owners moved in, but now the neighborhood showed signs of wear. I followed my phone app to the address Jenna provided, past the Boys and Girls Club, past blocks of apartments, along the winding roads of this quasi-suburban neighborhood. A tattered Black Lives Matter sign stood its ground in one yard. Halloween skeletons and cobwebs remained in others from the holiday a few weeks past. I pulled into Jenna's driveway and parked beneath a basketball hoop full of fallen leaves. On the way to the door, I stepped cautiously around colorful popsicle-stick crafts drying on the pavement. "My kids have recently discovered glue guns," Jenna said as she welcomed me inside.

Now her children were at school and her husband at work. Jenna had carved out a couple of hours in her morning before writing a graduate school paper to talk with me. As we sat at her kitchen table cradling large mugs of tea in our palms, she told me she was studying to become a social worker. "I love littles," she said, referring to early childhood clients. "So much brain development happens during that time. I would like to do something with children and families, to prevent trauma from happening instead of just trying to fix broken people." We talked about the Black woman in her church whose work with families had inspired Jenna's career shift. The family cat drifted to sleep on Jenna's lap as she began to trace the life experiences that had brought her to this place—this church, this work, this neighborhood, this path in life.

As with most interviews, I began by asking Jenna to tell stories that would fill in the end of this sentence: "I would not be committed to racial justice in the way that I am today if not for . . ." The first story Jenna told occurred after her first year of college. She attended a weeklong leadership training led by a Christian student organization. Away in an unfamiliar space, feeling curious and brave, she selected a training session titled with an unfamiliar word—*Whiteness*.

"Going into that session, everything that they shared was new information to me," she recalled. "Like I had never heard of White privilege before. I didn't have any friends of color. And I had kind of thought racism was dead. I just didn't really think that it existed anymore." Prior to that session, she imagined the timeline of racism jumping from slavery to Martin Luther King Jr. to a present in which "we're all good," with nothing problematic in between. "I had never even considered my race," she said. "I was like, 'I'm just me. I guess I'm White. Like it's a box I check on forms and stuff.' Race had never been an issue in my life. I'd never had to really think about that."

The session hit Jenna like a wrecking ball. "It just shook me to my core. After that session, I went back to my room and just cried for hours, just kind of processing that my experience in the world was very much not everybody's experience in the world. It feels so ignorant and naive now, but that's where I was coming from. And so that kind of started the trajectory of understanding racism and working towards racial justice."

Jenna was experiencing what I call a *collision*—a moment when the learned White social imagination clashes with reality so forcefully that it prompts a conscious and visceral response.[1] Collisions are one of

---

[1] By implying that a consistent and identifiable reality exists at all, I make a claim that is not uncontested. For readers interested in exploring the degree to which verifiable reality exists and what bearing that question has on racism, I recommend the volume *Race and Epistemologies of Ignorance*, edited by Shannon Sullivan and Nancy Tuana, particularly contributions by Linda Martín Alcoff and Charles Mills. Mills explains that arguments against racism require an

three elements that appeared in the life journeys of nearly every White person selected for this study. Both people of color and White people told stories of collisions shaping their life trajectories. You have likely experienced collisions yourself and witnessed them in others. As we'll see, the ways that people are racialized—assigned to racial groups by their surrounding society—generate different frequencies and interpretations of those collisions. We'll focus on the jarring role that collisions play in prompting White people to question their responsibility in a race-affected world. However, collisions alone are insufficient to produce lasting change. In fact, these unsettling moments can lead to shallow and even harmful responses. If we want to build more resilient hopes and lasting commitment to racial justice, we need to be honest about what collisions can and can't do. In the coming chapters, we'll consider why collisions are essential but insufficient, and what else needs to happen to produce enduring change.

⸻

Once, as I was preparing a presentation for a group, I typed "collision images" into an internet search bar. I discovered a photo that has come to symbolize for me what I mean by collisions. Every time I show this image to an audience, there's a little pause, then a gasp, then an awkward chuckle. At the center of the image sits a car, noticeably smashed. It is lopsided, crumpled, and immobilized. What elicits the laugh is what appears to have caused the collision. On either side of the car are two thick cement walls, angled slightly inward so that they form a narrowing funnel. Through the gap ahead we see a beautiful landscape of mountains,

---

intellectual framework "in which truth, falsity, facts, reality, and so forth are not enclosed with ironic scare quotes. The phrase 'White ignorance' implies the possibility of a contrasting 'knowledge,' a contrast that would be lost if all claims to truth were equally spurious, or just a matter of competing discourses." Sullivan and Tuona write, "Successful analyses of racial and other forms of systemic ignorance must be able to demonstrate alternatives to them and thus cannot afford postmodern refusals of concepts of truth, reason, and reality." Charles W. Mills, "White Ignorance," in *Race and Epistemologies of Ignorance*, ed. Shannon Sullivan and Nancy Tuana (State University of New York Press, 2007), 15; Shannon Sullivan and Nancy Tuana, "Introduction," in Sullivan and Tuana, *Race and Epistemologies*, 4.

trees, and lake. The driver, with eyes on that scenic view, seems to have squelched any doubts about the feasibility of the passage and rammed forward with a determined optimism that the car would fit through the opening. And it almost did. But not quite. And so, here sits the car, wedged between cement walls. No amount of speed, courage, or hope could change the persistent reality that the walls existed in that place and time, and the car would not fit. That driver jolted to an abrupt stop.

This image represents what happens when a person follows a false imagination of reality until they collide with reality itself. Gentle bumping between imagination and reality happens all the time in both welcome and unwelcome ways. We find ourselves interrupted by the surprise reality of an approaching thunderstorm, a medical test result, or a message from a secret admirer. Much of the time, we casually adjust and carry on. But occasionally collisions occur with such force that the pain is so strong, the obstacle so firm, or the confusion so great that we are lurched into entirely new directions. Or a complete stop.

That's what happened to Allan when he paused long enough to drink a Gatorade at the border of his reality. Allan grew up in a White family in an affluent suburb of a large city. People in his community didn't talk much about the neighborhoods that lay just a short walk away. Their silence communicated, even to Allan as a child. Adults used coded words such as *iffy* and *sketchy* to describe the spaces beyond certain corners, as if to soften the prejudiced implications of the words they implied: "dangerous," "poor," and "Black." By the time he reached high school, Allan knew which corners marked the lines between "his" places and "other" people's places. He knew that Black and Latino people lived on the other side of those borders, and he knew their worlds were somehow different in an undesirable and unmentionable way. He knew these things without having to think about them. He could not remember setting foot past those imagined borders.

Allan moved elsewhere for college and, to his surprise, found himself invited to work with a student team tasked with developing an outdoor education center. Working with that team was the first time in his life that he had worked closely with Black, Asian, and Latino people. He didn't have words yet to name what he was learning. Little discoveries kept sneaking into his awareness. The stories these students told about their lives differed from his own, and the differences had a lot to do with the ways the world assigned meanings to race.

When he came back to visit his family one weekend, things felt familiar and yet different in a way he still couldn't name. One night he started walking. He strolled through the familiar streets of his childhood with no destination in mind. The farther he walked, the more a certain niggling curiosity interrupted his thoughts. What lay beyond the borders? Did people beyond those borders have similar stories to the friends of color he was meeting in college? He arrived at a corner that he knew formed a juncture between worlds. No signs marked the boundary, but people around here could tell. He stopped. From that corner he could turn left and enter a Black neighborhood, turn right and enter a Latino neighborhood, or turn back home to his White neighborhood. At the corner sat a gas station.

He stood outside the gas station and said to himself for the first time, "This is constructed. There's a reason why people told me not to cross that line, and there's a reason why these communities are next to each other. I've driven through here, but I've never really interacted." He walked into the gas station between these three neighborhoods and bought a Gatorade. He walked out. He stood sipping his drink, paying attention.

A man standing outside the gas station greeted Allan in Spanish. Allan understood enough to keep the conversation alive, so he returned the greeting. The man said, "Hey, let me tell you about my experience." Allan was pretty sure the man was drunk, but they both stayed put. The man said he had fled Colombia and never managed to get documents, but he made it here, and he was grateful. They talked for what seemed like hours. The Gatorade was empty, and still they talked. The man invited Allan to his apartment. Allan followed him for a visit.

"And then I went back home," Allan recounted with a shrug. Choices opened in his imagination that he hadn't known were choices.

We'll pause Allan's story there before returning to it in a later chapter.

When Allan crossed the border between neighborhoods, what he encountered was not some unprecedented incident occurring for the first time in history. The people he met and their experiences had been there all along. To Allan, what made these discoveries so troubling was not that they were new but that they were *not* new, and yet they were new to him. His imagination of reality had never included this. The cement walls were there. He had not seen. People told him not to think about those walls. Now he had driven straight into the walls.

|||||||||

Imagining is one of the most basic human behaviors. Our bodies have certain ways of perceiving the world, including a neurological system wired to our five senses, but the information we take in does not come close to providing everything we need to know to function. Nor can we make use of all the sensory information bombarding us. To fill in the gaps, we constantly imagine. As I write this, I imagine that the pattern of light sifted through my eyes indicates there is a curtain beside me. My memory of how houses are built indicates that there is a window behind that curtain. I further surmise that the pattern of vibrations in my ear indicates a tapping sound, and I recognize it as rain splashing against that window. I have spent many hours in this chair and heard rain many times, so I am probably right. But I could be wrong. It could be my husband outside spraying the house with a garden hose. It could be a swarm of insects I never knew existed beating their wings against the window. It could be a firefighter plane dumping a load of water on our neighborhood. If I were wrong, I would remember that moment.

So too, we function in daily life not only by imagining our physical settings but by imagining our social settings. We imagine what others will do, will not do, and should be doing. We imagine the reasons they make choices and whether they have choices at all. The cues that train us to imagine our social world come from society itself. We learn not only by observing people's behavior but from a superabundance of meaning-making processes through which we interpret the significance of those behaviors. As anthropologist Clifford Geertz famously wrote, humans are suspended in webs of significance that they themselves have spun.[2] We crave meaning and thus live attuned to symbols, narratives, and discourses that make "ordinary, everyday experience comprehensible."[3] We depend on each other to interpret our life experiences, and we do this whether we choose to or not. Society hands us meaning upon meaning, whether we scroll through social media, chat at a coffee shop, or, in the case Geertz wrote about, place bets on a village cockfight. We have an insatiable and pragmatic desire to find patterns, evaluate, moralize, and figure out how to fit into our social world.

As we imbibe and digest a constant flow of information from our social world, each individual develops what's called a *social imagination*—a way of imagining society. The greatest influence on our own personal social imagination comes through the *social imaginary*, that is, a shared and pervasive framework that the society around us gives us to understand society. Thus our social imagination involves our own cultivation of information, but that cultivation happens as we absorb feedback from the dominant social imaginary surrounding us.

Sociologists, anthropologists, and philosophers have long known that humans go through much of their lives unaware of the untruths about society they soak up from society itself.[4] Indeed, the work of divulging

---

[2]Clifford Geertz, *The Interpretation of Cultures: Selected Essays* (Basic Books, 1973), 5.
[3]Clifford Geertz, "Notes on the Balinese Cockfight," *Daedalus* 101, no. 1 (1972): 23.
[4]Among the many social scientists who have explored this dilemma, Karl Marx in the late nineteenth century used the term "false consciousness" to describe distorted beliefs about social inequalities. In the early twentieth century, Antonio Gramsci expanded on Marx's work, considering how scholars and activists might convince people to question their culturally infused misperceptions of society, which he referred as hegemony. See especially Marx, "The Economic and Philosophic Manuscripts of 1844," in *The Marx-Engels Reader*, 2nd ed., ed. Robert C. Tucker (Norton, 1978), 66-125; Antonio Gramsci, *Gramsci's Prison Letters: Lettere Dal Carcene: A Selection Translated and Introduced by Hamish Henderson* (Zwan, in association with the

inaccurate hegemonic assumptions about society is something of a raison d'être for social science itself.[5]

When groups of people live according to a shared social imaginary, they bring into existence a world that conforms to it. Whether or not a pattern exists, people who believe it exists will make decisions according to that pattern. As sociologists William Isaac Thomas and Dorothy Swaine Thomas wrote in 1928, "If men define situations as real, they are real in their consequences."[6] It takes a lot of work to unlearn a pattern, and even more work to unmake that pattern once it's been built into society. If the social imaginary says, for example, that White people make better lawyers than people of color, everyone living according to that imaginary will make adjustments in their behavior ranging from tiny to egregious. If guidance counselors, college admissions committees, clients, judges, and fellow lawyers all think and act according to that social imaginary, they bring into existence further evidence that seems to confirm the pattern. Social imaginaries have an indomitable ability to become self-fulfilling prophecies.[7]

Because a social imaginary is built out of ideas we catch from each other, whoever has more power to be heard will have greater influence over the social imaginary. And because people with power tend to want to retain their power, social imaginaries often reinforce rather than disrupt power hierarchies. This happens as a default process—it doesn't take ill intent for people to preserve the ways they see the world, their hopes, their dreams, their expectations, by sharing those with others.

Edinburgh Review, 1988); Jean-Paul Sartre, *The Imaginary: A Phenomenological Psychology of the Imagination*, trans. Jonathan Mark Webber (Routledge, 2010); Charles Taylor, *Modern Social Imaginaries* (Duke University Press, 2003).

[5]In the words of anthropologist Signithia Fordham, "My raison d'être as an anthropologist is to analyze (and make visible) cultural patterns in order to render conflict and tensions less problematic and, in the process, to understand and illuminate hidden or masked behaviors and practices." Fordham, *Downed by Friendly Fire: Black Girls, White Girls, and Suburban Schooling* (University of Minnesota Press, 2017), 13.

[6]"Thomas Theorem," *Oxford Reference*, June 14, 2024, www.oxfordreference.com/display/10.1093/oi/authority.20110803104247382.

[7]Robert K. Merton, "The Self-Fulfilling Prophecy," *The Antioch Review* 8, no. 2 (1948): 193–210.

And when some people have more power than others to project their imagination, the social imaginary heads in their direction.

That's what happened as racism took shape in the Western world from the sixteenth century to the present. Humans have been hating, stereotyping, and jostling for control against those they perceive to be "Other" for as long as humans have been human, but racism isn't just your everyday, run-of-the-mill outgroup prejudice. It's a whole system of beliefs and institutions built to reinforce a particular set of ingroup and outgroup relations. That system ranks one group over other groups. Various versions of racism have occurred throughout history, but in the white-supremacist version that suffuses much of the world today, people who identified themselves as White ranked themselves over people they deemed to be Black and various other racial categories. The social imaginary that upholds the system imagines those racial groups to be based on essential human differences in biology, genetics, morality, culture, and aptitude. The race system not only places Whiteness as the superior racial category; it ranks all individuals and groups on a hierarchy from Blackness to Whiteness. Along that continuum the race system deems some groups, such as Asian Americans, to be "model minorities," admirable and acceptable so long as they don't surpass White levels of success. Model-minority beliefs disguise the discrimination against Asian Americans and the diversity of experiences within that vast label. Meanwhile, the race hierarchy creates conditions that pit non-White racial groups against each other in struggles for job opportunities, immigration rights, and other opportunities to move up the hierarchy.[8]

---

[8]Throughout history, the shifting ways in which minoritized groups become pitted against each other have reflected the economic priorities of White landowners, employers, and workers. As just two of many examples, early White colonizers compared the supposed cultural aptitudes for grueling labor across Indigenous North American and African ethnic groups, while similar comparisons often play out today between Black and Latin American workers in the United States. Franco Barchiesi, *Precarious Liberation: Workers, the State, and Contested Social Citizenship in Postapartheid South Africa* (University of KwaZulu-Natal Press, 2011); James Edward Ford III, "On Blackness and 'The Gift,'" Gift of Black Folk Panel, September 17, 2024, Baylor University, Waco, TX; Ruth Gomberg-Muñoz, *Labor and Legality: An Ethnography of a Mexican Immigrant Network* (Oxford University Press, 2011); Christine Jeske, *The Laziness Myth:*

The system did not emerge accidentally. It came about at a particular time and place because it benefited people of certain European descents. During the seventeenth and eighteenth centuries, Europeans accrued the military might, excess capital, and technological developments enabling them to forcefully and systematically steal from, kill, and exile Indigenous inhabitants in an expanding portion of the world. That abundance of stolen land would be profitable to the extent that it could be cultivated, which required a cheap and controllable source of labor. Chattel slavery and indentured servitude of peoples from the Americas, Asia, and especially Africa provided the cheap labor to expand European profits, largely through nonessential goods such as sugar, coffee, and tobacco for European consumption. The United States government ratified and crystalized race hierarchy through laws and court cases, including the Fugitive Slave Act of 1793, the Indian Removal Act of 1830, the Anti-Vagrancy Act of 1855, the Anti-Coolie Act of 1862, the Dawes General Allotment Act of 1887, *Plessy v. Ferguson* in 1896, the Immigration Act of 1924, the Japanese American Internment Executive Order of 1942, and innumerable Jim Crow laws designed to segregate and disenfranchise non-White people. Redlining, sundown-town terrorism, and local tax models shaped housing, education, and employment patterns, which in turn shaped generational income patterns. Written into these structural systems are feedback loops that become self-perpetuating. Just as a system of roads, once built, will continue to shape future developments and beliefs about normalcy for as long as no one actively destroys the road, the system of racism will influence the built environment and culture in perpetuity unless it is actively dismantled.

From the start, Europeans needed not only money and military to set the race system in motion; they also needed a system of ideas to justify it. In other words, they needed a social imaginary to uphold the race

---

And Other Narratives of Work and a Good Life (Cornell University Press, 2022); Gerald M. Sider, *Lumbee Indian Histories: Race, Ethnicity and Indian Identity in the Southern United States* (Cambridge University Press, 1993).

system as normal and appropriate. The social imaginary that has maintained the race system is called the *White imaginary* because it was designed by White people to benefit White people, and because it perpetuates ideas about what this category of "Whiteness" means in society. For more than three centuries, nearly all the world has been influenced by that White imaginary, even beyond communities where White people live.

Because Christianity was the dominant and default religion of Europeans during the centuries when racism was taking shape, Christianity offered building blocks in the edifice of the White imaginary. And that White imaginary in turn infiltrated Christianity itself in ways that many Christians absorb unconsciously.[9] As Jemar Tisby writes, "From the beginning of American colonization, Europeans crafted a Christianity that would allow them to spread their faith without confronting the exploitative economic system of slavery and the emerging social inequality based on color."[10]

For White people, most of the time the White imaginary—that social imaginary brought into being mostly by and for White people—conforms to their own experience in society. It's made to do so. The White imaginary can feel to them like an accurate fit for the signals they receive from people around them. Most days they don't have to question whether the White imaginary describes the social world as it is or should be. In Allan's case, words for racial groups were hardly spoken, but he picked up a White imaginary through the patterns of places his family did not enter, appearances of people in those spaces, and descriptors such as *iffy* attached to places and people. And as far as he could tell as a child, that social imaginary worked fine. Meanwhile, for people of color in the adjacent neighborhoods, it certainly didn't work.

---

[9]See, for example, Willie James Jennings, *After Whiteness: An Education in Belonging*, Theological Education Between the Times (Eerdmans, 2020); Jennings, *The Christian Imagination* (Yale University Press, 2010).

[10]Jemar Tisby and Lecrae Moore, *The Color of Compromise: The Truth About the American Church's Complicity in Racism* (Zondervan, 2019), 39.

The White imaginary comes about because White people have for centuries had power to dominate the discourse about the social world. They speak and act that imaginary into being, and for the most part, they believe it. But they are not the only ones who can adopt that social imaginary. No one is immune from picking up information about the racial imaginary, including people of color. The difference is this: For most people of color, the White imaginary conflicts with their lived reality on a nearly constant basis.

In the stories I heard from people of color, memorable collisions tended to happen earlier in life than for White people. During collisions, they often had close friends and relatives prepared to help make sense of what happened. By adulthood, they had grown highly cognizant of the differences between the social imaginary perpetuated by White people and an alternative social imaginary that more accurately described their own racialized experiences. W. E. B. Du Bois calls this clashing of messages experienced by Black people *Black double consciousness*: "It is a peculiar sensation, this double-consciousness, this sense of always looking at one's self through the eyes of others. . . . One ever feels his two-ness . . . an American, a Negro; two souls, two thoughts, two unreconciled strivings, two warring ideals in one dark body, whose dogged strength alone keeps it from being torn asunder."[11] Double consciousness is not only a Black phenomenon but an experience of many people of color.[12]

When I spoke with people of color about experiences that led to their own involvement in racial justice efforts, they described collisions of double consciousness that were painful, personal, and frequent. When I asked one Black woman to respond to the prompt, "I wouldn't be committed to racial justice if not for . . . ," she responded immediately, "I was born." Others responded with phrases such as, "too many to count,"

---

[11]W. E. B. Du Bois, *The Souls of Black Folks* (Dover Publications, 2016), 2.
[12]See for example, Vinay Harpalani, "Racial Triangulation, Interest-Convergence, and the Double-Consciousness of Asian Americans," SSRN Scholarly Paper, March 17, 2021, https://doi.org/10.2139/ssrn.3806339.

"where to begin," or "How much time do you have?" They had spent their lives consciously developing an imaginary of race because the dominant social imaginary included messages that did not match their daily lived experiences. When they heard messages like those Jenna or Allan grew up hearing—that racism ended with the Civil War, and people in non-White neighborhoods were distasteful—those messages clearly did not match their own lived experiences.

As I was writing this chapter, I attended a talk by theologian Matthew D. Kim, author of several books about race and Christian faith. He told the audience a story from his childhood in which he encountered the White imaginary. As a child in a White Midwestern neighborhood, he recalled, "I always thought I was White." Then one memorable day, his father stood beside him at a mirror and said, "Look at yourself. What do you see?" Matthew stared wordlessly at his boyish reflection. His father continued. "To the dominant culture, you're Korean, and you will always be Korean. Not American." Matthew's father trained him that day to recognize a White imaginary that treats "Asian" as perpetually foreign, regardless of how many generations pass since emigration. Like many Asian Americans, Matthew's experience navigating this exclusionary White imaginary was complicated by also feeling shut out from Korean nationality, language, and culture. He grew up hearing messages of insufficiency and unbelonging from two directions, telling him that he was neither Korean nor American enough. In his book *Finding Our Voice*, Kim reflects on this formative story, saying it took years to understand how instead as a Korean American he could "celebrate our hybrid, hyphenated, both/and, bicultural, liminal, or perhaps even third-culture self-confidence—a distinct voice and experience reserved by God just for people like me and perhaps you."[13]

Matthew didn't just learn from his father at the mirror one difference between the White imaginary and his reality; he learned that collisions

---

[13]Matthew D. Kim and Daniel L. Wong, *Finding Our Voice: A Vision for Asian North American Preaching* (Lexham, 2020), 10.

would repeat throughout his life. He learned to recognize differences between the safe space of mutual understanding in his own home versus the questionable dominant world outside. Like many Black children who receive "the talk"—an older adult's counsel on how to behave in potentially life-threatening race-inflected situations—Matthew learned that cognizance of race would be for him a matter of sanity, safety, and survival. For people of color, collisions between the White imaginary and reality tend to powerfully shape their life course from a young age because they are frequent and personally consequential.

For people of color, collision memories are characterized by *constancy*. In contrast, White collisions are marked by *rarity*. Both bring their own forms of cognitive force. As I tabulated interviews for this research, I looked for evidence not only of what types of experiences occurred but also evidence of *why* people had come to see those experiences as formative. In the case of collisions, I believe that rarity is part of what makes them powerful pivot points for White people. Often when White people described collisions, they expressed shock not because the incident happened but because they had lived so long without knowing such incidents happened regularly. When Jenna returned to her room after the talk about Whiteness, she cried not only because she saw that racism was real but because she hadn't seen it sooner.

The White imaginary does not accurately describe reality. This leads to a backward situation in which the very process of learning about society can inadvertently increase people's ignorance. Scholars call this an *epistemology of ignorance*—an inverted system of knowing that directs people away from truth and toward ignorance, through both willful and structured processes. White epistemology of ignorance produces "the ironic outcome that Whites will in general be unable to understand the world they themselves have made."[14] As philosopher Marilyn Frye writes,

---

[14]Charles Mills, *The Racial Contract* (Cornell University Press, 1997), 18. Mills also writes even more strongly, "Imagine an ignorance that fights back. Imagine an ignorance militant, aggressive, not to be intimidated, an ignorance that is active, dynamic, that refuses to go quietly—not

> Ignorance is not something simple: it is not a simple lack, absence or emptiness, and it is not a passive state. Ignorance of this sort—the determined ignorance most white Americans have of American Indian tribes and clans, the ostrichlike ignorance most white Americans have of the histories of Asian peoples in this country, the impoverished ignorance most white Americans have of black language—ignorance of these sorts is a complex result of many acts and many negligences.[15]

Because the White imaginary trains White people to believe they are genuinely seeking truth even as they absorb ignorance, a simple desire to learn is not enough to turn White people toward racial justice.

That's where collisions come in. Collisions are the outside impetus that kicks people into reexamining truth. Each collision I heard people describe was transformative because it was *nonagentic*—that is, it happened *to* a person, not by the choice of that person. In the grammar of the moment, the White individual became the object of the verb, not the subject. Collisions force a White person to become a respondent acted on by the world rather than an actor creating a world conformed to their wishes. Notice that through most of Allan's account, he didn't yet expect or desire to become a person who would care about racial justice. He made a few intentional choices along the way—accepting an invitation to join a club and taking a walk to the neighborhood border—and he came with some degree of curiosity, but he didn't know where those choices would lead. People often think of their own collision stories in passive voice. Allan *was invited* to join the multiracial working group in college. Allan *was greeted* by the Colombian man. Jenna *was invited* to attend a retreat. She *was shaken* by what she heard. They did not choose this, didn't want it, and wouldn't know how to find it if they had.

---

at all confined to the illiterate and uneducated but propagated at the highest levels of the land, indeed presenting itself unblushingly as knowledge" (13).

[15]Marilyn Frye, "In and Out of Harm's Way: Arrogance and Love," in *The Politics of Reality: Essays in Feminist Theory* (Crossing, 1983), 118.

This way of experiencing the world as a nonactor defies deep assumptions and can be profoundly uncomfortable. Children learn in grammar classes not to use passive voice. They learn that a story without a protagonist actively advancing the plot is a boring story. So too, the White imaginary trains White individuals to believe that above all else, they must have agency in the world. More agency is always better. They hear slogans such as "you can make it if you try," "the world is your oyster," and "hard work pays off." If you have the will to solve a problem, you can solve it.

Racial justice trainings can inadvertently reinforce the message that agency is the greatest asset of White individuals. I attended trainings that urged White people to take a stand, do something, change something. At the end of one interview with one racial justice educator, I asked what she would most like me to include in this book. "Don't let it be just a book that you read," she said. "Make it a call to do." I loved that advice, and true to her request, you will find in this book many ways to take action against racism. But in certain contexts, emphasis on immediate action can reinforce rather than unsettle the White imaginary. When I traced back through life stories from interviews, I realized that White people I spoke with spent a lot of time in nonaction. They needed to learn how to be acted on. In collisions, they were jolted out of their familiar position of control. Within a new nonagentic position in the social world, they were becoming accompanists rather than commanders.

Is it then up to people of color to be the agents who change White people? Both people of color and White people I met wrestled with how to transform White people without further encumbering people of color. Too often, organizations expect people of color to carry the burdensome, unremunerated, and at times painful work of educating White people about racism. In that work, people of color may face the manipulative responses of White people, or unearth traumas of prior experiences that then become an object of display for someone else's gain. White people too often reinterpret stories about resilience to manufacture evidence that racism is not so bad after all. When people of color call out racism, they face the risks of being questioned, disbelieved, or punished for their honesty. The title of Black British author Reni Eddo-Lodge's book powerfully conveys the decision many people of color make when asked to take responsibility for White people's transformation: *Why I'm No Longer Talking to White People About Race*.

In some collision stories, people of color paid these sorts of costs. Often the White person would not recognize that cost until years later, if ever. However, the roles individuals of color played in White people's collisions ranged everywhere on a spectrum from acutely hurtful to imperceptible. Some collisions happened when White people were distant observers, such as attending a class or watching the news. At other times they interacted directly with people of color. Allan said later about his encounter with the Colombian man he met at the gas station and his neighbors, "They didn't have to entertain me. But they did." One part of his response, which we'll return to later in the book, involved gratitude: "I have always been really thankful for that."

It's important to keep in mind, however, that collisions do not necessarily involve a decisive action by a person of color, either. Much of the time, individual social imaginations change without anyone making an active choice. Change does not happen simply through isolated acts of education. Each of our lives is the result of countless chains of cause and effect.

The social imaginary can be compared to a glacier on which you have set up a little home to live. From your vantage on the glacier, the motion is scarcely discernible, and yet everything you feel and see depends on that ice flow. Glaciers follow ruts traced through decades and centuries. They carve paths as they go, forming the grooves where future glaciers will slide. No single person chipping away with a pickaxe or blasting a blowtorch will make much difference to a glacier. And yet, the path of a glacier does change. Usually it happens imperceptibly, through the buildup of a multitude of tiny snowflakes, the innumerable bumps in the terrain, and the thawing and freezing of season after season. Only occasionally does a glacier move suddenly and dramatically. A crack opens up. Your house jolts violently. Perhaps a wall crumbles. If you wait long enough where a glacier meets an ocean, you might witness a calving—a giant ice block crashing into the sea with a force that can rock boats for miles around.

Likewise, sometimes people can make choices to place White people in contexts where collisions are more likely, such as intercultural settings. The social imaginary is not made of inert ice and rock but of human practices and beliefs, which means we each not only ride the glacier but also constitute it. The glacier path is redirected by major social events such as pandemics and assassinations as well as subtler shifts such as introducing new elementary school history books. But at an individual level, much of our life course depends on that glacier. Most collision stories I heard occurred without anybody orchestrating them. The social world was doing its thing. An individual was doing their thing according to their White imagination. Then crash.

||||||||

On a warm summer afternoon, I sat across from Dennis in his office. More than most people, Dennis had spent a lot of effort tracing the causes of his commitment to racial justice, but those causes still remained elusive to him. Before our first meeting, Dennis chose to send me a document he had written about the key events of his journey. When we met, he walked me through a timeline of collision-type events throughout his youth and early career. The first story happened when he was a teenager, staying for one week with a Black family in Chicago as part of a program designed to educate youth about racism. His hosts were the first Black people he had significantly interacted with, and, looking back, he could see his naiveté. One evening, neighbors visited, and the conversation shifted in a direction Dennis didn't choose.

"We're all sitting around having a beer together," he recalled, "and they talked about what it was like to be Black and what it was like to be dealing with White people. And it was really uncomfortable. Like, whoa. And they said, 'This is not personal with you.' But it sure felt personal."

That was the first of several collision stories Dennis told. He found himself in a conversation outside the African American History and Culture Museum in Washington, DC, with a woman personally affected by the Tulsa race massacre. Another time he witnessed a Black coworker's response at the moment she learned O. J. Simpson was acquitted. He had never heard of the Tulsa race massacre and hadn't understood why O. J. Simpson's trial mattered to Black Americans. "All of a sudden it became very personal," he said. "It was just like, *this is real.*"

I asked Dennis what led him to sign up for the Chicago program, and his face took on a wistful expression. "Why did I go in the first place? I wish I knew." He paused but couldn't find an answer. "I've tried to dig back into how this all happened. I don't know." He became stuck on this question, telling me about unsuccessful efforts he had made to dig back through records of events in his life, trying to understand the causes of his life course. Perhaps the inscrutability of causality was what made these memories so poignant for Dennis—he had not asked for them. They were not his own accomplishment. They were the beginning of a strange and painful kind of gift.

Like most people I talked with, Dennis experienced many collisions across his lifetime. The White imaginary is multifaceted, and so are collisions. In the next two chapters, we'll look at four types of collisions. None of these is sufficient on its own to compel people into lasting commitment to racial justice—there are two more elements in the journey yet to go. But each type of collision can carve away chunks from the glacier of the White imaginary.

SIX

Colliding with Ranking and Invisibility

PEGGY AND EARL GREW UP in southern Georgia at a time when most White people weren't talking about segregation as a thing that should end. Most weren't talking about segregation at all. They were busy benefiting from it.

"I grew up in the most racially charged environment you can imagine," Earl said. "It was totally racially segregated. The population of this little Southern town was 10 percent Black. I went to the White school. It was small, but all twelve grades. It was a good school. There was another school, a Black school. It was one room, unpainted, basically a shack. Just grades one through seven. If you wanted to go above seventh grade, you had to get a bus and go to the next county. And I saw nothing wrong on any of that at the time." Earl was young when the *Brown v. Board of Education* court case outlawed segregated education. "Both my parents were schoolteachers. It was unimaginable that we can go to school with Black kids. It was unthinkable that this could happen to us. It was just normal. The normal way of life."

His wife, Peggy, also grew up in the South. Her earliest memory of paying attention to race happened when she was about eight years old. Every day she would ride the city bus through the city where she lived on the way to school. One day as she was sitting with two friends, the bus approached a stop. Through the window, Peggy could see a Black woman standing at the bus stop, dressed neatly and, as far as Peggy could tell, on her way to work. The bus approached. The driver turned and saw the Black woman, then accelerated, leaving the woman behind.

"I was really distressed," Peggy recalled. "I said to my two friends, 'That was really bad. The bus didn't stop for that Black lady.'" Instead of sharing her concern, the friends scolded Peggy, "You never call a Black person a lady."

"At that point something clicked. It doesn't mean I became passionate. But there was an awareness beginning."

Peggy and Earl pointed out that these sorts of stories from Georgia in the 1950s were the sort that Northerners and White young people today use to distance themselves from the supposed bygone days and far-off places of racial terror. But the lesson Peggy and Earl learned in the intense segregation of the mid-twentieth century South were the same lesson I heard people describe encountering in their own ways through decade after decade: that racist societies subtly and unavoidably rank human beings on a scale from White to Black, on which White equals good and Black equals bad.

In the previous chapter, we saw that collisions matter. They happen to people without their choosing, causing confrontations with realities that do not conform to the White imaginary. In those moments, an unanticipated reality becomes vividly *real*, and in the jarring intractability of that reality, some fragment of lie falls away from the White imaginary. In this chapter and the next, we'll consider what exactly White people collide with—what unrealities does the White imaginary present? We'll look at four premises of the White imaginary that conflict with reality. Each White person I interviewed told some story of a collision, but they did not necessarily bring up collisions with each of the four premises. As we'll see in later chapters, White people learned about these aspects of the White imaginary not only from collisions but also in more gradual and intentional ways.

In this chapter we'll consider two lies of the White imaginary: the ranking system of race and the invisibility cloak of Whiteness. The following chapter will introduce two more types of collisions. But let's start with that image of humanity that justified building separate schools for White kids and Black kids, or leaving a Black woman behind at a bus stop. It's an image on which race is founded, and one that remains irrevocably seared into the social imaginary to this day, even as it hides in plain sight.

COLLIDING WITH RANKING

When I teach about racism in my classes, I show images from eighteenth- and nineteenth-century books and posters aiming to map out the categories of human races. Some trace out four categories, others nine, twelve or more. Some point to distinctive bodily features—lip size, hair texture—while others attempt to correlate humans with the mammals and birds living in continents and geographic regions. We learn about Carolus Linnaeus, the influential Swedish biologist whose *Systema Naturae* in 1735 introduced the binomial taxonomy system still used today for sorting kingdoms, phyla, class, and further subcategories of plants and animals. In the same text, he included a taxonomic ordering of the human species into four "varieties." He matched each group to a continent and categorized each according to hair type and skin type, and also a corresponding temperament ranging from the "crafty, lazy, and careless" African to the "acute and adventurous" European. Forty years later, German naturalist Johann Friedrich Blumenbach published a similar taxonomy attempting to match his own five varieties of humankind to skull anatomy and skin pigment. By the late nineteenth century, social scientists in the newly forming discipline of anthropology had absorbed a theory of humanity called unilinear evolutionism. Their aim was to sort humanity into the order they believed to be a single evolutionary line from "savage" to "barbarian" to "civilized." Enthralled with the idea of ordering existing cultures on a scale from lesser to more evolved, they began traveling the world to gather artifacts, skulls, and bones, often from recently deceased people. Their civilized category, unsurprisingly, bore an undisguised resemblance to the people who wrote the theory.

Students express horror at the blatancy of racism in these centuries-old records. Heads shake. Eyes stare mournfully. Brows furrow. "That is so racist," they say. The horror is palpable. Stories like these can become pat-yourself-on-the-back excuses to shift the blame to somebody else. "Clearly, we're nowhere near that bad now." I then ask students to talk about where they've seen human beings ranked by racial hierarchies today. Without fail, their stories pour out. The mission trips and development projects designed to tell "poor Brown people" how to solve their problems like White people do. The debates over welfare systems that hinge on the question of whether "some people" are too lazy or ungrateful to deserve welfare. The everyday discrimination built on assumptions that White people are better qualified. Do we still learn to rank human beings according to racial systems from Black to White, inferior to superior? Oh yes, we do. A few categories across that hierarchy have shifted (Jewish and Eastern European people becoming absorbed into the category of White, for example), but the ordering of the system has remained largely unmodified. What has changed are the techniques that White people use to hide that system, even from themselves.

One basic function of the White imaginary is to teach a standard for classifying and ranking bodies along a spectrum from Black to White. At the same time, it ranks everything associated with those bodies. In other words, the White imagery teaches us to racialize—to sort according to racial categories. This process is utterly absurd, and yet it remains so infused in socialization processes from childhood to adulthood that people rarely have any awareness of learning it at all, any more than people remember learning to distinguish left from right, up from down. White people rarely have to snap into conscious awareness of how that classification works and what it does. Until they do.

Around the time in her life when Hannah put on the blackface Halloween costume described in chapter one, she experienced a collision moment. She stumbled on that hierarchical human-sorting system of race, lurking in her own subconscious.

Hannah was studying linguistics in graduate school. One afternoon she sat in her usual seat in the lecture hall, listening to what she thought would be another ordinary lecture. Midway through the lecture the professor wrote the word *ask* on the board and asked the class, "How many of you are bothered when people pronounce this word 'aks'?" Hannah raised her hand. Looking around, she saw most students in the room raising hands. Then the professor explained that this phenomenon of reversing the order of sounds like *k* and *s* in a word is a natural and common linguistic practice called metathesis. Hannah thought to herself, "Metathesis is a fancy word but it doesn't legitimize mispronunciation." As a future teacher, Hannah planned to correct mistakes like that.

But the professor's next move was stunning. She wrote another word on the board and asked everyone to read it in unison. *Bird*, Hannah read along with her hundred classmates. Then the professor asked if anyone could guess what the word's original pronunciation was in Old English. After a pause, the professor answered, "Brid."

Hannah recalled, "I will never, ever forget the slow roll of humiliation I felt when I silently connected the dots." Metathesis happened in her own language. It wasn't a sign of a lack of intelligence or failed language learning. It was just another way language could happen to develop in a group of language speakers. She learned that the pronunciation "aks," along with patterns such as dropping certain final consonants and removing present-tense "be" verbs, is part of a speech pattern that is the primary language of many Black Americans.[1] Until the 1970s, linguists referred to the speech pattern as "Nonstandard Negro English." Even after

---

[1] Before becoming associated with African American English in the nineteenth century, *aks* was widely used by speakers of all races across the US. The pronunciation has roots in Old English and Germanic languages over a millennium old. In 1535, the first Bible written in English worded Matthew 7:7 as, "Axe and it shall be given you." Amanda Cole, Ella Jeffries, and Peter Patrick, "Ask or Aks? How Linguistic Prejudice Perpetuates Inequality," University of Essex Blogs, March 11, 2022, www.essex.ac.uk/blog/posts/2022/03/11/how-linguistic-prejudice-perpetuates-inequality.

a group of Black scholars in the 1970s proposed renaming the speech pattern "Ebonics," it was largely treated as a failure to learn "correct" grammar.[2] But by the mid-1990s—around the time Hannah attended graduate school—linguists were drawing on a wide body of evidence to argue that Ebonics—also called African American Vernacular English and Black Vernacular English—follows grammatical rules that are as systematic as standard English or any language. Ebonics is no more or less "correct" or "grammatical" as a language. As Hannah stared at the words *bird* and *brid* on the board, she realized she had believed Black people spoke an inferior language because they somehow could not or would not learn "normal" grammar. She told me, "I burned with shame and cried quietly in my seat. I didn't talk to anyone about it at the time. I don't think I told anyone for about ten years." The collision took her completely by surprise. She had not signed up for a class on racial justice, and here she was smashing into a White imaginary where she had least expected it.

Hannah had stumbled into one of the myriad ways in which the White imaginary trains people to see Blackness and Whiteness as opposite ends of a spectrum from bad to good. As philosopher George Yancy writes, "Whiteness sets itself up as the thesis. Blackness, within the dialectical logic of Whiteness, must be the antithesis."[3] Whiteness has correct grammar, Blackness has incorrect grammar. Whiteness is smart, Blackness is dumb. Whiteness is safe and acceptable, Blackness is dangerous and deviant. Written into the meaning-making processes of these categories is an insistence that the two are distinct, and Whiteness is the superior. And yet, as Hannah discovered with the single word *bird*, reality is otherwise.

▌▌▌▌▌▌▌▌

---

[2] See John R. Rickford, "What Is Ebonics (African American English)?," November 2019, https://pressbooks.ulib.csuohio.edu/understanding-literacy-in-our-lives/chapter/5-3-3-the-superficial-and-deep-ebonics-communication-and-perception-research-essay/.
[3] George Yancy, ed., "Introduction: Fragments of a Social Ontology of Whiteness," in *What White Looks Like: African-American Philosophers on the Whiteness Question* (Routledge, 2004), 9.

Even as many early anthropologists were building the racist theory of unilinear evolutionism, a handful of social scientists were hard at work disproving the theory. In the late nineteenth century, a Haitian scholar named Anténor Firmin was invited to attend a gathering of French anthropologists. At the meetings, he seethed as he realized they were spending their energy trying to compile evidence that Black people like himself were inherently inferior. He went on to spend years learning the principles of this newly blossoming field called anthropology in order to debunk the unilinear evolutionary model. Using the very tools of those French anthropologists, he wrote a carefully researched anthropological tome arguing, as its title states, for *The Equality of the Human Races*. French speakers systematically ignored his book, and English speakers left it untranslated for nearly a century. Likewise, Black scholars including Frederick Douglass and sociologist W. E. B. Du Bois in the United States churned out scholarship exposing flaws in the racial system. Each was received with a shifting mixture of curiosity, criticism, and silence from many White scholars in their lifetimes.

A handful of non-Black anthropologists began joining in the work of debunking unilinear evolutionism and its racist paradigm in the early twentieth century. Franz Boas, born to a Jewish family in Germany, spent months learning the language and customs of Inuit people in the Canadian Arctic. In that setting, the complexity and ingenuity of their ways of life stunned him into a career of dismantling the hierarchical view of humanity. He advocated a new approach to studying human difference, which he called cultural relativism—understanding people from within their own cultural setting without judging according to an outsider perspective. He went on to spend much of his long career attempting to reorient anthropology toward recognizing the equality of all people. Unexamined prejudices would continue to seep into his work, but he set a disciplinary precedent of deconstructing racism using cultural and biological evidence, and of collaborating with and training

Black, Indigenous, and female scholars, including Zora Neale Hurston and Ella Cara Deloria.

By the civil rights era, anthropologists and sociologists had spent decades proving that "races" are arbitrary groupings of human beings, with no basis in finite genetic delineations or inherent traits such as intelligence or docility.[4] By the decades following the civil rights movement, most White Americans knew that it was incorrect—or at least impolite—to refer to non-White people as inherently inferior. And so today, many White people can recognize such race-based bodily classification schemas—called biological racism—as false. Nobody is setting up a fair or a museum exhibit to teach the public that White bodies are born inherently superior to bodies of people in other races. Having learned to scoff at the claims of biological racism, most Americans believe that they and the people around them are no longer racist.

But a problem remains. At the same time, people can see the remaining differences among racial groups. They read statistics showing, for example, that Black people are more likely to experience poverty, Latino people are more likely to work in low-paying manual labor, or Indigenous people are more likely to have poor health outcomes. This presents a dilemma to the White imaginary. How could these differences remain if racial groups are not born inherently different in capability?

To be clear, decades of research demonstrates that racialized differences in income, test scores, and other life outcomes stem from cumulative effects of historic and ongoing racism. Non-White people are more

---

[4]While traits commonly associated with race such as skin tone and eye shape are passed down genetically, race itself is not a meaningful genetic category. Genetic trends across populations are clinal—that is, gradual, without meaningful breaking points that could suggest sharply drawn categories such as Black and White. Further, the traits that catch the attention of observers depend on the socialization of observers. Two people who are racialized as belonging to a common race by those around them do not necessarily have any more in common genetically than each would with another person who is racialized differently—indeed, their own parents or siblings could be racialized as belonging to another race. Nor are any racial groupings more or less "evolved." Genetic lines continue evolving at the same rate. Adaptations such as light and dark skin arise in response to climatic conditions, and each has spontaneously developed at multiple times and places in the span of human history.

likely to live in neighborhoods with inadequately funded schools and stagnant property values, and less likely to be selected for advanced-placement courses, job interviews, and promotions. Rather than receiving inherited wealth to invest for retirement, their early-career income often goes toward financially supporting family. Meanwhile daily microaggressions have measurable effects on their emotional and physical well-being.[5]

But the flawed post–civil rights White imaginary offers another explanation: There must be something inferior about the *culture* of non-White people. Knowing that biological racism is wrong while simultaneously recognizing that ongoing racial inequalities exist, many people embrace a culture-based explanation of racial inequality, called *cultural racism*. Alternatively, they dismiss racial phenomena as a temporary lingering effect of past racism or as a normal outcome of meritocracy.[6] Through tacit dismissals and cultural racism, racism hasn't ended; it has just gone incognito. Among Christians, cultural racism can lead to trying to solve racism by converting people of color to Christianity or training them in what White people believe to be Christian culture. The focus becomes supplying people of color with good Christian mentors who are either White or blending in with White culture. Through the 1970s and 80s, colorblindness became the dominant mode in which White people—especially White Christians—engaged with people of color. The habit of racializing others and ranking others did not go away; it just burrowed into the realm of things polite people weren't supposed to talk about. Thus the White imaginary today tends to deny that racialized bodies should be ranked, even as it continues to subtly rank everything

---

[5]For more on these topics, see, for example, Clarence C. Gravlee, "How Race Becomes Biology: Embodiment of Social Inequality," *American Journal of Physical Anthropology* 139, no. 1 (2009): 47-57; Devah Pager, *Marked: Race, Crime, and Finding Work in an Era of Mass Incarceration* (University of Chicago Press, 2007); Derald Wing Sue et al., "Racial Microaggressions in Everyday Life: Implications for Clinical Practice," *American Psychologist* 62, no. 4 (2007): 271-86; William Julius Wilson, *More Than Just Race: Being Black and Poor in the Inner City* (Norton, 2009).
[6]Eduardo Bonilla-Silva, *Racism Without Racists: Color-Blind Racism and the Persistence of Racial Inequality in America*, 3rd ed. (Rowman & Littlefield, 2009).

associated with those bodies according to the same hierarchy. Opportunities to collide with that system of ranking still abound. As do opportunities to collide with the next false belief of the White imaginary—the colorblind lie.

COLLIDING WITH INVISIBILITY

Bill, a White man in his late fifties, spent much of his adult life in predominantly Black spaces. He had worked for a predominantly Black church, taught high school students at risk of dropping out, married a woman of color, and raised their multiracial children. Like Allan, he could clearly recall the day he crossed a racialized boundary. There he collided with the lesson that race was kept strictly invisible and silenced, even as it determined the confines of his existence.

Bill attended elementary school in the early seventies in what he called "a border neighborhood," where both White and Black kids attended. When he was seven years old, Bill became close friends with a Black classmate named Ivan. One day Ivan invited Bill to play at his house. Ivan's house was "on the east side, which was crossing the border." The two second graders walked in the door of Ivan's house, cheerfully hatching plans to play football and do whatever second graders do for fun. But Ivan's mom took one look at Bill and asked him sternly, "What are you doing over here? Does your mom know you're here?" Bill shook his head. In his family he was expected to come straight home after school, but he knew there was some leeway in that rule—he'd played with other neighbors after school before. But something was different this time—something he didn't understand. Ivan's mom called Bill's mom, and she immediately came over to take Bill home. On the way home, she scolded him, "Don't do that. Come straight home from school. You can't just go over to his house." Bill could tell she was alarmed, but she said nothing about race.

Only looking back years later did he figure out this was a racially charged incident. He hadn't just crossed a border; he had crossed a racial border. He had entered a space that adults considered different somehow, and different in a bad way. It wasn't long before Bill started noticing clues that things were going wrong on this other side of the border. "Where there should be grass," he remembered seeing, "it was all dirt and broken glass."

Bill wouldn't put together until years later all the reasons that the other side of town had dirt and broken glass instead of grass, but he learned one thing that day: Adults paid attention to who crossed that line. He was supposed to stay on the "better" side where he belonged. But at the same time, he wasn't supposed to speak of the line. It existed and at the same time didn't exist. He was seven years old, but already he could feel there was something evil about this situation.

In scolding Bill for crossing a racialized border while simultaneously not speaking aloud the system of race that defined that border, Bill's mom was training him in a second aspect of the White imaginary: It disguises the fact that Whiteness is a category at all. It treats Whiteness as the invisible, unmarked normal. Even as the White imaginary divides people according to a hierarchy of racial categories, it paradoxically also teaches that humans are all the same. It assumes that whatever White people experience is pretty much what other people experience too. It conjures the illusion that Whiteness does not really exist as a category. Spaces like Bill's side of the border don't have to be called by the word *White*; they're just plain, ordinary spaces. What's White is strategically left unlabeled as just *normal*.

The White imaginary weaves a cloak of invisibility around Whiteness, not so much by what is said as by what is not said. Colliding with this aspect of the White imaginary can happen as people begin to notice how often labels linguistically mark the race or ethnicity of non-White categories while the corresponding White category has no label. A class in "Black history" versus just "history." A book about "Asian theology" versus simply "theology." A shelf of "ethnic hair" products versus just shampoos. Whiteness is the standard beside which all other groups become "other." The White imaginary creates what George Yancy calls "an elaborate social subterfuge, leading both Whites and non-Whites to believe that the representations in terms of which they live their lives and understand the world and themselves are naturally given, unchangeable ways of being."[7] Whiteness has what's called *normativity*—it sets European and Euro-American people, customs, and experiences as the standard for what is and should be normal.[8]

As seven-year-old Bill learned, he and his White friends were just "friends." Only Ivan was a "different" friend, one for whom different rules applied. He was experiencing what's been called *selective race cognizance*.[9] He was supposed to put people into categories but not consciously question those categories or reflexively admit that he also has been categorized.

Many White people I spoke with collided with the unmarked invisibility of Whiteness through a relocation experience when they became the numerical minority in a predominantly non-White space. Studying abroad, attending a predominantly non-White church, or being included in a non-White friend group often catalyzed these discoveries. In these settings, they confronted the reality that their own way of being in the world was simply one way of being—not the normal. They saw that they too had culture. They too were racialized. They too had traditions. These

---

[7] Yancy goes on to explain, "Whiteness fails to see itself as alien, as seen, as recognized. To see itself as seen, Whiteness would have to deny the imperial and epistemological and ontological base from which it sees what it wants (or has been shaped historically) to see. Whiteness refuses to risk finding itself in exile, in unfamiliar territory, an unmapped space of uncertainty in the form of both knowing and being.... To refuse this process, Whiteness denies its own potential to be Other (to be 'the not-same'), to see through the web of White meaning that it has spun." George Yancy, ed., "Introduction: Fragments of a Social Ontology of Whiteness," in *What White Looks Like: African-American Philosophers on the Whiteness Question* (Routledge, 2004), 11, 13.

[8] Mills explains White normativity in this way: "Ethnocentrism is, of course, a negative cognitive tendency common to all peoples, not just Europeans. But with Europe's gradual rise to global domination, the European variant becomes entrenched as an overarching, virtually unassailable framework, a conviction of exceptionalism and superiority that seems vindicated by the facts, and thenceforth, circularly, shaping perception of the facts. We rule the world because we are superior; we are superior because we rule the world." Charles W. Mills, "White Ignorance," in *Race and Epistemologies of Ignorance*, ed. Shannon Sullivan and Nancy Tuana (State University of New York Press, 2007), 25.

[9] Eileen O'Brien, *Whites Confront Racism: Antiracists and Their Paths to Action* (Rowman & Littlefield, 2001), 55.

things were not just something "other" people had in ethnic studies classes, cultural fairs, or ethnic food sections of a grocery store. They began to see, as one person put it, that "Whiteness is a thing." The racial system is not just a categorizing system that labels "other" people. They too go through life being racialized.

Often collisions happen when White people are dislocated in some way—moved either physically or socially into spaces where their race or culture is not the majority. In the book *Teaching Community: A Pedagogy of Hope*, Black scholar bell hooks reflects on what sorts of pedagogies foster resilient struggles against racism. She intersperses in the book several conversations she has had with White individuals who have worked alongside her on this topic. Among those she quotes is Parker Palmer, a Quaker scholar of education, faith, and democracy. He defines dislocation as happening when "we are forced by circumstance to occupy a very different standpoint from our normal one, and our angle of vision suddenly changes to reveal a strange and threatening landscape." He goes on to explain how these experiences, while seemingly threatening at the time, have been transformative in his life. "The value of dislocation, like the value of disillusionment, is in the way that it moves us beyond illusion, so we can see reality in the round."[10] hooks contends that, in this process of moving beyond illusion about race, White people are rediscovering something that, at one level, they have already known all along.

> Individual white people, moving from denial of race to awareness, suddenly realize that White supremacist culture encourages White folks to deny their understanding of race, to claim as part of their superiority that they are beyond thinking about race. Yet when the denial stops, it becomes clear that underneath their skin most White folks have an intimate awareness of the politics of race and racism. They have learned to pretend that it is not so.[11]

---

[10] bell hooks, *Teaching Community: A Pedagogy of Hope* (Routledge, 2003), 21.
[11] hooks, *Teaching Community*, 26.

Dislocation is a starting point to take off the cloak of invisibility surrounding Whiteness and see what is already present.

One reason that the invisibility of Whiteness is a problem is that it creates an unbalanced, unreciprocated directionality in the knowledge people have of each other. The White imaginary teaches that White people can feasibly and deservedly acquire an understanding of people of color that those people cannot reciprocate toward White people. In a stark example of this, from May to October of 1893, over twenty-five million visitors strolled through downtown Chicago past zoo-like "living dioramas" of human beings from around the world. People from at least eighty nations were made to spend the summer in the mock village, complete with huts, teepees, and wigwams built according to the imaginations of the fair organizers. The event, called the Chicago World's Columbian Exposition, was designed to celebrate the progress of humankind at the four-hundred-year anniversary of Christopher Columbus's arrival in the Western Hemisphere. At the center of the fair, massive white buildings—dubbed "the White City"—displayed new technologies intended to illustrate the progress of humankind.[12] For the entertainment and supposed education of fair visitors, people on display in the international sections shivered through spring temperatures in their flimsy fake housing, then sweated through the heat of summer in supposed traditional clothing. Fair leaders demanded that the Inuit people in the displays wear warm fur clothing. When they refused, they were locked in a shed as punishment. Eventually many Inuit people formed their own company and set up an independent exhibit outside the fairgrounds, but many others from around the world stayed, in part because they would receive passage back home only when the fair concluded.[13]

Fair organizers scheduled daily activities to entertain and educate visitors. A Javanese Village included eighty dwellings where three

---

[12]David F. Burg, *Chicago's White City* (University Press of Kentucky, 1976).
[13]Jim Zwick, *Inuit Entertainers in the United States: From the Chicago World's Fair Through the Birth of Hollywood* (Infinity, 2006).

hundred people from at least eight separate Pacific islands and languages lived for the summer, performing acrobatics, juggling, and "medicine man" acts in two theaters. Egyptian women danced, West African people conducted ceremonies cloaked in mystery, and Arabian people offered camel rides. These activities often blurred the lines between performance and a stark realism. The Office of Indian Affairs set up a space where Indigenous school children who had been taken from their families were made to sit and study. On at least one occasion, someone in the displays died. As friends and family performed mourning rituals, crowds looked on. Fair organizers made arrangements for bodies to be transported to the Smithsonian Museum, where craniologists could study them for clues to rank these bodies in the progression of human evolution. Inuit babies born at the fair were given names by White Chicagoans, including a boy named "Christopher Columbus Palliser" and two girls called "Columbia," one of whom lived only one week.[14]

Records from the time of the Chicago World's Columbian Exposition register little if any concern from White visitors over this mock display of human diversity. Ironically, one woman attending the event reportedly cried out in horror while watching a wildly inaccurate staged cannibalism ritual performed by Dahomeyan people, "Make it stop. We are Christians!"[15] She saw no conflict between her Christian faith and her own participation in an event that confined, misrepresented, denigrated, and dehumanized non-White people for the enjoyment of White viewers. She could take for granted the normalcy of White people casually examining the bodies and even intimate life experiences of people of color in order to see, learn, believe, and take whatever they desired.

---

[14]Burg, *Chicago's White City*; Curtis M. Hinsley, "Anthropology as Education and Entertainment: Frederic Ward Putnam at the World's Fair," in *Coming of Age in Chicago: The 1893 World's Fair and the Coalescence of American Anthropology*, ed. Curtis M. Hinsley and David R. Wilcox (University of Nebraska Press, 2016), 1-77.

[15]Charles King, *Gods of the Upper Air: How a Circle of Renegade Anthropologists Reinvented Race, Sex, and Gender in the Twentieth Century* (Doubleday, 2019).

Those zoo-like displays were a microcosm of what White people have done beyond and since the confines of the world's fair. Museum curators have collected body parts and sentimental objects to dissect and display. Police have spent disproportionate time in predominantly Black and Brown neighborhoods for surveillance. Unethical medical experimentation on Black people, with harmful and deadly results, has been rampant throughout history.[16] Social scientists have collected data to study and monitor Black and Brown lives, reinforcing the belief that the "problems" of society will be located there. In everyday actions, White people have presumed the right to touch Black hair, ask personal questions about racial trauma, and otherwise interrogate Black and Brown experiences without reciprocity.

The White imaginary trains White people that they have the right to see people of color with what scholars have described as a one-way *gaze*. Such a gaze peers into the life of an Other to know and control that Other, while imagining themselves to be invisible to the Other. Like a prison watchtower with dark glass through which the observer can see but not be seen, racial privileges are often designed so that White people see—or believe they have the right and the ability to see—into Black lives at will.[17] Those gazed on internalize the feeling of being always potentially under surveillance, which shapes their own subjective behaviors toward keeping their self in line with the one watching. Like a plantation slave master claiming the right to oversee the lives of enslaved people from work, to church, to home, the White imaginary instills in White people a belief in their right to know at will. One way to exercise power over an Other is to know of them without being known in return.

---

[16]Harriet A. Washington, *Medical Apartheid: The Dark History of Medical Experimentation on Black Americans from Colonial Times to the Present* (Doubleday, 2006).

[17]Michel Foucault, *Discipline and Punish: The Birth of the Prison*, 2nd ed. (Vintage Books, 1995); Frantz Fanon, *The Wretched of the Earth* (Grove, 1963); bell hooks, "Representations of Whiteness in the Black Imagination," in *Black on White: Black Writers on What It Means to Be White*, ed. David R. Roediger (Schocken Books, 1998), 38-53; Jacques Lacan, *Seminar XI: The Four Fundamental Concepts of Psychoanalysis* (Norton, 1978).

People of color do of course peer into the lives of White people as well. Enslaved people on plantations knew, as have oppressed people throughout time, how to protect portions of their lives from oppressor gazes and how to peer back into oppressors' lives. For people of color, studying the White Other has often been a necessity. As Charles W. Mills writes, "Often for their very survival, blacks have been forced to become lay anthropologists, studying the strange culture, customs, and mind-set of the 'white tribe' that has such frightening power over them, that in certain time periods can even determine their life or death on a whim."[18]

Consider, then, why the gaze at the opening of this book was so jarring to Hannah. She used the word *gaze* and described it as "super focused." It was a look she could recall seeing on the faces of people of color only a few other times in her life. She didn't phrase it this way, but it was what anthropologists have called a "reversed gaze," from a Black person assessing a White person's past and future possibilities, rather than a White gaze holding power over a person of color.[19] And it was a moment when her Whiteness could not be shielded from full and conscious visibility. In the very act of putting on dark makeup for a Halloween costume, Hannah had been conscious of difference in skin tone between herself and Florence Griffith Joyner. But in the moment, she had made the decision as if race—the social construct of meanings and experiences surrounding that skin tone—did not exist. As if Whiteness did not exist. And now, here at the table with her friend, she collided with how wrong she had been.

Racial hierarchies and the invisibility of Whiteness are not benign happenstances. They have real effects. Those effects are not fair, and that unfairness brings harm to some as well as advantages and culpability to others. In the next chapter, we'll consider what happens when the White imaginary collides with those two realities—injustice and culpability.

---

[18]Mills, "White Ignorance," 17-18.
[19]Mwenda Ntarangwi, *Reversed Gaze: An African Ethnography of American Anthropology* (University of Illinois Press, 2010).

SEVEN

Colliding with Injustice and Culpability

Laura went through her first years of high school still unable to see through the invisibility cloak of Whiteness. "It didn't even occur to me that I was different somehow from anyone else," she said. It wasn't until senior year that something happened that would, in her words, "haunt her." Laura was one of three captains of the pompom squad, all of whom were White. All the captains joined the coach in evaluating the new recruits who auditioned for the squad. Four Black girls auditioned that year. "They were really good," Laura remembered. "I mean, they were *great*. They could dance, they could follow directions." Meanwhile a number of White girls tried out, and some were clearly less qualified than the Black girls. Laura filled out a scorecard ranking the girls accordingly and gave it to the coach, a White woman.

When the coach posted the list of girls who made the squad, none of the Black girls were on the roster. Laura and the other White girls serving as captains were shocked. "We kind of looked at each other like, 'Wait a second. They were actually good. What? And you picked these couple of girls that were terrible? Huh?" Laura and the two other captains decided to quit in protest. They reported the incident to the athletic director, asserting that racism had skewed the coach's decision. Laura recalls the director's response: "That's not possible." The director refused to believe them, gaslighting away their clear evidence that racism occurred.

Through the experience, Laura caught a vision behind the veil that treats Whiteness as a nonentity. And she also saw something else: injustice. Until then, she had known a few Black, Asian American, and Latino and Latina students in her classes. She supposed there were some cultural differences between their experiences, but she wouldn't have been able to name what those differences entailed. This incident alerted her that what differentiated their lives was something other than culture alone. Their society was racializing them differently—assigning racial categories and associated meanings to each of them. It was not treating them fairly.

COLLIDING WITH INJUSTICE

Laura's experience with the pompom squad was one of many stories White people told of their first recollections of being deeply troubled by an incident of racial injustice. Sometimes these encounters with injustice were unsettling to them because they happened to people they knew personally. Six White people recommended for this study mentioned having dated or married a person of color, and two had adopted a child of color. Several others mentioned having a best friend of color at an early age. For others, a collision with injustice was difficult to ignore because it had dominated the news cycle. Whatever their generation, the stories followed a similar pattern of watching the news of tragic deaths of Black individuals and wondering how to stop this. Emmett Till, Martin Luther King Jr., Rodney King, Michael Brown, and George Floyd all came up in interviews. Other times a collision with injustice stuck because a White person was a part of an institution where the injustice occurred. Several mentioned finding themselves in leadership at a workplace, club, or church dealing with the fallout of a racist incident. For any of these reasons, the tangible effects of racism in individual lives became salient to them. Like Jenna, who felt "so naive" looking back, for many people the impact of the experience was amplified by their surprise they didn't learn this sooner.

Collisions with injustice alert people that race is not morally neutral. It is not balanced in its consequences, affecting White people a bit one day and people of color the next in roughly equal significance. People collided with the reality that a racialized society incurs economic and psychological penalties on non-White people. Eventually they may learn to take this idea a step further, noticing that the injustice of the race system harms not just people of color but everyone. When a society distributes resources unequally by inhibiting opportunities for a portion of the population and spreading lies about that process, the society suffers as a whole.

One common way that White individuals begin to notice the injustice caused by racism is through experiences of injustice based on other social dimensions in their own life. As Laura talked about her response to the discrimination directed against her Black classmates, she recalled also the times she had experienced discrimination directed against herself and her family. Her father had often told her stories about his upbringing as an Irish American kid in rural America. "We were treated like poor dirty kids," he had told her. "And so you will treat people kindly. You will treat people with respect." Later she would see parallels between the racism she observed and her own experiences of sexism. When men distrusted her leadership at work and in her church, she paid attention to her own responses and grew in empathy for people who experienced racial and ethnic discrimination. Such experiences are called *overlapping approximating experiences*—experiences when a person's own form of social discrimination leads to understanding or empathizing with the subordination of another subordinated group.[1] Several women I interviewed mentioned approximating experiences with sexism. People also mentioned experiences with poverty and class discrimination. One man traced the beginning of his concern about racial injustice to his own painful experience of being bullied in middle school. People who know

---

[1] Tiffany Hogan and Julie Netzer, "Knowing the Other: White Women, Gender, and Racism," unpublished manuscript, University of Florida, Department of Sociology, 1993, 175-76; Mark R. Warren, *Fire in the Heart: How White Activists Embrace Racial Justice* (Oxford University Press, 2010).

what injustice feels like from an insider perspective have a starting point for taking it seriously when it happens to someone else.

But not every approximating experience produces empathy. I often have had conversations with White people who see their own hardships as reasons to dismiss racism. When White people narrate their own life stories as individually motivated triumphs over poverty or other hardships, it can be all the more difficult to understand how people of color or other socially subordinated groups continue to experience the effects of subordination. Without an awareness of the invisibility aspect of the White imaginary covered in the previous chapter, approximating experiences can cause White people to be less, rather than more, empathetic. Philosopher Janine Jones suggests that White people's "inability to form the belief that they are Whites" detracts from their ability to empathize "because they are unable to import an ingredient essential to empathy: an appreciation of their own situation."[2] Here we see how collisions fit together—colliding with the invisibility of Whiteness can help people make sense of collisions with injustice. As we'll see in the next chapter, not every lesson has to be learned through a collision (and that's a good thing). Nor does every lesson have to happen in a particular order; nor is a lesson done and checked off the first time it occurs. But one way or another, a long-term commitment to racism is going to involve coming face-to-face with injustice.

Collisions with injustice offer many people a starting point for recognizing that racism is not just an interpersonal problem but a social problem. If racism were just a problem of individuals being cruel to each other, the solution to racism would be training in how to be nicer to each other. In the behavior of Laura's coach toward the girls who auditioned for the pompom squad, there was no absence of niceness. The coach treated the girls with politeness and respect during their audition. The

---

[2]Janine Jones, "The Impairment of Empathy in Goodwill Whites for African Americans," in *What White Looks Like: African-American Philosophers on the Whiteness Question*, ed. George Yancey (Routledge, 2004), 70.

athletic director was calm and kind in demeanor when he denied that racism had happened. Racism occasionally manifests in interpersonal cruelty, but it is not ultimately a problem of individual animosity from one person to another. It is, rather, a problem in the arrangements of society more broadly.

Collisions with injustice allow people to confront the ways the social imaginary treats the effects of racism as if they were problems at an individual level. In a White imaginary, Laura could go befriend a Black girl and encourage her to try harder next time, and all would be well. But Laura discovered that the problem was bigger than friendship, kindness, or even the efforts she and her fellow captains made to advocate for justice. There was something going on that was bigger than any one, two, or three of them.

One analogy I find helpful for understanding how racism is a social rather than merely interpersonal issue is the image of a torn cloth. Racism is a tear in the fabric of society. Like the cloth forming a shirt or a parachute, a tear in one place can compromise the utility of the entire article, having consequences beyond its immediate location. As the aphorism "a stitch in time saves nine" reminds us, a small tear left unattended is also often likely to spread. Society is like a woven fabric made up of many threads of individuals, institutions, nodes of connection, and interactions. Racism is like a rip shooting across that fabric. As it shreds the fabric, it interrupts any and all essential functions of society.[3]

Humans need societies. We cannot survive in isolation. Societies are broader than communities, extending far beyond the people we ever see or know, encompassing people who touch our lives without our ever realizing it. Society includes my mother and father, who greeted me the moment I was born, and the teachers who guided me through elementary

---

[3] Among the many scholars who have referred to society as a fabric, Martin Luther King Jr. uses this image in his Letter from a Birmingham Jail: "We are caught in an inescapable network of mutuality, tied in a single garment of destiny. Whatever affects one directly, affects all indirectly." King, "Letter from a Birmingham Jail," African Studies Center—University of Pennsylvania, April 16, 1963, 2, www.africa.upenn.edu/Articles_Gen/Letter_Birmingham.html.

school, and the distant workers who grew the peach I ate for breakfast, and the person long before me who invented the keyboard I type on at this moment. Through society, we meet our physical needs, such as shelter and food, and through society we also find meaning. Society is a carrier of goods and also of culture, of ideas, of belonging, of joy. And racism organizes society in a way that leaves these functions weakened or worthless.

The White imaginary emphasizes the capacities of individuals to be free, active agents driving their own lives. It relies on *antistructuralist* explanations for the human life course, downplaying the influence of social structures and culture on human lives and ignoring the many unintended consequences of decisions. In the 1990s, sociologists Michael Emerson and Christian Smith studied comprehensive survey and interview data and found that antistructuralist explanations of racial inequalities were more pervasive among White Christians than in the White population more broadly. White Christians tended to believe that, because individuals were held accountable to God for their own free will, their lives unfolded independently of social structures. In believing that relationships mattered, many Christians expected interpersonal interracial relationships to offer a complete solution to racism.[4] Decades later, in 2019–2020, researchers replicated similar survey questions. They found these same antistructuralist beliefs still holding strong among White Christians.[5]

But if racism were merely a matter of individual White people needing to renounce the sinfulness of discrimination, they could solve racism through heartfelt repentance and some kindly interactions with individuals of color. Likewise, if inequalities in health, education, and wealth outcomes across racial groups were only a matter of needing to renounce some sins, simply converting people to Christianity and redirecting their

---

[4] Michael O. Emerson and Christian Smith, *Divided by Faith: Evangelical Religion and the Problem of Race in America* (Oxford University Press, 2001).
[5] Christina Barland Edmondson and Chad Brennan, *Faithful Anti-Racism: Moving Past Talk to Systemic Change* (InterVarsity Press, 2022).

behavior would be enough to solve those inequalities. But as we'll see in the coming chapters, the structural causes of racism require more than a mere change of heart. Contact between people of color and White people alone does not necessarily cause White people to unlearn their stereotypes and biases.[6] The "just make diverse friends" approach to addressing racism not only fails to solve racism; it often exacerbates its effects by putting people of color in closer contact with White people who are oblivious to their biases. In collisions with injustice, White people experience jarring discoveries that racism has consequences that hurt, and those consequences will not be solved through friendship and interracial social contact alone.

COLLIDING WITH CULPABILITY

When White people collide with the reality of racial injustice, they face the troubling fact that people of color have suffered. In some circumstances they also face an even more troubling fact: They—White people—caused that suffering.

The White imaginary teaches that Whiteness is not only normal; it is innocent. In the White imaginary, racists are anomalies or caricatures. They are snarling men marching through the darkness with lynching ropes in a bygone era, or Southern belles asking "Mammy" to rub their aching toes, or swastika-tattooed skinheads with Confederate flag bumper stickers. Surely the racists are not their own families, coworkers, or fellow Christians. And surely not themselves. With this imaginary, the solution to racist incidents such as police brutality or racist graffiti is to search out an individual on whom to pin the blame, have a stern talking-to with that individual, and perhaps implement some bias-awareness training to prevent other individuals from doing these terrible things again. The rest of the

---

[6]Emerson and Smith, *Divided by Faith*; Mary R. Jackman and Marie Crane, "'Some of My Best Friends Are Black . . .': Interracial Friendship and Whites' Racial Attitudes," *The Public Opinion Quarterly* 50, no. 4 (1986): 459-86.

White population can settle deeper into self-assurance—*I'm glad I'm not like that*. They can believe themselves to be what philosopher Janine Jones calls "goodwill Whites."[7]

Often, collisions happen when individuals are confronted by their own culpability. Like Hannah discovering her own prejudice against Black Vernacular English, people are shocked to find racism in their own lives.

Collisions can also happen when people are forced to reckon with the culpability of other White people, especially those they love and respect. A White man named Robert hit that point as a teenager growing up in the American South in the 1950s. As a child, he adored his father. "Dad was a genius," Robert said. His father had started a company that took their family from poverty to multimillionaires during Robert's lifetime. "I grew up in a very privileged kind of little capsule of all-White—" Robert paused before saying the final word in the sentence, gesturing scare quotes: "*Christians*." Robert now believed that his childhood church was no reflection of Christ. His pastor and other church members used the n-word regularly. His dad used the word to describe his Black employees, even while speaking directly to them. Robert recalled that in his father's company, "needless to say, Black employees did the hardest, dirtiest work in the factory." His parents described the Black employees who cleaned their home as "like family," projecting a White imaginary of themselves as benevolent caretakers for needy people. But slowly it dawned on Robert that there was nothing benevolent in his parents' behavior.

Robert eventually faced a crisis. He wanted to see his parents, pastors, and church members as good mentors. But how could they be good if they treated fellow humans in this way? "I loved my parents, and they loved me very much. I had a loving family," he recalled. But something didn't add up. Finally, he decided to gather up his savings and travel as

---

[7]Jones, "Impairment of Empathy."

Colliding with Injustice and Culpability

far away from home as he could. He headed across the globe to spend the next three years traveling through Africa and the Middle East, searching for role models of a different sort from his family. Robert began a process of rebuilding his identity, precipitated by the discovery that the people closest to him—his own mother, father, church, and adult mentors—perpetuated a system he now considered evil.

For White Christians, the imaginary of White innocence can take on a uniquely Christian flavor. On one hand, Christians learn to self-examine themselves. They learn to expect to find sin lurking in their own hearts at every turn. Christians have been told to take the log out of their own eyes before removing the speck from their neighbor's eyes. They have been told not to be like the Pharisee proudly boasting of his good behavior but to be like the tax collector who stood before God asking for mercy for his sin (Matthew 7:3-5; Luke 18:9-14). And yet, there's a feeling of holier-than-thou that just keeps creeping into Christian culture. The weekly rhythms of confession and absolution of sin, the habits of soaking up sermons and trainings to follow Christ's example, and the pleasant fellowship with smiling Christian people after church can all contribute to a sense that "surely we Christians are good people."

Many White people who collide with the culpability of the historical church or their own congregation decide to leave the church. Some, like Robert, search for new church communities, often among people of color. Some never return. Many people I spoke with had friends or acquaintances who had made that choice. Some were on the verge themselves. As a woman we'll meet in a future chapter put it, injustice in the church leaves them "jaded," with "more than one foot in agnosticism."

When White people experience a collision between the fantasy of White innocence and the reality of White culpability, it can provoke *cognitive dissonance*—a mental disturbance caused by the feeling that one's beliefs and actions contradict each other. Most people go through life assuming that they are, at least most of the time, pretty good people. In order to uphold that belief in a setting where one's entire group bears a culpability for injustice, social groups construct elaborate edifices of beliefs to maintain the fiction of innocence.[8] When those accumulated beliefs shudder and fall, the crash can be forceful indeed. Collisions with injustice and culpability are genuinely emotionally troubling. They provoke deep emotions, and those emotions often manifest in tears, angry outbursts, or other forms that affect the people around them. In recent years, much has been written about the phenomenon called "White tears." The phrase refers to times when White individuals who experience the types of collisions described in this chapter respond with tears, but those tears serve to direct attention away from the suffering of people of color and back toward the White individual themselves. This becomes a problem particularly in settings where people of color speak up about the injustices done to themselves, and rather than focusing energy on righting the injustice, a group shifts their attention toward comforting the White people experiencing sadness at the fresh discovery of the situation.

For these reasons, White people going through collisions can be exhausting and disruptive to the people of color around them. While a White person is processing their shock and horror over injustice or defending their innocence, the people of color around them are likely experiencing the situation very differently. As we saw in chapter four, people of color tend to experience collisions more often and earlier in life, and they are more likely to have been around other people of color who lead them through that process. Thus the naiveté and defensiveness with which White people experience collisions run precisely counter to collision experiences among people of color. When a group responds to a collision by meeting the felt needs of White individuals—needs to

---

[8]As philosopher Lina Martin Alcoff writes, "If it is true that most people prefer to think of themselves as moral or at least excusable in their actions, then in unjust societies those in dominant and privileged positions must be able to construct representations of themselves and others to support a fantasyland of moral approbation." Alcoff, "Epistemologies of Ignorance: Three Types," in *Race and Epistemologies of Ignorance*, ed. Shannon Sullivan and Nancy Tuana (State University of New York Press, 2007), 49.

process their shock, emote their grief, or rearrange their assumptions of culpability—the group is very likely to miss entirely the needs of the people of color at that moment.

That's not to say that White people should never respond to collisions with tears of sadness or anger. Tears are often an unavoidable bodily reaction to collisions. Several of the people I interviewed mentioned crying, in the right circumstances, as a valuable stepping stone toward transformation. When one White woman mentioned "crying buckets of White tears" over a movie she'd seen about racism, I asked her to talk more about what she thought about White tears. She had worked as a professional facilitator of diversity, equity, and inclusion trainings, and was ready to explain the ways she teaches other White people about what to do with emotions as they learn. "White tears," she said, "are centered in that moment and don't serve any other purpose." Crying in this way is performative—it's an expression of a person feeling stuck in an uncomfortable situation and looking for a way out, and tears offer a way to garner sympathy. When White people use tears to make someone else responsible for their own feelings, especially if that someone is the person of color who was most affected by the racism in the first place, "that's a problem." But White tears, she reiterated, are not the only way White people cry. There's such a thing as justified crying. "This is upsetting, heavy work," she said frankly. "And you're going to cry."

Collisions can provoke not just momentary bouts of emotion but slower processes of grieving and lament. We'll return to the topic of lament in the final section of this book, but people need not wait to lament until they have a comprehensive understanding of racism. Sometimes the spontaneous involuntary emotions provoked by collisions need to be acknowledged as normal bodily responses as people readjust their imaginary of self and society. Collisions will be troubling. That's what makes them transformative.

Collisions, as we've seen, confront people with a reality that conflicts with the White social imaginary, doing so powerfully enough to evoke a conscious and visceral response. Collisions typically feel as though they come from without, happening *to* a person without their anticipation. They catch people off-guard in ordinary settings—a day with a friend, joining a club, taking a required class, meeting a stranger. Their power is in startling people to pay attention, and they jangle people's social imagination enough to knock some pieces off the White imaginary. These moments say, *Look. Pay attention. Things are not as they seemed. Rearrange your cognitive pathways. Unlearn the lies you never even knew you believed.*

Important life changes can begin from collisions. Collisions alert people that there's a problem. People begin to see how hierarchy, White normativity, injustice, and culpability, all symptoms of a racist society, have shredded the fabric of society. If you've related to some of the collisions in this section, you're on your way toward seeing why the rest of the book matters.

But hold on. We're still only a third of the way into the process. There's a lot that collisions don't do. They alert people to the problem, but they don't tell people much about how to solve that problem. Often the initial response to a collision is to do something that makes the problem worse, not better. Collisions don't tell people how to fix the problem in the future, nor do they tell people what to do about the harm already done. Nor do they tell people how to have hope. Collisions tend to wipe away hope, not restore it. Without some other elements in their journeys, collisions can be little more than an intense ride at the amusement park: much rattling and exhilaration through the ups and downs of the moment, but all within the confines of safety precautions and restraint systems. Then back home again at the end of the day.

Collisions alone are ephemeral. Often when people recounted their earliest collision stories, what followed was a leap ahead of several years before the next notable step in their journey. Allan said after telling his story of drinking a Gatorade with the Colombian stranger, "And then I went back." Lasting change requires something more. Collisions are a shock treatment of training in nonagency, but change will require learning how to use one's agency. It will also require knowing what needs to change and how to make that change. That means seeing the full scope and depth of the problems both surrounding and within yourself, asking what people have tried in the past to change those problems, and assessing the cost of implementing solutions. It's going to be a troubling route forward. If you were packing for this journey, you'd want to take along an extra ration of hope. But even then, there's tough news ahead—the hope that most people pack for the journey isn't the kind they need. Their hope goes stale, and to make room to replace it with hope that lasts, they're going to have to empty a lot of baggage out of their packs.

PART 4

Asking a Lot of Why

EIGHT

Big Problems

IF YOU LIVE VERY LONG in this world, you discover that some problems are *big*. Maybe that discovery comes on the dark night when you admit you need professional help. Maybe you sat with a loved one while their body trembled through detox. Maybe you spent years goading some institution to change its course on some seemingly small but essential issue, and nothing changed. Maybe you saw a marriage fall apart, struggled to dig yourself out of debt, or dropped out of school. Maybe somebody you love was wounded in a way that won't heal in the way time supposedly heals all wounds. You've tried praying, you've tried being the nicest or toughest or smartest person in the room, and you've tried building a coalition of other good people. You've exhausted every resource you can find and have still come up short. Maybe you have an idea of what needs to happen but can't find a way to make it happen, or maybe despite all your trying you still don't even know what needs to happen. Maybe nobody does.

Some problems are big. The only way through big problems is to dig deeper and wider, searching out the tendrils and roots that feed that problem from spaces beyond what you originally imagined. This work is the second of the elements I saw in the lives of people pursuing racial justice for the long haul: *asking why.*

Collisions, as we have seen, are moments when people stumble on immediate effects of racism in ways they cannot—at least in that moment—ignore. But people have a remarkable capacity to go back to denying ideas and realities that don't match the frameworks of their social imaginations. Asking why means taking the time to rebuild new frameworks. It enables people to trace the causes and effects of racism across place and time—across history, nation, planet, and down to the present day. It involves looking at a problem through many disciplinary lenses—economics, theology, sociology, ecology, and more. And it requires learning from many experts from many walks of life.

People who start asking why questions soon discover that racism is too big a problem to untangle alone—it won't be solved by a weekend event or a perfectly designed program. Racism is locked into place through the ordinary systems we take for granted, not just tucked away in the hearts of caricatured, mean-spirited racists in urban alleyways or rural hollows. It's not just happening in the flare-ups of racial "incidents" that show up in newspapers and company meetings. Racism spreads through all of society as subtly as dye into a glass of water, and it's not going to be cleaned up with a swipe of a spot-remover pen or with the right amount of "likes" on social media platforms.

Recall the story of Allan, who collided with reality when he drank a Gatorade with a Colombian man at the border of his neighborhood. In the last chapter, I left off that story with Allan saying, "And then I went back." He had that one surprising encounter, and then he returned home. But his story didn't end there. A seed of curiosity germinated. He wanted to know more. "Now I wanted to talk to people in the public housing project," he said. People in his classes. In more neighborhoods. His curiosity sprouted new branches. In the next phase of life, he said he kept walking up to people saying, "Tell me. Please tell me. What is it like to be here?"

And people talked. Ten minutes from his house, he learned more than he ever imagined. "I was like, why? What blinders and what structures were put on me so that I wasn't interacting with the folks that lived ten minutes away from me? And now I am. And I'm learning about myself, and I'm learning about this whole structure of White supremacy that's been put in place." Allan's White imagination didn't just disappear in one collision moment. It took years of intentional exploration to figure out what lies he'd believed and what truth could replace those lies.

In this section, we'll look at how White people begin asking big why questions and where that exploration leads. As with collisions, we'll see important changes happening through this element of the process. Whereas collisions tend to happen to people, taking them by surprise, asking why requires agency. This phase occurs through one active choice after another. In that process, people are not just accumulating new information; they are also unlearning false ideas absorbed earlier in life. They come to see the fullness of the White imaginary—the lies it taught, how it protected those lies, and what those lies did. But we'll also see that these two elements together—collisions plus asking why—are still insufficient to guarantee lasting change. These experiences together strip away the delusional hopes that characterize the White imaginary, and when we get through this part, we're going to need to consider how people find a sturdier hope.

|||||||

To see how this element works, we'll dig into the story of a White woman named Megan. She used a phrase that seemed to encapsulate a certain period of life that I heard described by one White interviewee after another: "asking a lot of why." For Megan, her "asking a lot of why" phase happened while living and working in a predominantly Black and Hispanic neighborhood in a program designed to teach about social injustice. As an intern, she lived and ate together with other outsiders like herself as well as long-term insiders from the community. During the day they volunteered in the community, and local mentors led them through regular learning sessions. "We were given the curriculum of books we were going to read and things we were going to study and pay attention to," she explained. She said those sessions kept the why questions at the forefront of her mind. In a given day, she might work alongside a Hispanic neighbor who casually recounted a near-death border-crossing story, then join a book discussion about the history of immigration policy with a group of young volunteers like herself along with a leader from the local neighborhood. One day she stood in line at a post office with an acquaintance who pointed out that every Black and Hispanic person in line had been asked to show an ID card. Megan, the only White person in line, was not carded.

This was not Megan's first encounter with racism. Collision-type incidents, one after another, had already led her to choose this step of learning. Growing up in a White neighborhood, one day she noticed that her family had many friends on the block but never spoke to the one Black family in the neighborhood. One summer Megan got a job picking fruit, and she listened to the stories of migrant coworkers for whom fruit picking was a means of survival, not just a way to earn some summer cash between years of college. "When I graduated college I was looking for—" She paused to consider her next words. "What was I looking for? Well, I knew I needed another place to get out of my bubble."

Megan found that escape from her bubble through this program. She wanted to live in a place where "most people didn't look like me." And she wanted time to linger in her questions. As a twenty-something just out of college, a year in one place felt like a long time. "I think it could have been easier to dismiss it if it had only been like a three-month program. Like, 'Oh, that was interesting,' and then just forget about it. But because we stayed with it, getting to know our neighbors over that stretch of time, it's not as easy to forget."

A few years later she joined another organization that similarly combined intentional community, cultural diversity, activism, and learning. After the death of George Floyd, she began meeting regularly with a group from within the organization she worked with to talk more specifically about racism. "There were ten of us who were doing that twice a week for a few months," she recalled. The organization was already oriented toward justice-related work, but they dug deeper into challenging questions about why the organization had always been majority White and had a White-dominated power structure. She noticed herself gradually becoming more comfortable talking about race. "It became more of like a lunch-table conversation."

Some of Megan's strongest memories of her first year in the urban learning program involved working with kids in an underresourced neighborhood where she lived. "I guess it's easier to judge adults than it is to judge kids," she reflected. "We spent a lot of time with kids. The kids just came over to our house all the time. And I was wondering a lot about like why they're in the situations they are. Why? Why are these sweet kids the ones who are experiencing this? They're eating Cheetos all day, and their dad comes home and is not kind to them, and mom is working nights, and, and . . ." Her voice trailed off for a moment. "So I was asking a lot of why."

As Megan spent years asking a lot of why, her questions stretched outward from those interactions with kids, following trails across the history and legacy of her city, country, and world. In the years that followed, she continued working amid social groups that supported her learning. Megan's encounters with the White imaginary went from momentary shocks to a steady unraveling. Asking why tends to intensify during some periods of people's lives, but it's not a phase with an endpoint. It's a process whereby the momentary swell of passion found in collisions can become a consistent, habitual posture of openness.

There is no list long enough to name every lesson that people encounter in this process of asking why. It would require more than an entire book just to explain why kids in an underresourced neighborhood ate Cheetos for lunch. People who take time to learn about injustice are learning not just a set of isolated facts but the overarching fact that there is always more nuance and more context to be found. They learn how to zoom in like a camera narrowing to the veins on a single leaf or deeper still to the microscopic cells of a leaf. And they also learn to zoom out, from leaf, to tree, to forest, country, earth, and universe. They do this again and again, turning 360 degrees. Asking why is not an over-and-done event; it is a posture that people take on.

<hr>

"Why" questions about racism tend to lead into at least three areas of discovery: structures, culture, and morality. Structural learning involves seeing the ways that enduring institutions and social systems affect individual lives, even without individuals in those systems making active choices to maintain the systems. For Megan, this meant learning that the children "eating Cheetos all day" came from families where wealth was hard to accumulate and even harder to pass between generations because of factors such as discrimination in bank lending, real estate, hiring, and education. She also learned that traumas associated with racism—anxiety, food insecurity, inconsistent sleep, and insufficient health care—shape human bodies down to the level of craving and digesting calories. Other interviewees described learning about policies and systems of incarceration, housing, immigration, trade, military, and education. They learned how social structures carry enduring effects across generations by studying the history of sundown towns, racial-restrictive covenants, redlined neighborhoods, Japanese internment camps, the Mexican American War, chattel slavery, and colonialism. Learning about social structures involves not only learning a list of historical events but also training oneself to see patterns in the way those structures are formed, reinforced, resisted, and rebuilt.

Deep learners also learn to recognize the effects of culture—both in themselves and others. Megan's learning about culture was kick-started by two years living in India as an outsider adapting to other people's cultural systems, but not everyone I met with learned about culture through an immersive experience. Some had learned about cultural patterns through books and other resources while interacting with people of differing cultural backgrounds in their own communities. Learning about culture needs to happen at an intellectual level—identifying ways that misunderstandings, biases, and discrimination hinder communication across diversity—but also at an experiential level—learning to adapt one's own behaviors in accordance with cultural surroundings, recognizing that culture is more nuanced than a list of values or ethnic-group labels. Cultural learning involves building practical skills to get over the awkwardness of hanging out with people who respond to the world in different ways.

A key lesson of cultural learning is that dominant cultural groups disproportionately influence the cultural formation of subordinate groups. As subordinated cultural groups find ways to cope with the trauma of subordination, sometimes those adaptive techniques unintentionally reinforce people's own oppression. At the same time, subordinated cultural groups often grow in emotional, moral, and social fortitude as they resist oppression. When White people start learning about the damage done by racist social structures, they sometimes develop an image of people of color as somehow damaged, pitiable, or fragile. Learning about culture can help counteract this tendency, pointing to the ways people of color go on loving life and thriving every bit as much as anyone.

Third, asking why involves exploring the moral questions of what to do about racism. For Christians, this means putting all this learning about structures and culture into conversation with Christian faith. Like many people I spoke with, Megan didn't mention Christian faith when she began describing the earliest transformative experiences in her life. Most of the collision and asking why experiences I heard could have happened to Christians or non-Christians alike. Often people's early encounters with diversity or injustice seemed to drive them to theological questions more than the other way around. But in time, learning about racism leads to moral questions, and for Christians in this research, that meant exploring biblical and theological concepts. Megan loved biblical passages portraying God as an active peacemaker. She identified parallels between the injustices in her present world and the injustices found in the Bible—injustices against Israelites, the poor, ethnic outsiders, and against Christ himself. She saw God as a peacemaker who moved toward injustice, not fearing it but overcoming it through Christ's presence in the world as the ultimate peacemaking act. Like many of the people I interviewed, she believed that seeking justice was an essential calling for Christians because it is modeled after the fundamental character of God.

Other Christians brought up stories of Jesus' interactions with people of marginalized class, gender, and ethnic groups. Jesus taught that the kingdom of God was at hand and that this kingdom was unlike any that people had ever imagined. God's kingdom overturned and dismantled hierarchies of dominance and subordination. The poor, women, children, sick, disabled, and other social outcasts were leaders when it came to receiving God's coming. Others pointed to the exodus account—how God rescued Israelite people from Egyptian enslavement. They saw in that account not just a one-time escape from injustice but the beginning of a longer story in which God gives people a new design for society where all people can live in the holistic flourishing known as *shalom*. Several mentioned *imago Dei*, "the image of God," the Christian belief that humans in all their diversity are each created to reflect God. Others highlighted that the apostle John's prophetic vision of the end of time includes "people from every nation, tribe, people and language" worshiping God together (Revelation 7:9), a healed world in which God sanctifies rather than eradicates ethnic diversity.

As these Christians learned to see the scale of racism, they contextualized racial justice within theological frameworks: God's abiding love for the full diversity of humanity, God's active pursuit of justice, and God's overturning of unjust human systems. These doctrines and stories contributed theological underpinnings to their widening conceptions of racial justice. The particular content of why questions varied somewhat from person to person, and no individual had to know everything on a list to qualify, but they had adopted a posture of learning built on a belief that history affects the present, that social structures and culture affect individuals, and that injustice requires moral discernment.

In grade school, most children take classes in mathematics every year from elementary school to graduation, plus more if they continue into college. But when it comes to learning about racism, few people have more than an occasional story in elementary school, maybe a monthlong unit in high school, or an entire college class. The learning most people get about racism is like a scant introduction to subtraction and multiplication when there's calculus to be learned. People get PhDs to understand racism, and even then they're still learning. Asking why is a lifelong habit. One of the oldest couples I interviewed had just signed up to attend a weeklong learning trip to the National Memorial for Peace and Justice in Alabama. They knew they still had more why questions to ask.

|||||||||

It's no accident that much of Megan's process of asking why happened while she lived among Black and Latino/a communities during early adulthood. For White people, being around people of color in this life stage can play a central role in a process of political and religious identity formation. To understand how this works, it's worth summarizing the work of Michele Margolis, a sociologist of religion and politics. By studying panel data surveys and interviews of young people as they moved through life stages, Margolis found that young people tend to form political affiliations at an earlier life stage than religious affiliations. Political affiliations form during adolescence and early adulthood, at a stage when people tend to be pulling back from forming religious affiliations. By the time their religious identities are crystallizing—usually when they are choosing life partners and starting families—their partisan choices have already taken a strong enough hold to now have a strong influence on their religious decisions. Because political affiliations form first, they set the direction of religious identities more than vice versa. And, importantly, the current dominant political messages direct people in opposite religious directions: Republicans point people to greater religiosity, and Democrats steer people toward lesser religiosity.[1] This helps explain why left-leaning White Christians in my research felt like such outliers. Being both religious and left-leaning regarding race-related issues, they found themselves at odds with national trends among White people. As we'll see in the next chapter, they often found themselves estranged from both religious social groups and political social groups—a lonely and precarious place to be.

But here's what many people in my study discovered by accident: African American religious and political identities match up in a different direction. Margolis found that African American Democrats do not experience the same pushback for being Christian as White Americans. Thus when African Americans formulate their religious affiliations in early adulthood, their social circles treat Democratic Party affiliation and Christianity as self-reinforcing rather than conflicting.[2] It makes sense, then, that when White people in their politically formative adolescent life stage and later in their religiously formative young adult life stage interact with African American church settings, they encounter a different current from what they feel in White church settings. Several White people I spoke with mentioned learning from African American communities how to integrate Christian faith with a political commitment to addressing racism.

Black churches are not the only groups that provide a subculture in which young people see Christian faith lived out in connection with an

---

[1] Michele F. Margolis, *From Politics to the Pews: How Partisanship and the Political Environment Shape Religious Identity* (University of Chicago Press, 2018).

[2] Mangolis offers several reasons that Black Christians tend to align with Democratic politics. She notes that African American religious traditions diverged from other denominational groups as a direct result of racial discrimination, and thus, for African Americans, religious identity is more closely associated with racial identity. Within the historical circumstances of racism, Black churches placed a greater theological emphasis on themes of injustice, exploitation, resistance, and communal alliance than did White churches, whose theology focused more on individual sin, repentance, and piety. Black Protestants are more likely than White Protestants and White Catholics to openly discuss politics in church, and African Americans are more likely than any other racial or ethnic group in the US to be religious.

activist response to racism. Such currents have existed within White Protestantism throughout the history of race relations in America. People in my research often found comfort and encouragement through connections to subgroups within the larger church in which racial injustice was taken seriously. The formative settings that White people mentioned included Quaker abolitionists; Catholic social movements; InterVarsity Christian Fellowship and its triennial missions conference, Urbana; Evangelicals for Social Action (now Christians for Social Action); Koinonia Christian Community and the organizations it founded, including Habitat for Humanity and Jubilee Partners; and justice-focused groups at Christian colleges including Wheaton College and Eastern University. In such groups, White people found supportive subcultural settings with people who shared beliefs in both Christian faith and political advocacy against racism.

|||||||||

People of color also spend a lot of time asking why questions about racism. As we saw in previous chapters, collision experiences tend to happen more frequently and at earlier life stages for people of color than for White people. Likewise, exploring the structures of racism often weaves into everyday life for people of color, rather than only occurring in intentional learning settings. However, being exposed to learning about racism on a regular basis does not necessarily afford people of color opportunities to consider the ways social systems work in a wider scope or how racism affects people with experiences that differ from their own. Several people of color who lived or attended school in predominantly White settings were especially attuned to the ways they had needed to seek out learning opportunities when the teaching they received about race in formal learning settings was limited or outright misguided.

Luis, the Latino pastor who described the ways his congregants hope, recounted how he had gone through much of his life responding to racist incidents by laughing it off. He shrugged it off when he got put into a remedial math class without being tested. The problem seemed resolved when his highly educated parents petitioned the school to get Luis into an advanced course that fit his abilities. He laughed when a White neighbor saw him mowing his own lawn and asked how much he charged, assuming Luis must be a hired worker. The neighbor apologized afterward, and Luis thought to himself, "Sure, it would have been nice if the guy knew better, but he was a good man and he made a mistake." Luis laughed when a police officer asked him to step out of his car while he was on a date with a White girlfriend to ask whether the White girlfriend was there against her will. Luis wasn't in danger of being deported, and his girlfriend didn't make a big deal of it either. "I kind of used to laugh, you know, and not care about it," he said, "in part because I knew who I was." He thought of his response as a "Christian thing—I know my identity in Christ, and I don't care." But these stories added up. He started noticing, "Hey, this happens a lot." It was unsettling.

One day Luis was telling some of these stories to a Black friend, and the man challenged him. "You know, Luis, the problem is that when this happens to you every day or once a week for the past fifty-some years, you're done laughing about it."

"That's when I realized we can't just laugh about it anymore," Luis said. His realization had two parts. First, even though he had experienced discrimination as a Hispanic man, he realized he needed to learn about racism against other groups. "The truth is, these things were not happening to me every day or every week, but this Black friend was experiencing this over and over and over." Second, he realized that these kinds of incidents were not just isolated or accidental. They would not go away on their own. "People shouldn't just put up with those things," he said. He embarked on a journey of actively learning about racism and using his influence as a community leader to guide others in that journey.

As Luis realized, people of color are not necessarily exposed to the experiences of people of other racial minorities. They too have learning to do in this area. In many interviews, people of color mentioned shifts in their lives as they learned to take seriously the forms of racism against other groups—a Black man learning to speak out against anti-Asian racism, a Latina woman identifying anti-Black racism in her organization, and so on.

At the college where I teach, every student is required to take at least one course that fulfills a "diversity in the United States" requirement. Sometimes students of color ask why they need to fulfill this same requirement as White students. Many of them come into these classes much more familiar with diversity than their White classmates. A common shortcoming of courses on diversity is that the offerings in a given college or city all start at the same starting point—a point often designed for White people with little exposure to race. In the same way students in math classes would be poorly served by having every math course begin with addition, people need more options than a Racism 101 course. Learning about diversity deserves a scaffolded and complex curriculum. In a well-designed curriculum, people of color will also grow in understanding about how society works. Students of color do not share one homogeneous experience, so the process of asking why often involves identifying ways that their own racialized experiences are both patterned and individualized. They learn about intersectionality—how racism intersects with other areas of domination and subordination in society including ability, gender, sexuality, citizenship, and class. For some, deeper learning means delving into particularities in their experience such as being multiracial, being racialized differently from siblings, being adopted, growing up in predominantly White spaces, or growing up outside the United States. A well-taught class on race should challenge and stretch people of color as well as White people, because pursuing racial justice long term will require of anyone a robust understanding of history, psychology, culture, and social structures.

Answering why questions is where a lot of antiracism training focuses, and rightly so. At least nine out of the forty White people in this research mentioned a college class as a formative part of their journey. More than three times as many—thirty out of the forty interviewed—mentioned trainings led by nonprofit organizations, workplaces, or churches. Of these, at least nine—almost one-quarter of all White participants—had joined longer immersion programs such as the one Megan attended, lasting months or years. Another ten White interviewees mentioned living abroad as a key part of their journey. Such opportunities to intentionally learn from many experts can have lasting effects.

The city of Madison offers a plethora of race-related trainings, perhaps because the University of Wisconsin–Madison causes the city of Madison to attract a disproportionate number of people who are inclined to pursuing learning opportunities. Those that I attended as a participant-observer during my research included a two-day conference, a six-month cultural and racial awareness training for White Christians, a multiweek training designed for workplaces, and a Madison-based nine-week Black history course. Based on publicity materials and estimates from program planners, I estimated that these programs in total attracted at least five thousand attendees that year.

Research suggests that diversity, equity, and inclusion trainings do have measurably positive effects for both White people and people of color. For programs that do not meet their stated aims, often underfunding is a significant factor. Programs described as "diversity, equity, and inclusion" vary widely and are typically highly adaptable.[3] Contrary to the misinformation that has been widely disseminated about such programs, researchers have found that most such programs do not lead to divisiveness, shaming privileged groups, or hiring underqualified employees. As one scholar summarized, "DEI initiatives, at their core,

---

[3] Shaun Harper, ed., *Truths About DEI on College Campuses: Evidence-Based Expert Responses to Politicized Misinformation* (USC Race and Equity Center, 2024), https://race.usc.edu/wp-content/uploads/2024/03/Harper-and-Associates-DEI-Truths-Report.pdf.

emphasize belongingness, critical thinking and community engagement, cultural recognition and celebration, and institutional accountability for needed cultural transformation."[4]

Intellectual learning undoubtedly plays a role in equipping White people to address racism. When I asked people of color to describe what can go wrong in White people's attempts to pursue racial justice, often they brought up examples in which White individuals or groups lacked learning. A Latino man named Gabriel said he'd been thinking a lot lately about the importance of "intentionality in learning." He had been a part of a predominantly White church, and in the wake of a series of racist incidents, several church members of color decided to convene a group to work on steering the church toward being more racially and culturally inclusive. The group included mostly people of color and a few White individuals. After months of meetings, the group became mired in disagreements about both the diagnosis of the problem and possible solutions to the problem. Multiple members of the group eventually left the church. Gabriel described the problems he had witnessed: "I think there are White brothers and sisters that just think Black folks are still stuck in something in the past. Well, how about asking *why* they are stuck in something that hasn't changed much? Why don't you ask yourself those questions? And go find out the answers and not assume that your perspective is all there is. Why are you just making broad statements? I think for White folks, it's important to just know that there are realities that are not theirs. And so learn about those. Ask questions and learn history. And do it with humility. Take a humble posture of just learning and asking. I think that itself would go such a long way."

One point of tension in Gabriel's church had been how to respond to George Floyd's death. Some church members had taken part in demonstrations after Floyd's death, while some White church members condemned the demonstrations. Black leaders in the city had spoken up

---

[4]Lori Patton Davis, "Truthful Response," in *Truths About DEI*, 15.

about the validity of feeling angry at injustice, and White church members in Gabriel's church homed in on the word *anger*, saying anger was a sin. "It's sad to me—it's really sad to me—that a lot of White brothers and sisters will look at what's currently happening in our country and immediately just have thoughts and ideas and judgments without much relationship with anyone who's different than they are, and without even knowing or understanding a lot of the history. No one gets to where they are out of a vacuum. You can't look at people rioting and people screaming in the streets and being angry or being frustrated and just say, 'Well, they're just angry, frustrated people.' Nothing happens in a vacuum. So why aren't they asking themselves *why*? Why aren't they just even asking themselves simple questions? Like, why are Black folks angry? Not just going to the conclusion, 'They are just angry.' Well, why? Did you ever ask yourself? Did you ever try to search out the why?"

Given the emphasis that Gabriel and other interviewees placed on asking why, one might conclude that intellectual learning is the centerpiece of transformation. Indeed, much energy goes into teaching White people about racism, and of the three elements I'll cover in this book, I believe this is the one that gets the most attention and resources. We are fortunate to live at a time when resources for learning about racism abound. Recent years saw a surge in movies, websites, and trainings that explain the effects of racism for learners of all ages. When organizations aim to address racism, often their go-to action point is to train people to understand a little more about racism. Learning about racism has certain advantages that make it a convenient action point. It is, to some degree, measurable, either through number counts of people trained or assessments of whether trainees met learning objectives. It is also to some degree scalable—a course can be taught more times per year and to more students; a book and a movie can be distributed to more consumers. Teaching and learning also happen to some degree on demand. Whereas in most cases no one can cause a collision to happen to someone else or even oneself, individuals and institutions can opt in to learning or teaching as an intentional choice. Learning also spreads across many years of a person's life, which can make it seem like a more substantial part of the process than the momentary collision points that can seem like only optional blips along the longer stretch of learning.

But I'm convinced that collisions and asking why play separate roles, and these roles interlock in at least two important ways. First, as I pointed out earlier, asking why requires agency on the part of the learner, while collisions involve a release of agency. Both are important lessons for White people who have been socialized with an inflated view of their own power to control their selves and surroundings.

A second way in which these two elements fit together is that collisions personalize the social, while asking why socializes the personal. Recall Dennis, the man who was jolted into awareness of racism by listening to Black families describe racism during a visit to their home. He said it felt "personal." Collision moments often have the force to snap people into attention by personalizing the social. Collisions bring racism to a local level, which is the level at which people are used to conceptualizing the world. People of color have long recognized that intellectual arguments alone will not be sufficient to motivate change. As Black sociologist W. E. B. Du Bois said in a speech in 1934, "For the last two decades, we have striven by book and periodical, by speech and appeal, by various dramatic methods of agitation, to put the essential facts before the American people. Today there can be no doubt that Americans know the facts; and yet they remain for the most part indifferent and unmoved."[5]

To the other extreme, however, if people can conceive of racism only at the individual level, their solutions to racism will be limited to smoothing interpersonal interracial relationships. They will fail to understand how racism's deep danger is not merely the momentary slights of racist individuals but the effects of those slights when multiplied by the thousands. A collision is like picking up a shell on a beach for the first

---

[5]W. E. B. Du Bois, "A Negro Nation Within the Nation," *Current History* 42 (1935): 266.

time and feeling a surge of wonder. Asking why is like putting years of effort into learning to recognize the patterns of waves, tides, sands, migrations, seasons, and evolutions that brought that shell to the shoreline.

Sometimes in my classes, I hear students say, "You can't argue with experience." It's a conviction that often surfaces when young people recount their own life experiences around racism. Some use the phrase as sure proof that racism matters, and others to argue that racism does not matter. Experience is one basis of deciding what is true—an epistemology. Other possible epistemologies could be based on faith traditions, scientific methods, or artistic renderings. For the many people, and perhaps especially among Gen Z, the epistemology of *experience* tends to eclipse all others. But personal experience makes flimsy proof when it comes to learning about how society works. Learning about racism requires taking seriously each individual experience, and also looking beyond that micro situation to the context and patterning that surrounds it. One experience is not necessarily representative of wider trends. Each individual experience matters, but when it comes to understanding society, one experience is only one data point—no bigger or smaller than anybody else's data points. That you know your own data points in rich detail doesn't make your experience any more common or probable than the data points of individuals whose details you don't know.

Asking why involves finding new data points by hearing from a larger and more diverse pool of life experiences. Collisions offer tangible evidence that can jolt people into believing that a point of data they had previously denied does indeed exist. Asking why expands people's trust that even more data points are real, even when they cannot personally experience those data points. It's a common trope that "statistics" are lifeless and impersonal. But statistics, when used with a careful attention to what they actually portray, offer essential guideposts for understanding the world we live in. The combination of seeing statistics and seeing the individual examples of those statistics can powerfully motivate people to action.

Collisions and asking why can happen in either order. Each can beget the other. There was no consistent pattern in whether White interviewees traced the start of their transformative journey from a collision or from actively learning about racism. In Megan's case, a series of collisions prompted her to sign up for a yearlong cultural immersion program in which she could focus on learning about justice. Other times collisions happened nested within intentionally designed learning settings, as when Megan's friend in her program pointed out the discrimination happening in the post office line, or Hannah learned that Black Vernacular English is not grammatically inferior.

But learning about racism alone doesn't necessarily produce life change. White people who actively choose to learn about racism do so for a variety of acknowledged and unacknowledged reasons, some of which have little to do with addressing racism. Trainings assigned in workplaces can have neutral or even negative effects if they give participants a false sense that completing the training means completing their dealings with race, rather than empowering people to address the institutional causes of harmful outcomes for people of color.[6] Other times individuals sign up for trainings to gain approval from others, to feel like a moral person, or to fit in with a group. As a Black woman who led organizations through diversity and equity trainings said, "I see people pitfalling into that 'check the box' thing all the time, like, 'Well, I did the training! Done.' Instead, it's a practice, it's in your everyday living, in your everyday thoughts."

---

[6]As mentioned earlier, programs that use the terms *diversity*, *equity*, and *inclusion* typically include more initiatives than just training individuals. The research on diversity, equity, and inclusion programs has found mixed outcomes—some programs are more effective than others—and program design matters. Elizabeth Desnoyers-Colas, "Talking Loud and Saying Nothing: Kicking Faux Ally-Ness to the Curb by Battling Racial Battle Fatigue Using White Accomplice-Ment," *Departures in Critical Qualitative Research* 8, no. 4 (2019): 100-105; Patricia G. Devine and Tory L. Ash, "Diversity Training Goals, Limitations, and Promise: A Review of the Multidisciplinary Literature," *Annual Review of Psychology* 73 (2022): 403-29; Hahrie Han, *Undivided: The Quest for Racial Solidarity in an American Church* (Knopf, 2024); Elizabeth Levy Paluck et al., "Prejudice Reduction: Progress and Challenges," *Annual Review of Psychology* 72 (2021): 533-60.

People who walk away from race-related trainings without changing their lives abound. Important to keep in mind, though, is that many of the White people I interviewed had been those people in past seasons of their lives. Years and decades passed when they couldn't recall doing anything related to racial justice. Looking back, they often couldn't pinpoint any reason that they had left behind what they learned about racial justice during those stages; they just never had the opposite—a compelling reason to stay. Avoidance was easier. So they took the easy option.

Because here's the thing—White people can walk away. Unlike people of color, White people can choose to have a conversation on race one day and then not think about it again for months. As we saw earlier, Whiteness is the invisible, unnamed standard of normalcy, and White people in a majority-White and White-dominated society don't have to assimilate to fit in racially. They are what everyone else is supposed to assimilate into. Aside from isolated collision moments, they can recede into White enclaves and make it through life feeling fine about their racial identity. Even with as many as five thousand people attending racism-related trainings in the city of Madison in a year, several people of color I interviewed still struggled to think of any White individuals they would recommend for this study. Clearly a lot of White people could walk away from these trainings without making significant positive changes. One Black man described the difference between his experience and White people's experience. "A lot of White people want to start thinking about racial stuff and then take a break. I can't never stop. As much as I'd like to stop, I can't. It's a constant thing. That's because of the White environment I live in. I never get a break."

Staying on the journey once you've begun to ask why is inherently tough. For many White people, it's easier to "take a break." For some, it will be a long or endless break. In the next chapter, we'll consider why it's so difficult to stay on the journey.

NINE

Pitfalls to Perseverance

IN THE LAST CHAPTER, we saw that learning about the wider systemic causes of racism is a crucial part of White people's transformative journeys. In this chapter we'll consider why learning alone is not enough to propel lasting change.

"I feel like I've kind of like tapped out on some stuff." Lynn and her friend Anna, both White women in their forties, chatted casually on Anna's porch. The day was unseasonably warm. We sipped glasses of ice water and munched snacks from bowls Anna brought to share. Their families had both moved into this neighborhood over a decade earlier. They met through church, and both shared a desire to join in a historically underresourced and diverse neighborhood. Their kids attended public school together, sometimes as the only White kids in their classes. They often sat on porches and around dinner tables with other neighbors, processing life in their city. I had come to interview Anna, and as we were chatting, Lynn had stopped by to offer Anna's kids a ride to a birthday party later that day. When Anna introduced us and described my research, Lynn was intrigued. Ten minutes later, she was settled into a chair on the porch fully engaged in the conversation.

In many ways, Lynn's life paralleled a lot of White people in this study. She grew up in a Christian family in a White neighborhood where people didn't talk about race, then faced some troubling discoveries about injustice in college. She joined a summer-long internship designed to train young people to address social injustice, and the combination of living in a non-White neighborhood plus theologically grounded training left her unsettled. She met people who had persevered in this work longer than her lifetime. A question consumed her: How could they keep pushing against unjust systems for so long without getting discouraged?

"I was working with people who had been in it for the long haul, and I'd ask them, 'How do you keep it up? How have you been doing this so long? You burned your draft card in, like, 1969? And you're still going? And you still somehow believe that the moral arc of the universe bends towards justice? Like, how?'" She could already tell there was something different between their staying power and hers. "I was like, 'I'm having trouble. I'm twenty-two, and I'm already struggling. So how do you, like, *sustain* that?'"

I smiled, assuming this was her lead in to a discovery she had made since. "So here we are twenty years later, and now *you're* the person who's been at this longer," I prompted. "What would you tell your former self about how to sustain that?"

Her response was quick. "I don't know if I'm the best person to ask that. I feel like I have not sustained it in some ways." That's when she admitted, "I feel like I've kind of like tapped out on some stuff."

Her "tapping out" involved shifting to a career that didn't deal with injustice as directly as her previous work. It also included what she called a "pause" on Christianity. She called herself "jaded," with "more than one foot in agnosticism." Anna laughed at her playful wording, but the story was all too familiar. Each of us knew others in her situation. "My jaded default at this point is like, 'Christians have nothing to contribute to this conversation. Christians botched it from start to finish and should probably just like, tap out. Take a bye. Take a bye for this millennium.'" I felt the raw hurt beneath her joking.

She told more of her journey. This wasn't the first time she'd wrestled with how to hope for Christianity, justice, or their combination. "When I was in college, I was in a resistance phase," she said. "I was figuring out who I am and who I'm supposed to be. When I look back on it, it feels cringy to me."

"That's common," I said. "A lot of people don't know what to resist. They're trying to figure out where to begin."

"Yeah, well, I began everywhere!" We laughed again as she mimicked the angry voice of her former self. "*I hate all of this. And I think you're all wrong.*" At the time, she thought of herself as "breaking things down." Looking back, she uses a word that has since come into common use: *deconstruction*. Somehow the pieces that broke apart for Lynn in that season never seemed to fit back together.

Lynn was attending a Christian college in September 2001, when terrorists destroyed the World Trade Center. She remembered the confusion and horror as classmates filed into an impromptu chapel service that afternoon. The chaplain began the service by leading the college in "A Mighty Fortress Is Our God," a hymn full of battle imagery and references to God being "on our side." In other contexts, the lyrics might be a metaphor for spiritual battle, but on that day it seemed to Lynn to be chosen as a justification for nationalistic militarism. Lynn was disgusted. She listened to the chaplain banging out triumphalist anthems, thinking, *This is bad. This is really bad.* Finally, a professor stood up and voiced what she felt. "He was like, 'Can we please sing a song of lament? We need to lament.'" This word, *lament*, was new to her, and it felt right.

The following year, Lynn joined an organization striving to prevent the United States from going to war in Iraq. She described that year as "formative because it *didn't* work. The war started. And has been ongoing ever since. That felt like a huge blow." She believed now that this failure was just the lesson she needed. "As young activists, it was useful to feel how sometimes you put your whole heart and soul into it and the wrong thing still happens. And it really helps with the ego and that attitude that thinks, 'I can stop a war.' Actually, sometimes you can't."

Sometimes you can't. Then what? Do you sing a song of triumph to refresh your energy? Do you lament? Do you tap out? Do you persevere?

In this chapter, we explore pitfalls that White people encounter as they try to turn their learning into persistent advocacy for racial justice. Even when people have experienced both the motivating shake-ups of collisions and the slow growth of asking why, they lack some important pieces to make this journey sustainable for the long haul. Before we consider how the third element combines with these two, let's take a tough look at four pitfalls that White people consistently told me they had encountered as they tried to become advocates for justice: (1) gaps between knowledge and embodiment, (2) uncertainty around complexity, (3) loneliness, and (4) fear of guilt and shame. Together, these break down delusional ways of hoping, leaving people uncertain how to hope or whether there is any hope at all.

GAPS BETWEEN KNOWLEDGE AND EMBODIMENT

As we saw in the last chapter, asking why involves developing a posture of continual exploration about structural, cultural, and moral aspects of racism. Through this process, people learn a shared repertoire of ideas. They can become adept at talking the talk.

But here's the rub: *Intellectual learning is not the same as embodying.* When White people begin trying to embody new ways of being a part of their social systems, they discover that people of color are not the only people constrained by cultural and social systems—they too are led by society down pathways they may not choose. Anthropologist Vincent Crapanzano describes the dilemma well in his ethnography of White South Africans prior to the end of apartheid.

> In the popular imagination, the dominant—"the establishment," "capitalists," "imperialists," "the upper classes," "the rich"—are often cast as though they were immune from social, cultural, and psychological constraint. How often is "the imperialist" characterized as a ruthless exploiter without conscience! If he were only that, he would have been far more successful in his exploitations. Such a view fails, of course, to recognize the constraints on the dominant.

To be dominant in a system is not to dominate the system. Both the dominant and the dominated are equally caught in it. One has the advantage; the other does not.[1]

Intellectual teaching about racism can provide White people with a kind of behavioral rulebook. People new to this learning tend to absorb that rulebook as a binary set of dos and don'ts. Do let people of color lead. Do acknowledge Indigenous caretakers of the land. Do lean in with curiosity and intention when learning about racism makes you feel uncomfortable. Don't expect people of color to be your personal educators or recount their trauma for you. When called out for your own racist behaviors or complicity, don't redirect the attention to your feelings or intentions.

Knowing these dos and don'ts is not the same as developing an embodied way of being. Anthropologists use the word *habitus* to describe the set of inclinations and tendencies that come naturally to a person due to the totality of circumstances passed down to them through their social world.[2] Habitus doesn't change overnight. A handful of classes, a book club, and a podcast will barely make a dent in a habitus.[3] We learn a habitus through a continual process of trying one action after another, responding to the feedback of the world around us and, through that back and forth, slowly accumulating tendencies in our emotions, perceptions, and habits. People exposed to similar social circumstances will share a similar habitus. They will seem to follow the same rules even without being able to name those rules, like a jazz orchestra without a conductor. In this way, every individual improvises their own creative life course, but each does so in unconscious accordance with a habitus formed out of the

---

[1] Vincent Crapanzano, *Waiting: The Whites of South Africa* (Vintage, 1986), 20.
[2] In a longer explanation Pierre Bourdieu defines *habitus* as "systems of durable, transposable dispositions, structured structures predisposed to function as structuring structures, that is, as principles which generate and organize practices and representations that can be objectively adapted to their outcomes without presupposing a conscious aiming at ends." Bourdieu, *The Logic of Practice* (Stanford University Press, 1990), 53.
[3] Robin DiAngelo is another scholar who explores the question of how Whiteness shapes habitus. She explains the concept for which she is best known, White fragility, as an aspect of the habitus that White people learn, in which they are unable to tolerate even minimal stress related to race. DiAngelo, "White Fragility," *International Journal of Critical Pedagogy* 3, no. 3 (2011): 54-70.

path they have come from. Habitus helps explain why groups within society—such as socioeconomic groups or racial groups—often carry on in similar trends across time even without obvious forces instructing them to do so, like a train laying down its own tracks as it goes.[4]

In some ways, trying to change one's habitus is like learning to dance. Imagine yourself on a dance floor. The act of improvised dancing is a complex process of building something out of all the inputs you receive through every dance you have ever witnessed or tried, as well as every smile or smirk on the faces of people watching. Dancing involves conscious thought as well as unconscious moderating of what feels right in your own body. Different people on the same dance floor are absorbing some of the same inputs, but they are also processing those inputs through differing histories. A man whose past experiences add up to a message of "I hate dancing and I'm bad at it" will likely beeline off that dance floor. Another just took her first dance class and she's trying out some new moves, but in her head she is still counting one, two, three-and-four in her head to get it right. A man next to her might be repeating the same three dance moves he's been using since that one great memory of a cute friend smiling at him at the high school prom. Whatever moves each makes, they are filtered through all their experiences of dancing up until that point. If they keep coming back, their movements will undoubtedly change over time, but they will still thread incrementally forward from their past experiences. They can't merely think their way into dancing. Nor can people think their way into a new habitus that works against racism. Intellectual learning does not necessarily translate into new ways of acting, and when it does, it can take a long time to feel natural.

UNCERTAINTY AROUND COMPLEXITY

Even when training about racism gives people advice about active steps to take, no one can purchase a shortcut into a habitus that will enable

---

[4] Bourdieu, *Logic of Practice*, 57.

them to consistently, effectively, or effortlessly handle race-related situations. As one woman put it, "My Whiteness comes with me in all spaces." This woman told me about a dilemma she faced during a time when she had just begun actively learning about racism. She was invited by a Black acquaintance to join a gospel choir where she would be one of only a few White singers. At first, she loved the experience. "I loved singing that music. It was a pure joy to be there." But the more she read about race, she found herself caught in a contradictory web of dos and don'ts. "After learning more about my Whiteness, I just didn't feel like it was the right thing to do. I didn't want to ruin a safe space where they could come and just feel like they could be themselves," she said. "Whiteness comes in there with me. So I stopped participating." She didn't want to force Black people to adapt to her, and she didn't know any way to avoid that except to leave. "I just didn't want to take the risk. And I never asked anybody—I never said like, 'Do I change your experience, or how does it feel to have me here?' I just was like, 'I'm just not going to take the chance.'" Like many White people, she began to see herself as a safety threat in non-White spaces, and she didn't know how to embody anything else.

At the time of her dilemma about whether to join a Black choir, this woman might have benefited from hearing the caution I heard from one Black leader: "There will be 'danged if I do, and danged if I don't.'" Part of the reason it's hard to move from learning about racism into doing something about it is that there's not always one clear best path. If racism trainings give a set of rules, people will still need to contextualize those rules. And contextualizing requires dealing with seeming contradictions.

Confusion about how to navigate dos and don'ts within their own contextualized situations presents a serious challenge to many White learners. Pete was a White man whose account of his life story included many of the same elements as Megan's story. He had been shaken by some initial collision points talking with people of color about their experiences with racism, and he had benefited from professors, authors, and speakers who directed him to further learning. As a college student, he spent a summer volunteering in an urban immersion program in a predominantly non-White neighborhood. The summer was "a very moving experience" for him and "challenging in good ways." But it also left him unsettled. He began the program thinking, *Oh, we're going to come in and hopefully make a difference.* By the end of the summer, he realized "how much we didn't know, how much we had to learn, and how much we had." Most unsettling was the discovery that what he thought was an act of generosity—volunteering—was part of the chasm of difference between himself and the people whose lives he wanted to improve. People in the community kept marveling that he could take a whole summer off without pay. "They're like, 'Wait, what? You're volunteering your time?'" Those conversations poked holes in the simple moral codes he believed at the start of the summer. Now he faced a contradiction: If you don't volunteer, you're selfish. If you do volunteer, you're privileged. What then?

I've often fielded questions from White students wrestling with danged-both-ways contradictions in their early years of racism awareness. How can you give generously but not think of yourself as a White savior? How can you see all the wrongs White people cause but not be driven by White guilt? How can you create safe spaces for people of color but not treat people of color as fragile or pitiable? How are you supposed to follow and learn from people of color but not expect that they take on the burden of educating you or spending their valuable time on you? How do you learn empathy for racism by paying attention to other areas of subordination you might experience, such as gender, disability, sexuality, or religion, but never imply that, by knowing about these, you know how racism feels?

Often these conflicts leave people paralyzed. Not wanting to offend anybody, people come to believe that the only alternative is not to intervene at all. Young people in my classes are often familiar with the title of the influential book by Steve Corbett and Brian Fikkert: *When Helping*

Hurts.⁵ But contrary to the intent of the book, they have become hyperaware of the pitfalls of trying to improve society, so much so that they believe helping only and always causes hurt.

In his controversial book *Woke Racism*, Black scholar of linguistics John McWhorter critiques the wave of antiracism education that he claims has created "a collection of tenets that, stated clearly and placed in simple oppositions, translate into nothing whatsoever." His list of contradictory tenets includes: "When Black people say you have insulted them, apologize with profound sincerity and guilt," but simultaneously "Don't put Black people in a position where you expect them to forgive you." "Silence about racism is violence," but also "Elevate the voices of the oppressed over your own." "Show interest in multiculturalism," but "do not culturally appropriate." And "Support Black people in creating their own spaces and stay out of them," but also, "Seek to have Black friends."⁶

For McWhorter, this all translates into "nothing whatsoever." But I'm convinced that these contradictions add up to something more than nothing. Based on what I heard from people who had grappled with these contradictions for years and decades, I believe that rather than translating into nothing, these contradictions point to a typical, run-of-the-mill, big problem. The nature of big problems is this: They demand careful contextualization and more why questions. Instead of writing off a seeming contradiction as an excuse to give up, a contextualized approach asks, "In what situations is one side of this contradiction appropriate and in what situations is the other?"⁷ For example, a person can show interest in multiculturalism while also learning how to recognize the problematic forms of cultural appropriation that occur when people

---

[5] Steve Corbett and Brian Fikkert, *When Helping Hurts: How to Alleviate Poverty Without Hurting the Poor . . . and Yourself* (Moody, 2009).

[6] John McWhorter, *Woke Racism: How a New Religion Has Betrayed Black America* (Penguin Random House, 2021), 8-9.

[7] Psychologist Michael Billig argues that by paying attention to everyday ideological contradictions such as these, people can learn to think more clearly. Billig, *Ideological Dilemmas: A Social Psychology of Everyday Thinking* (Sage, 1988).

with power and privilege profit from the cultural traditions of those they dominate. Learning to contextualize takes not just knowledge but wisdom. It also takes a willingness to learn from others with perspectives different from their own. Those things don't come quickly. At some point it can all just feel like an impossibly confusing web of questions.

LONELINESS

Learning about racism changes the way White people see the world, which can make it difficult to fit in with people who don't see the world that way. Many described times when they began to feel like outsiders among White communities and culture. Often this happened while they were beginning to search out more diverse communities, but they hadn't yet found a home in those communities either. Learning to belong in a community where they're not the majority is challenging for many White people. Precisely because of the normativity of Whiteness, many have little experience being in the minority. They may feel they're bumbling along awkwardly. This can be a lonely season.

I sat one sunny afternoon on a patio outside the home of a White couple named Tanya and Martin in a predominantly Black neighborhood where they had lived for over a decade. They told me how much they had enjoyed living there—getting to know neighbors, sending their children to neighborhood schools, and sharing their home with non-White renters. "It's been great," Martin summarized. But to their parents, their choices had never quite made sense. "They thought we were weird," Tanya said.

Later, when I listened to the recording of our conversation, I realized they had used the word *weird* ten times in one hour of conversation. Their White friends thought they were weird. When Tanya and Martin moved there, at first their neighbors' behaviors had seemed weird. Soon they realized that, from the perspective of their neighbors, they themselves were weird. "The more you're exposed to other cultures," Tanya said, "and the more your own culture is the minority, the more you're like, 'Wow, this doesn't actually make sense. Actually we are pretty weird.'" Martin said he thinks a lot about how ignorant they were.

But being weird can get tiring. When I asked about the challenges they felt in living in their neighborhood, Martin and Tanya spoke about what else comes of finding yourself "weird" to your family, your neighbors, and even to yourself: loneliness. "It's definitely made it more difficult to connect easily with White people," Martin said. At the same time, they had come to terms with the reality that their Whiteness would always be a part of their interactions with neighbors, no matter how long they lived there. "I say this gently," Tanya said, "because I haven't made a huge effort lately to try and connect with people, but actually, I've found it really hard to build real friendships. And I know the tendency is that people here tell each other, 'Don't trust White people. White people will change and turn on you.' And I think that feeds into it. And our whole history. And just the transient nature of the community. But I often feel like it's harder because of the color of our skin to connect with people, because there's an assumption about us." She paused, and in a moment of self-awareness, shifted into a joking tone. "I realize, it's *so* hard to be White. It's really tough!" She didn't mean to complain about being White, knowing that people of color experience a similar loneliness being in the minority on a regular basis. In a more serious tone again, she reiterated, "But I would like to feel more connected and have more meaningful friendships."

Martin cut in. "The odds of that happening if we were in a White suburb are also pretty low." Tanya agreed. That's just the thing—they didn't fit in with people of color, and they didn't fit in with most White people anymore either. They had entered a liminal space, and it was hard to find people like themselves in that space. Tanya and Martin were figuring out how to be a new kind of outsider. Often White people mentioned finding a White mentor or close White friend who played an essential role in their journey. Tanya and Martin had each other, and for some seasons they had other White friends who were similarly committed to racial justice, but some of their closest friends had moved away. There is a leaving behind that comes with learning, and sometimes there's no assurance of how, or even whether, a sense of belonging will ever return.

FEAR OF GUILT AND SHAME

The awkwardness that many White people feel in their early attempts to embody what they learn about racial justice is not without cause. They are navigating their way through real harms affecting real lives. And they make real mistakes, despite whatever good intentions they bring. Even when their minds are hyper-aware of racism, White people are still positioned in societal places and bearing deeply ingrained ways of being that can cause microaggressions and other forms of harm against people of color. Sometimes their mistakes are relatively harmless and laughable. One White man recounted that when he worked alongside a Black pastor for the first time, he was concentrating so hard on following the Black church tradition of referring to people with "Brother" or "Sister" before their names that he accidentally referred to a highly respected male pastor as "Sister." He recounted the story with self-depreciating humor, and in the years since, he had told the story as a way to lighten the embarrassment and awkwardness other White people feel in early encounters with people of other ethnic and racial groups. But not all the blunders I heard made such lighthearted stories.

A Black woman named Joyce recounted a time she was working in a community organization alongside a White woman. Joyce had a PhD and many years of leadership experience in Black and underresourced communities. This White woman was also well-versed in the social issues their organization was addressing, but Joyce started to notice something strange in this White woman's interactions. "She seemed so uncomfortable with me." One day Joyce decided to confront the White woman directly. "Finally I said, 'What is it? What? What is the problem?'" The woman responded, "Well, you know, I've never worked with a Black person who had the kind of credentials that you do." In retelling the story, Joyce raised her eyebrows and paused to let the moment sink in. Today she makes a point of telling White people, "You won't learn anything by going to help those poor kids somewhere else, like the Salvation Army or afterschool program. All it's going to do is reinforce what you already believe about them. What you have to do is see if you can be in some kind of equal-status relationship." Very few of the White people I talked with had grown up around people of color in equal status to themselves or their families.

Awkwardness like that of Joyce's White coworker may be more common in early efforts at racial justice, but the disheartening reality that White people face is that no amount of experience or training ever produces antiracist perfection. In fact, at least early in their journey, their efforts to address racism generally put them into more contact with people of color, which means more opportunities to make mistakes and see the effects of their mistakes.

Collisions and asking why lead to encounters—and often long, deep, scary encounters—with inadequacy. Beverly Tatum, a psychology scholar who has written extensively about race, identifies the "guilty white" model of racial identity characterized by "the heightened awareness of racism and the accompanying shame and embarrassment about being white," which "interferes with one's ability to take effective action to interrupt the expressions of racism."[8] Drick Boyd, a White professor of urban studies at a Christian college, writes about seeing students in his classes paralyzed by the guilty White complex. "I have found that in my courses that there often comes a point where White students feel caught between an overwhelming sense of guilt and shame for the history of White racism from which they have benefitted while feeling powerless as to how to proceed in a way that does not perpetuate existing racist policies and laws or cause offense to Persons of Color they

---

[8]Beverly Tatum, "Teaching White Students About Racism: The Search for White Allies and the Restoration of Hope," *Teachers College Record* 95, no. 4 (1994): 471.

know through casual interaction. For many of my White students this is a point at which they feel stuck between the awareness of their need to change and confusion on what or how to change." Too many White students become bound by "guilt and hopelessness."[9]

Fear of guilt manifests in multiple ways. One way White people try to manage a fear of guilt is by building walls to protect their positive self-image, creating a protective shell of pride. Trying to be a great advocate for racial justice can itself become a centerpiece of pride. "Allies are the worst," one man of color commented to me. His tone was sarcastic, but there was also a thread of seriousness in his message. He explained that sometimes in the surging desire to be on the right side of injustice, newly trained White allies leap into indignant condemnation at the slightest sniff of racism. Other times they overstep the slow, consistent work of more experienced people and advocates.

As another man of color pointed out, White people "need to move beyond a hierarchy of wokeness." In their desire to be people of action, White learners can latch onto the action of calling out individuals who don't conform to the rules they've learned. Facile finger-pointing can promote the public perception that racial justice work is nothing more than an obsession with canceling and calling out others. Examples abound of mob-like drives to ostracize and shun the racist offender du jour. While such efforts occasionally lead to important changes in institutions, along the way they can create bitter opponents who might do more harm to the institution in the long run. There is a tempting path of proving one's legitimacy as a "good" White person by comparing one's self to whomever seems slightly more racist. But it's an ugly and unsustainable way of being.

For others, fear of guilt manifests not in pride but in self-loathing. As White people become more aware of their individual and collective involvement in racism, they can so fully imbibe an awareness of wrong that

---

[9]Drick Boyd, *Disrupting Whiteness: Talking with White People About Racism* (Arch Street, 2021), 5-6.

it becomes a source of shame—a belief that they not only *do* wrong at times but that they are fundamentally flawed.[10] They believe the lie that their racist actions and their participation in racist systems necessarily makes "racist" their primary identity. As we'll see in the coming chapters, finding a way out of guilt and shame is a critical turning point for White people who develop persevering hope.

The way out of the guilt or shame will not come by reaching a point where they never have to be wrong again. No one ever becomes immune to making racist mistakes. In fact, as I write this, I can recall not one but three microaggressions I've caused just in the past two months. The track record is that bad. First was the day I attended a gathering of Christian women from many churches. The event was hosted at a Black church. As I placed fruit and a donut on my plate in the breakfast line before the event, I chatted with a Black woman in line beside me. Assuming that members of this Black church had provided the breakfast, I asked her, "Did you help set up for this event?" She responded ever so politely, "Actually, I'm the speaker today." I looked at her heels, her satin shirt, her perfect hair. Seated near the kitchen were women wearing aprons who presumably had set up for the event. This woman was the keynote speaker, the guest of honor, here to receive an award. I had mistaken her Black body for "the help."

A few weeks later, I attended a separate event in which I mistook one of the few Asian women in the room for another Asian woman, as if the only important distinguishing characteristic between them and every other participant was the continent their ancestors came from. A few weeks after that, at a community event I mistook a Black woman who had come to volunteer for a recipient of aid.

In each misstep, I knew immediately that I'd committed another quintessential microaggression. Microaggressions are "brief and

---

[10]For at least one informant, writing by Brené Brown was helpful in distinguishing between shame and guilt. Brown, *The Gifts of Imperfection: Let Go of Who You Think You're Supposed to Be and Embrace Who You Are* (Hazelden, 2010).

commonplace daily verbal, behavioral, and environmental indignities, whether intentional or unintentional, that communicate hostile, derogatory, or negative racial slights and insults to the target person or group."[11] The term *microaggression* can be misleading—the reason they are so troubling is that they are the surface-level manifestations of patterned harms reaching back across decades or centuries. Microaggressions inadvertently communicate to people of color that they do not belong, are second-class citizens, or are untrustworthy. The very fact that they are subtle and constant makes them all the more significant in impact. Microaggressions are incessantly fatiguing for those targeted by them because it's impossible to pinpoint exactly how much bias was involved—was that a racial incident or just an accident? Was that intentional, and if so, does that matter? If this has happened a thousand times before, is it worth saying something this time? Is the likelihood of backlash for speaking up worth the risk? Racial battle fatigue builds up over time as people of color are mistaken for blue-collar workers, foreigners, welfare recipients, the other person of color in the room, or caricatures of themselves.

I know. This is all cringeworthy. I can still feel my gut tensing at the memories. Each time these things happen, I apologize. I name what happened. I try to name why it's not okay and say I'm working on doing better. People respond with kind words like "It's fine," because that's often the easiest way to survive microaggressions. I try to say, "Thank you, but I still want to do better." Often we make an awkward exit from the conversation. I want to crawl under a table. I wonder whether it would be better if I had not showed up at all.

I have earned a PhD and written now two books on racism. I attended many trainings on racism for this research, and many more over my own professional and personal journey. I have years of experience living and worshiping in interracial and intercultural settings. I teach

---

[11]Sue et al., "Racial Microaggressions in Everyday Life," 273.

about racism as my profession. I offer these examples from my own life not to make myself look worse (or somehow better) than anyone in the study but as evidence that intellectual learning does not produce immunity from doing racist things. Not for me and not for any White person in this research.

The memories of guilt that White people in this research carried were often heavy and painful. Causing a person of color to unnecessarily lose their job. Seeing people die in international wars provoked by their own US government. Failing to visit sick and dying acquaintances out of awkwardness or shame. Again and again, just standing by and doing nothing—not knowing what to do, not finding the courage to do what they knew to do.

Native American author Mark Charles and Asian American author Soong-Chan Rah argue that as White people participate in causing harms against people of color, they experience a particular form of trauma that lacks a name. "Could whites, even as perpetrators and beneficiaries of trauma inflicted upon people of color, also experience a trauma that is distinct from the trauma experienced by people of color? Could white Americans, privileged and empowered, be responding to the reality of trauma in their lives?" They suggest that one way to understand such trauma would be to treat it as a complex repeated form of the psychological condition called participation-induced traumatic stress (PITS), which occurs in people who have participated in causing someone else's trauma.[12]

White people who want to address racism will need to spend time around people of color. That means the likelihood of causing harm and seeing the effects of that harm will increase in the short run. If a White person wants to feel like they're not doing anything wrong, their best option is probably to surround themselves with no more than one person of color at a time and a lot of White people who know less about racism

---

[12]Mark Charles and Soong-Chan Rah, *Unsettling Truths: The Ongoing, Dehumanizing Legacy of the Doctrine of Discovery* (InterVarsity Press, 2019), 172-73, 175-76.

than they do. Getting out of that White enclave to find ways to deal with racism will mean becoming vulnerable enough to try new interactions. Some will go well and some will go badly, and probably more will go badly than anyone would like. White people can see the effects of their actions more clearly when they're around people of color, and that can be tough on everyone. At some point every White individual who seeks out opportunities to deal with racism is going to need an answer to the question: Wouldn't this space be better off without me?

And they will not find a simple answer to that question. There are a lot of reasons for White people to give up trying to address racism. Sometimes those can even seem like good reasons. Loving reasons. Racism-aware reasons. Reasons that people of color might agree with. What then?

Racism is so, so big. It's a *social* problem, and that means no one *individual* can make it go away alone. You and all your friends can't make it go away. You can't even change yourself. You're steeped in a racist society, and no matter your training or your experience, you're going to do racist things sometimes, and maybe a lot of the time. Maybe you think you're going to be different from all the rest because you've got a plan and you're not like those other people. Good luck with that. Even if you were to somehow manage to get it all down perfectly, how are you going to fix all the harm that came before you? And how are you going to share that with enough other people to make the change stick? And whether it's somebody else or yourself who lets you down the next time, what are you going to do? Are you going to trudge ahead on your lonely road of self-perfection, self-recrimination, and self-flagellation? If you're White, what are you going to do with all of that guilt? If you're a person of color, what are you going to do with all of that hurt?

As we saw in earlier chapters, Whiteness offers people a certain imagination of the social world. That imaginary trains people to see Whiteness as the normal, unmarked category while ranking non-White Others in a hierarchy. It denies the harm of racism and the culpability of individuals and systems causing that harm. Social imaginaries form our frameworks for interpreting the present and our visions of the future. In other words, social imaginaries are the scaffolding of hopes. When we disassemble our social imaginaries, we also disassemble our hopes.

The processes we have discussed so far—collisions, asking why, and the pitfalls people navigate along the way—all are very effective at stripping away hope. When you know just how big the problems of racism are, and that you are culpable in perpetuating those problems, and that sometimes you'll feel alone in tackling those problems, and that you're going to get it wrong again sometimes, well, it's hard to hold on to a conventional, optimistic hope. In the absence of those old habits of hope, people face discomfort and disillusionment strong enough to drive away even the most well-intended and strong willed.

If microaggressions are brief and commonplace daily indignities that communicate hostility, then perhaps we could say that there's also such a thing as *microdiscouragements*—the brief and commonplace daily encounters that communicate reasons to give up hope. The power of microdiscouragements, like microaggressions, is in the space between feeling and certainty. One speculates constantly whether there might be a course of action to neatly explain this all away. *Perhaps I've only imagined this to be so bad. Perhaps it's just me and my oversensitivity. Perhaps I'm the crazy one.* When faced as just one incident at a time, microaggressions and microdiscouragements aren't so bad, but there's always a looming sense that they add up to something more. There are many techniques for holding at bay that "something more." You can ignore it, deny it, put on a cheerful face, or speak a platitude. If you want to save yourself from facing that something more, you don't tell a friend who experienced the same thing. You don't risk finding out whether there's really something happening here and whether this is indeed a pattern. You stop asking questions about the bigger picture. You don't question whether there's any end in sight. If you want to get through the day, you don't go there.

But going "there" is where truth is found. The truth is that racism still happens. There's a flood of that truth just beyond the flimsy walls of the delusional hope that people build around themselves. All the survivalist, repressive techniques and denial tactics in the world are just patches on those walls. If we want to find freedom, we'll have to open the door, let that mucky truth flow in, and see what happens next.

PART 5

Responding to Grace

TEN

What to Do with Guilt

LET'S RETURN FOR a moment to the place this book began. Recall the story of Hannah, who darkened her skin for a Halloween costume and then, years later, casually mentioned that experience to a Black friend, Mark. She said their conversation across the table together was the most charged moment of her life. Mark faced her with what she called "a certain kind of gaze."

If we freeze that gaze like a paused film, we might see on the faces of Hannah and Mark each a kind of horror. For Hannah, it's the horror of discovering that she has done something wrong. She believed herself to be a kind, well-intentioned, and socially aware person. Mark's gaze has shattered that self-image. Her horror is in discovering that she is not who she thought she was.

On Mark's face is a horror that, from what Hannah can tell, seems an expression of disappointment that she is next in a long progression of people doing the same wrong thing. He knows the history. This is more than an innocent, one-time mistake; it's evidence that this society has raised one more White person to disregard what it feels like to be Black. He has dealt with White people enough to read much of what Hannah sees in herself—that she believes herself good, that she hates discovering her actions were not. He does not want to be here. Neither of them do. But here they are.

But Hannah noticed two more things in Mark's face besides horror. The first was love. "I know he loves me deeply, right?" Their families had been friends since she was a child. This was not a relationship that either expected to give up on that night. There was a commitment there, a willingness to find a way through this.

The second thing she saw in his face was hope. "I think there's a little part of them that has hope, you know? That this stupid White girl might learn something, like she might just learn something. But then, like, *do you dare even hope for that?*" They were frozen in the precipice between the present horror and an unknown future. What would it look like to orient themselves toward that future *anticipating good*?

Sooner or later, everyone who tries to fix injustice will stand between horror and hope. Collisions and why questions unearth the horrors of half-rotted harms from long ago and new harms still fresh with stench. And those harms are stamped with culpability. Racism ultimately hurts everyone, but the balance of harm is not even—White people have harmed and taken more than they have healed and given. There is an existential question in this place between horror and hope: What do we do with harm?

This is a complicated question at an individual level, but even more so at a collective level. What can people, collectively, do about the debts accrued through wrongdoing across lifetimes and generations, harms woven into every thread of collective life? How do people break down the seemingly impassible walls of otherness, hurt, and incommensurability that cut between us?

Whether consciously or not, every person attempting to deal with social injustice acts out of some belief about the answer to this question. Some choose a "let bygones be bygones" response that silences history. Others operate with a "what's done can never be undone" approach, forever tethering their identity to wrongdoer or wronged. Others make a goal of quantifying and equalizing the debts, hoping to count and repay what's been taken across lifetimes. Others take the approach Benjamin recognized in the question at his conference—protect yourself from the Other because there is no pathway back to love. We are surrounded by people living according to each of these answers. That is why the response of people in this study was so startling.

If we unpause the story of Hannah and Mark, the way the next frame of that film unfolds will depend on their answer to the question of what to do about past harms. They might walk away, choosing to organize their lives on opposite sides of that wall of separation forever. Avoid confrontation. Keep things quiet. Tiptoe. Or they might take a more confrontational route. They might metaphorically "burn it all down." Trash the relationship, trash whatever systems and institutions they're enjoined by. Try to find a new beginning when the ashes cool.

Let's unpause and see what happened next.

In the moment of that gaze, both Hannah and Mark found a way to calm the fight-or-flight mechanisms that must have been sparking through their bodies. Perhaps that staying strength had something to do with this sentence of her recollection: "I know he loves me." Hannah recalled him saying slowly, perhaps with a sigh, "This is a teachable moment. Can I use this as a teachable moment?" She took a breath and listened. He explained why it's wrong for a White woman to put on dark makeup for Halloween. He gave her his honesty.[1]

Hannah told me she had seen that "certain kind of gaze" at other times. She said the moment with Mark made possible another story later, like an arc stretching across her life.

After graduating from the college where the Halloween party occurred, Hannah began working as a teacher in a public school. That work brought her into frequent interactions with students of color. Over time, her uncertainty about race-infused incidents began building up. On an

---

[1] Because I was unable to meet with Mark to confirm his interpretation of this story, we do not know how he would interpret this event. As the coming chapters will demonstrate, too often the actions of Black people have been interpreted as grace when they did not intend them to be so, which becomes particularly problematic when grace is misused as an excuse that lets White people off the hook. While I have chosen to relate Hannah's interpretation of these events, and I see these events as fitting within the definition of grace I use in this book—a freely given gift of his time and honesty that prompted a freely given but anticipated future response from her. Like all stories, this one is open to other interpretations.

especially trying day, she called the parents of a Black student about an incident in class, and the mother burst into impassioned frustration directed at Hannah herself. "It really rattled me. Part of it was just my own sensitivity, but there was a racial element there for sure. But I didn't have the wherewithal and the skills to see. I really was a mess afterwards. Like I couldn't sleep at night."

That night she scrolled through her phone looking for something over the weekend that might distract her. She noticed that an influential Black Christian leader was holding an event about how to address racism. She decided to attend.

"It was at the church." This was a strange space to her. Hannah had never been a church attender. "And just being in that church, something happened to me." She sat and soaked up the talk. "I get a little weepy thinking about it still. I was like, 'Wow, I don't know what's happening here, but I feel like I belong here. I feel like, there's something hopeful here.' Because I felt so horrible and I just thought, here's this Black man appealing to White people. Like, believing in White people that if you just, if you educate them and give them the space to do their best, that could really happen. And I wanted to be part of that."

Later she talked with the Black church leader about the school incident that prompted her to come to the talk. She half-expected him to chide her for what she knew to be her own blame. Instead, he took time to help her think through the incident from new angles. She said of that conversation, "I'll never forget the grace that he had with me in that moment. I didn't know what grace was, but when I look back at it, it's ever more profound, like understanding how effed up we actually are, and yet he still—" Here her sentence broke off and she gave a kind of awed headshake.

Hannah began attending that church. She became a Christian because of what she found there. Christianity was still new to Hannah when we met, but she had dropped one of the most spot-on definitions of grace I've ever heard: *understanding how effed up we actually are and yet still.* . . . Yet still, despite a context of utter undeserving, somebody who's been wronged offers a tangible demonstration of love. That's a pathway between horror and hope worth investigating.

|||||||

If Hannah were the only person who told stories of grace, I might have written these off as just nice moments in her relationship with new Black friends. But I heard stories like these in one interview after another. Often when people talked about these experiences, a softness came over their faces. Hannah teared up as she told me these stories, and she mentioned tearing up while talking to Mark also. To my surprise, as I looked back at other times when people cried during interviews, in almost every single instance, they were telling a story about undeserved grace. People of color brought up stories like these and talked at length about what grace and forgiveness should—and shouldn't—mean. In more than half of all interviews, people used the word *grace* or the related terms *mercy* or *forgiveness*. They also used terms such as *surprised, unexpected, undeserved, indebted,* and *forgiven* to describe stories like Hannah's. I realized that stories of grace drill down to the very core of the theological and practical questions that haunt anyone interested in racial justice, and I started paying attention to what made these stories unique.

Grace is a particular way to respond to the question of what to do about past harm. It happens at both an intellectual level—making meaning around events that might occur to anyone—and an active level—making certain choices in response to what happened. This combination of understanding grace and (importantly) *responding* to it is the third element that I saw evidenced in nearly every life account of White individuals recommended for this research. The two elements covered so far—collisions and asking why—happen to White people regardless of religious beliefs. When I asked people to describe differences between the ways Christians and non-Christians address race, they generally didn't talk about those two elements, except to say that Christians might be more doggedly resistant to accept their own culpability. But when it comes to this third element, grace, Christianity prompts a different course of action.

Grace is a central tenet of Christianity.[2] One might assume, then, that every Christian would have this element down pat. But as I'll go on to show, not everyone relates grace to the circumstances of racism in the same way. How people employ grace in the context of race matters. In this chapter we'll investigate what grace means through a combination of stories from my research, plus anthropological and theological explanations, drawing especially from theologian Miroslav Volf. In the next chapter, we'll see how people in this study believed grace relates to racism. In the pairing of these two, we'll find an answer to our question of how to hope.

| | | | | | | | |

Let's start by listening to some stories people told about grace.

Candice said she didn't think her journey fit "the usual mold." When I asked her what stories were pivotal to becoming a person recommended for this study, she said, "I feel like I come to this place from a different journey or lens. I didn't come into it because I was interested in racial justice. I came more from the relational aspect." She visited Mexico with her family when she was in high school. Walking into a market, she discovered that even with the little Spanish she learned in school, she could communicate enough to get by. People "put up with me," she said, seeing past her mis-conjugations and drawing her into playfulness and humor. "I just remember thinking this was amazing. I walked away feeling so energized and excited that I could connect with a person who from first glance was so different from me." That experience prompted her to keep studying Spanish and then study abroad in college. "It's the

---

[2]Of course it's not only Christians who use or appreciate grace. In an entire book dedicated to "how grace changes everything," Julia Baird insists that while grace is core to the Christian faith, "I want to draw the circle far wider, because we all know, instinctively understand and experience grace." Baird, *Bright Shining: How Grace Changes Everything* (4th Estate, 2023), 5.

relationships—that's where my heart is on fire and I'm passionate." So far her stories had all been about the warmth of hospitality and welcome. Her next story had a different tone.

"I have members of my family who are very, you know, racist. So it's been interesting just observing those dynamics," Candice continued. "My grandmother definitely had a fear of Black people." This grandmother spent the latter years of her life in an assisted-living facility with several African American caregivers. Candice recounted the kinds of racist remarks her grandmother would make, especially as her dementia worsened. Candice witnessed Black caregivers respond to her grandmother with a combination of truth and grace, and it astounded her. "They could tell her like it is. They would be able to push back and be like, 'Wait. Get it together.' They would speak directly, and yet they were loving and caring for her." This was more than just the friendly relationships across differences that Candice had told me about so far. These were tough, honest confrontations over racism combined with genuine care. "It just could make me tear up," she said, her voice cracking. "Because God just puts these people around her, and you could tell in the end she had an affection for them as well. I would kind of chuckle because I'm like, 'Okay, Lord. I see what you're doing. You're surrounding her by people who she has this fear of, and she has these deeply rooted beliefs, and it's almost like you're surrounding her with them and they're loving on her and they're caring for her. And she is in her worst!'" Candice's voice quieted as she recounted the last part of her grandmother's story. "And you know, the only person from that final care facility who came to her funeral was an African American woman."

Candice thought her journey of being drawn into interracial relationships through undeserved love wouldn't "fit the mold" of my study, but there was nothing unusual about it. Stories of an undeserved welcome showed up everywhere. Another White woman said of her experience of being welcomed into a Latin American church and community, "I was invited into a world that wasn't for me." A White pastor recalled being invited into a multiracial group of pastors addressing racism before he knew much about racism. Initially, he thought he must have done something to deserve the invitation. "And then I realized, wait a second, hold on. *I* wouldn't have invited me to this!" He realized that he was invited despite his bad record, not because of a good record. Each of these people knew someone had taken a chance on them that they didn't deserve. They saw their lives since then as response to that undeserved gift. "I take it so seriously," the White pastor said. "It is such an honor that we have this space and these relationships."

Some stories of undeserved hospitality happened between people who would become longtime friends, while others occurred in brief, passing encounters. Jenna, the woman who collided with the history of racism through a talk at a college retreat, said another very different pivotal moment happened during one of the darkest moments of her life. She had signed up to attend a weekend gathering of several church congregations, but no one else from her church signed up. Just before the event, she learned she was pregnant. Her previous child had been born prematurely and spent harrowing months in the hospital. Now a doctor prepared her for this pregnancy: "This child is going to be premature. It's 100 percent certain. And very likely earlier than your other child." He hinted at abortion. She wanted to feel joy over this child, but all she felt was terror.

With that news on her heart, she attended the weekend retreat. She found herself subsumed in loneliness, wrestling with God, and "feeling really heavy." One night while everyone was singing worship songs, the weight of it overwhelmed her. "I just kind of ended up breaking down and went up to the altar and was just crying out to God." At that moment, a group of Spanish-speaking women from another church came and surrounded her. She didn't speak Spanish, and they didn't speak English. "I never talked to them. They just came and wrapped their arms around me and were praying for me. And I was trying to communicate what was going on, but I didn't have to. They just saw a sister in need and they didn't know me from anybody. But they loved me and supported me in that. And it was beautiful."

A single story about grace might hit like a drop of water on a hot stone, leaving a quiet hiss as it evaporates into steam. But these stories patter one on another like rain, changing the temperature of the stone itself, forming rivulets and puddles. By my tally, all but three of the forty White participants told stories that fit the concept of grace. The buildup of stories like these had an effect on me. I wasn't planning to write about grace. I knew that advice about grace in the context of racism has so often gone wrong, and I'll talk more about that in the coming chapter. But if I wanted to be true to the data, I had to write about grace.[3] I felt a building awareness that whatever else may be true, *grace happens*. That fact does not deny another reality, that *injustice happens*. But injustice, collision, learning, grace, and hope all fit together like pieces of a puzzle, each giving meaning to the other. Without naming the injustice, grace has no substance. Without the possibility of grace, justice has no hope.

▌▎▌▎▌▎▌

What is grace?[4] Among Christians, grace is regarded as the centerpiece of the whole relationship between God and humanity. Grace is a central

---

[3]In her study of a church-based program designed to bridge racial divides, Hahrie Han also points to the centrality of grace in her findings. She chooses to title her epilogue "Radical Grace," commenting, "I started this project because I wanted to understand how people seeking to make change in something as complex as racial justice persisted in the work. . . . But as I got further into the research, I realized I was learning about much more. For the first time in my life, I developed a visceral understanding of the Christian concept of grace, the belief in unmerited favor from God." Han does not elaborate on how that concept played out in her study, but she hints that it originated with God and led to active responses: "For the people I met in Undivided, their deep, abiding belief in God's grace manifested itself as the courage to fight for one another's dignity." She pairs the word *grace* with *radical*, meaning "rooted," saying she discovered that "making change not only had to alter the roots of an unjust system, but it also had to be rooted in real people." Han, *Undivided: The Quest for Racial Solidarity in an American Church* (Knopf, 2024), 238-39.

[4]Anthropologists point out that people use and define *grace* in a variety of ways. Unlike theologians and philosophers, who tend to take a topic such as grace and zoom in directly to the question of what it truly means in its deepest ontological essence according to an argument of logic or biblical interpretation, anthropologists tend to start by zooming out and identifying the various ways humans make meanings around this topic. If you want to understand an object, you might hold it in your hands and describe it from every angle you can see, or you might ask

tenet—perhaps *the* central tenet—to Christian doctrine.[5] Grace, mercy, forgiveness, and repentance came up in music, liturgy, or sermons in every church I visited, regardless of denomination, racial and ethnic composition, or political leanings. Nobody in this research saw themselves as inventing a new or radical idea when they spoke about grace. Neither am I attempting in this chapter to present anything that hasn't been said by theologians and anthropologists who have spent years studying grace. But as we'll see in the next chapter, the ways in which Christians apply grace within the domain of racism do differ, and those differences matter. Therein lies a key difference between White people who build a lifelong practice of addressing racial justice and those who don't. But let's start with commonalities.

In this chapter I'll trace out a basic definition of Christian grace in four pieces: Grace is a gift that (1) occurs within a prior condition of indebtedness, (2) is given rather than demanded or deserved, (3) traces ultimately to God; and (4) anticipates response.

||||||||

Grace describes a gift given within a prior condition of indebtedness. Imagine you have a neighbor who keeps showing up to help you rake leaves and fix your lawnmower and drop off fresh vegetables. At some point all that kindness leaves you feeling you should do something in return, so you decide to bake them a pie to even out the relationship. But just as it's coming out of the oven, they show up at your back door with

---

somebody you consider an expert to tell you their thoughts about that object. Anthropologists aren't opposed to these ways of knowing, but we tend to metaphorically pass the object around. We watch it in the context of everyday lives of lots of different people, and we watch how their hands, eyes, memories, and practices apply more meanings to that object than we might have imagined. And we can use that process not just for a physical object such as a plow or a crucifix but for a nexus of ideas, such as grace or hope. Just as we saw in earlier chapters that we can understand hope by considering the many ways in which people hope, we can understand grace by considering both the variety and commonalities in the ways people understand and use this thing called grace.

[5] Anthropologists Edwards and McIvor, for example, make this claim. Michael Edwards and Méadhbh McIvor, "Introduction: The Anthropology of Grace and the Grace of Anthropology," *The Cambridge Journal of Anthropology* 40, no. 1 (2022): 1-17.

a bushel full of apples and an offer to clean your garage. It's over the top. A grace gift is a way of saying, "I'm not requiring you to repay this debt. We don't have to ever make this relationship reach zero. Let's figure out another way for this relationship to work."

John Barclay, a theologian well-versed in both the theology and anthropology of gift exchanges, calls grace *incongruous*. The recipient realizes they do not deserve to be treated in such a way. The gift is not a return of anything previously gifted.[6] To the contrary, grace comes to someone who already owes a debt.

Human relationships continually accrue unbalanced accounts, whether through material exchanges yet to be repaid or wrongdoings yet to be resolved. Grace occurs in the context of these unbalanced accounts. Humans live within unequal accounts all the time, but not all imbalances are necessarily *debt*. For people to see themselves as indebted, they must imagine that some rebalancing of accounts is possible. And for that to be possible, they must see each other as the sorts of people who deserve rebalancing. People who believe themselves to be existing forever on different hierarchical planes—as master and enslaved, high and low caste, or royalty and their subjects, for example—have unbalanced accounts, but they don't necessarily believe that their accounts can or should be restored. Debt "first requires a relationship between two people who do not consider each other fundamentally different sorts of being, who are at least potential equals, who are equals in those ways that are really important, and who are not currently in a state of equality—but for whom there is some way to set matters straight."[7]

In a now famous 1865 letter, Jourdan Anderson, a freed Black man, responded to his former master's request for Jourdan to return as a laborer. With a politeness that is almost humorous for its bold honesty, Jourdan brings those debts to light:

---

[6]John M. G. Barclay, *Paul and the Gift* (Eerdmans, 2015).
[7]David Graeber, *Debt: The First 5,000 Years* (Melville, 2011), 121.

At $25 a month for me, and $2 a week for Mandy, our earnings would amount to $11,680. Add to this the interest for the time our wages have been kept back, and deduct what you paid for our clothing, and three doctor's visits to me, and pulling a tooth for Mandy, and the balance will show what we are in justice entitled to. . . . If you fail to pay us for faithful labors in the past, we can have little faith in your promises in the future. We trust the good Maker has opened your eyes to the wrongs which you and your fathers have done to me and my fathers, in making us toil for you for generations without recompense.[8]

Jourdan's letter calls attention to the fact that dominant groups often do not see their own indebtedness.[9] Likewise today, if indebtedness is the starting point for grace, the starting point of indebtedness is the collision and learning that allows people to see the full humanity and deservingness of others.

Knowing that a debt exists does not necessarily mean knowing how to repay it. Many debts exist that have no practical way to be cleared through mathematical accounting. The human condition is steeped in imbalance. We constantly depend on support from others, from tiny favors such as handing someone a tissue to life-on-the-line services such as military protection. To demand that every exchange be paid back in full would be insulting, impossible, or both. In another famous story that unveils social expectations around debt, on his twenty-first birthday author Ernest Thompson Seton received a letter from his father requesting repayment for all the expenses accrued from the doctor who oversaw his birth through his childhood. Seton repaid the money and

---

[8] Jourdan Anderson, *To My Old Master* (Double D, 2012), Kindle ed.
[9] James Edward Ford III, scholar of Black studies, draws on W. E. B. Du Bois to list the many gifts that Black people contributed to the formation of the US. These gifts included their labor, songs of sorrow and joy, and political leadership, as well as ideas about the very meaning of a gift, including a belief that labor should produce spiritual returns rather than merely economic gain, and an insistence that gifts passed forward from ancestors—not only contemporaries—matter. James Edward Ford III, "On Blackness and 'The Gift,'" Gift of Black Folk Panel, September 17, 2024.

promptly left the family forever.[10] The incident reveals a pattern in human indebtedness more broadly: Paying off a debt completely allows for that relationship to end. That end might be favorable for both parties or might be painfully final.

Sometimes debts involve exchanging material goods. More often the thing exchanged is intangible, such as a debt caused by cruelty between individuals or groups. Debts over wrongdoings are hard to quantify, because wrongdoing typically can't be valued through market exchanges. How does one put a price on an insult? A racial slur? The long-term effects of being turned down for a cheerleading squad? The emotional energy it takes to explain that a Halloween costume can be racist? The theft of communally shared land? The enslavement of human beings?

Forgiveness is the subset of grace that deals with that indebtedness that comes specifically of wrongdoing. Just as grace happens only when people can acknowledge debt, forgiveness happens only when people can acknowledge wrongdoing. Forgiveness is not simply forgetting; it involves naming and condemning the wrong. As theologian Miroslav Volf writes, "To forgive is to condemn," and "to forgive isn't to shrug off."[11]

Grace, then, is a gift in the direction of someone materially or relationally indebted. Instead of a debtor making a payment to a creditor, grace is a creditor giving still more to a current debtor. The gift of grace does not necessarily match the value of the debt and doesn't necessarily claim to stand for all members of an offended group. But it comes with a willingness to acknowledge that even if the value of the debt may never be calculated or matched, the giver is initiating generosity toward that debtor.

The second defining characteristic of grace is that it can only be given by a free giver.[12] The recipient has not coerced the giver into giving it,

---

[10]Ernest Thompson Seton, *Trail of an Artist-Naturalist—the Autobiography of Ernest Thompson Seton* (Read Books, 2020).

[11]Miroslav Volf, *Free of Charge: Giving and Forgiving in a Culture Stripped of Grace* (Zondervan, 2005), 165, 167.

[12]Walter Brueggemann notes that this freedom is modeled after Christ's death. God—the infinitely free one—perfectly demonstrates the simultaneity of grace and freedom by choosing to give

nor has the recipient earned grace by doing something right or valuable. Both giver and receiver interact according to their own free will, not coercing or manipulating each other's behaviors. Because grace happens in direct defiance of the expected rules of accounting and repayment, it has the power to send a signal that the whole system of accounting is null. As anthropologist David Graeber observed about Christian forgiveness, "'Redemption' is no longer about buying something back. It's really more a matter of destroying the entire system of accounting."[13]

Third, Christians define grace as something that comes initially from God, not humans. Prior indebtedness to God is the baseline state of humans. Volf explains it in this way: "We live, not so much on a *borrowed*, but on a *given* breath. We work, we create, we give, but the very ability and willingness to work, along with life itself, are gifts from God."[14] There is no way for humans to give back what they have received from God, because any gift they might offer came first from God.

What humans can do, though, is respond to God's grace by becoming givers of grace. Humans imitate God's grace by using the power of God acting through them. "We give because we *are* givers, because Christ living in us is a giver."[15] God models grace to humans and provides the resources of love and material goods with which they extend grace to each other.

This pattern of God becoming the source and impetus to human giving applies not only to material gifts such as food but also to the immaterial gift of forgiveness. "God alone has the power to forgive," Volf explains. "And in Christ, God has in fact forgiven. Here we need to take the next step: Because God has forgiven, we also have the power to forgive. We don't forgive in our own right. We forgive by making God's forgiveness our own."[16]

Christ's own life: "The crucifixion articulates God's odd freedom." Walter Brueggemann, *The Prophetic Imagination*, 2nd ed. (Fortress, 2001), 95.

[13]Graeber, *Debt: The First 5,000 Years*, 83.
[14]Volf, *Free of Charge*, 34.
[15]Volf, *Free of Charge*, 66.
[16]Volf, *Free of Charge*, 196.

That does not mean that only Christians give grace or that grace happens only when people consciously relate their actions to God. Christians make sense of grace by tracing its source back to the God they believe in, but others might trace its source to nature, family, the universe as a whole, or no one at all. For Christians, tracing grace back to God means that even if humans give grace to each other imperfectly or not at all, they see God's grace still acting as the original impetus from which all grace begins.

Humans, then, do not shoulder the burden of generosity. God is the one who carries the weight of grace and forgiveness. Without this theological tenet, asking someone to extend grace might seem unfair or cruel. Why should one person give more grace than another? Why should someone who has already been harmed give more? But if God is the ultimate source of all gifts, the equation shifts. Christians believe that humans can give grace fearlessly and generously because they each continue to receive back more than enough through the goodness of God.

The fourth defining feature of grace is that it anticipates a response. Grace is not supposed to be the end of the story. It could be, but that's not how it's supposed to go. Just as a recipient can't demand or deserve grace, so also the giver can't demand or deserve a certain response afterward. There is freedom in giving grace, and there is freedom in the response. And yet grace prepares the ground for a response. It prepares the ground for a relationship that is qualitatively different from what existed before between giver and receiver. It anticipates a response. Without a response, something would be incomplete about grace.

Anthropologists for over a century have studied what happens when people give each other gifts.[17] One finding that has proven true across

---

[17]Graeber, *Debt: The First 5,000 Years*; James Laidlaw, "A Free Gift Makes No Friends," *Journal of the Royal Anthropological Institute* 6, no. 4 (2000): 617-34; Bronislaw Malinowski, "Tribal Economics in the Trobriands," in *Tribal and Peasant Economies: Readings in Economic Anthropology*, ed. George Dalton (Natural History, 1967), 185-223; Marcel Mauss, *The Gift: The Form and Reason for Exchange in Archaic Societies*, trans. W. D. Halls (Norton, 1990); Jonathan Parry, "The Gift, the Indian Gift and the 'Indian Gift,'" *Man* 21, no. 3 (1986): 453-73; Marshall David Sahlins, *Stone Age Economics* (Aldine, 1972).

cultural settings and time is this: Gifts seal relationships. In most circumstances, a person who receives a gift will feel a tug to give back something in return.[18] Gifts have a way of simultaneously communicating two seemingly contradictory messages: There is no need to repay, and yet the receiver *must* repay somehow, perhaps continuously, even when the value of the initial gift can never be matched.[19] That tug to give back sets in motion a kind of pendulum, and the motion of the pendulum creates a bond between people. When there is a frequent oscillation between one person being indebted to the other and vice versa, the back and forth of indebtedness works to seal the relationship. You pay for a friend's coffee, saying, "Next time you get mine." Here you've signaled that you anticipate there will be a next time, that the friendship will continue. At the same time, they've trusted you enough to not feel ashamed to receive. One-sided giving can signal a power imbalance. To always buy coffee for a friend might communicate that they are a charity case incapable of giving. But by giving with the anticipation of receiving, you give someone the dignity of being both giver and receiver. A week later, they might text you a favorite song that reminds them of you. Another day you call to let them vent about a tough workday. Then feed your pet while you're on vacation. The very incalculability of these gifts, the back and forth in the vicinity of zero without ever achieving zero, sends repeated messages that your relationship is interminable.

Something very different happens when people aim to land their exchanges at precisely zero equivalence. Imagine, for example, what happens if, as soon as you've paid for your friend's coffee, you ask them to pay you back to the precise penny. Or more awkwardly, you offer to pay them for time spent listening in conversation. You have sent a

---

[18]Settings in which the tug of responsibility doesn't occur often have to do with power or status inequalities, as when a parent's status is understood to be on another plane from that of a child, who needs not give back what a parent gives, or when an oppressive state takes from subjects without acknowledging an obligation to repay.
[19]Pierre Bourdieu, *Outline of a Theory of Practice*, Cambridge Studies in Social Anthropology 16 (Cambridge University Press, 1977), 191-95.

message that now you are even, the transaction is done. You have transformed the transaction from a gift to a commodity. In some settings, culture tells us that it's appropriate to commoditize coffee or listening, such as when paying a coffee shop barista or a therapist. But humans everywhere recognize differences between commodities and gifts. In a commodity exchange, whether you see the person again is irrelevant. This sort of transaction is like grasping the pendulum and, rather than pushing it so that it swings past its lowest point, placing it at the bottom of its arc. There is no more potential energy. The motion stops.

Grace is a way of jumping straight into an oscillating give-and-take relationship without having to clear away all the prior debts first. It says, "Let's start fresh with sharing as equals. Let's be people who attend to each other's needs here, there, and everywhere, rather than waiting for it all to be set right at once." Grace sets in motion a pendulum that has been stuck either unmoving or off-kilter to one side. If the recipient does their part, they'll respond, swinging it back to continue the motion. The recipient of grace is not meant to grovel in dependency to the giver thenceforth. Nor is the exchange an excuse to walk away unaffected. Instead, grace starts anew a simple motion of back and forth, as when a gift has been given between friends.

If you offer forgiveness on the condition that someone repents afterward, technically you have not given a gift of forgiveness. You have attempted to purchase or manipulate repentance. You have negotiated an agreement. While such negotiations can be useful, they are not the same as grace. Commodified and negotiated agreements are designed to be endpoints. The parties agree on a way of reaching equivalence, and in that equivalence, they can each walk away. Not so with grace.

Arguably, that's how love works. As Paul writes in 1 Corinthians 13:5, "[Love] keeps no record of wrongs." Paul doesn't say that love prevents or ignores all wrongs. He says that love isn't keeping score. There is a back and forth in love—asking for forgiveness, receiving forgiveness, granting forgiveness. Giving gifts, receiving gifts, passing gifts forward to someone else. Love is found in the perpetual motion, not in the calculating of who owes more to whom. Grace is a free gift with an anticipation that both giver and receiver will henceforth live in right relationship, passing grace forward in perpetuity.

There has been a long debate among scholars about whether such a thing exists as a "pure gift," meaning one with no expectation of reciprocity of any sort. If there is such a thing as a gift without obligations, grace as conceptualized by people in this study was not it.[20] Grace doesn't let people off the hook. It hooks them permanently into a lifetime of giving and receiving.

The possible responses anticipated by grace are many: acknowledgment, gratitude, paying forward, repentance, or restitution to an individual or social group. The first anticipated response is simply to receive. This may seem obvious, but there are many ways that people refuse gifts. A recipient might say they don't need or want the gift, or transform it from gift to commodity by immediately paying for it. Or they might take it without acknowledging there's a giver behind it.

A second anticipated response is gratitude. This might mean speaking the words "Thank you" or might be communicated in other ways. When a child opens a gift, if they jump up and down and throw their arms around the giver, their gratitude is clear.

Another possible anticipated response is to give. One might give back to the same individual, or to others in their social group, or to humanity more broadly. Regardless, the recipient becomes a giver themselves. Again, this is how grace works between God and humans: God gives life, forgiveness, and all goodness to humans, and humans become givers in response.

When the gift given is forgiveness, grace anticipates a particular response: repentance. To forgive is to acknowledge that wrong occurred

---

[20]Barclay and Parry argue, in fact, that this very debate is incompatible with the ways people thought of transactions through most of human history, and itself only an invention of modernist imaginations inclined to read every transaction as one of a mere two options: gift or market transaction. See Barclay, *Paul and the Gift*; Laidlaw, "Free Gift Makes No Friends"; Parry, "Gift, the Indian Gift"; Georg Simmel, *The Sociology of Georg Simmel* (Free Press, 1964).

and, second, to not hold that wrong against the perpetrator. Similarly, to repent is to name one's responsibility for a wrong and to receive the gift of forgiveness. These are separate acts. Sometimes forgiveness is offered without anyone responding in repentance. Sometimes repentance is offered without anyone responding in forgiveness. But each anticipates the other, and when the two come together, there's a kind of completion.

Finally, grace following wrongdoing also anticipates restitution. Often a precise, quantifiable restitution is impossible. Those harmed may be deceased or innumerable, or the value of psychological and physical harms may be incalculable by a market supply-and-demand process.[21] But even when restitution cannot be precise, it offers a direction to aim for. Volf writes, "We should *offer* restitution. We may not necessarily succeed at giving it."[22] Restitution could include financial compensation, returning what was taken, ongoing efforts to restore relationships, or creating memorials to honor victims.

This chapter has reviewed general principles of grace that are widely accepted among Christians. Where we turn next is to the question of how Christians with deep and lasting commitments to racial justice apply grace. In the context of racism, what makes grace so amazing?

---

[21] In his essay titled *On Forgiveness*, philosopher Jacques Derrida considers how to forgive wrongdoings spread across entire societies, such as the crimes against humanity committed under South Africa's apartheid system or the German Nazi regime. Even if costs could somehow be quantified, one faces the impossibility of determining recipients. "We are all heir, at least, to persons or events marked, in an essential, interior, ineffaceable fashion, by crimes against humanity." Particularly challenging are wrongs committed against those now dead. "Who would have the right to forgive in the name of the disappeared victims?" he writes. "They are always absent, in a certain way." Jacques Derrida, *On Cosmopolitanism and Forgiveness*, trans. Mark Dooley and Michael Hughes (Routledge, 1997), 29, 44.

[22] Miroslav Volf, *Free of Charge*, 121.

ELEVEN

Where Grace Meets Race

GRACE IN THE CONTEXT OF RACISM is a loaded topic. There is just so much that has gone wrong in the name of grace. Like hope, grace has impostor lookalikes. And so, before we arrive at how people in this research connected grace to racism, let's be clear about what they didn't do. We'll begin with three controversial stories.

First, consider the story of Brandt Jean. One night, a White off-duty police officer named Amber Guyger walked into his apartment. She claimed afterward she believed this to be her home own home despite it being the wrong floor of her building. Walking in, she saw Brandt's brother Botham Jean, a Black man whom she later described as "a silhouette." She assumed he was an intruder, pulled her gun, shot, and killed him.

Eighteen-year-old Brandt said he felt anger and hatred toward his brother's killer for months afterward. Then, at Guyger's trial, as he listened to the killer's testimony, he felt a desire to respond out of his Christian faith. Choking back tears, he read a statement forgiving Guyger, then embraced her in a long hug. Onlookers cried. A law enforcement organization made plans to give Jean an ethical courage award.[1]

---

[1] Doug Criss and Leah Asmelash, "The Problem with Always Asking Black People to Forgive," *CNN*, October 3, 2019, www.cnn.com/2019/10/03/us/black-americans-forgiveness-trnd/index.html; Ashley Killough and Madeline Holcombe, "Emotions Run High in and Outside of Courtroom After Amber Guyger Sentenced to 10 Years for Botham Jean's Murder," *CNN*,

Not everyone was so impressed.

One of the first observers to criticize this public display of forgiveness was CNN analyst Bakari Sellers, who tweeted, "Why do black folks always have to forgive? We can have a conversation about black folk and our unconscionable forgiveness in the face of hate and violence. I don't get it."[2] The internet exploded with debates about Black forgiveness. Many commentators interpreted Brandt Jean's actions as the latest iteration of a story White people have repeated to themselves for centuries: Black people are great at forgiving, so let bygones be bygones while White people get on with their lives. Besides, won't it make life easier for people of color if they stop worrying over the little things? Hand out forgiveness, along with a blindfold and a Band-Aid, and carry on.

Consider a second complicated story of grace and race. On June 17, 2015, in Charleston, South Carolina, an avowed white supremacist named Dylan Roof opened fire at a Bible study held in Emanuel African Methodist Episcopal Church, killing nine African American people. Afterward many family members of the deceased were quoted in news stories saying they forgave Dylan Roof. "I feel forgiveness in my heart," said one mother of a victim.[3] A sister said, "We have no room for hating, so we have to forgive."[4]

One week later, President Barack Obama traveled to the Charleston church to eulogize those lost. "This whole week I've been reflecting on grace," he said to a warm applause. He spoke of the grace of those killed, God's grace given to everyone, and the grace that those gathered could give each other by "recognizing our common humanity." At the

---

October 3, 2019, www.cnn.com/2019/10/03/us/botham-jean-amber-guyger-trial-wrap/index.html; Darran Simon, Ed Lavandera, and Ashley Killough, "His Hug of Forgiveness Shocked the Country. Yet He Still Won't Watch the Video from That Moment," *CNN*, December 6, 2019, www.cnn.com/2019/12/06/us/brandt-jean-botham-jean-forgiveness/index.html.
[2]Simon, Lavandera, and Killough, "His Hug of Forgiveness."
[3]Criss and Asmelash, "Problem with Always Asking."
[4]Elahe Izadi, "The Powerful Words of Forgiveness Delivered to Dylann Roof by Victims' Relatives," *Washington Post*, June 19, 2015, www.washingtonpost.com/news/post-nation/wp/2015/06/19/hate-wont-win-the-powerful-words-delivered-to-dylann-roof-by-victims-relatives/.

conclusion of the speech, Obama began singing "Amazing Grace." The crowd rose to their feet and joined the song.[5] The speech became instantly famous.

Again, not everyone was enamored. In a *New York Times* piece titled "Why I Can't Forgive Dylann Roof," professor and social commentator Roxane Gay responded to the flood of news stories about forgiveness and grace. "What White people are really asking for when they demand forgiveness from a traumatized community is absolution," she wrote. "They want to believe it is possible to heal from such profound and malingering trauma because to face the openness of the wounds racism has created in our society is too much." In Gay's analysis, Black people forgive not out of freedom but "because we need to survive."[6]

In the coming years, scholars continued analyzing what happens in race-inflected forgiveness incidents. Historian Isabel Wilkerson cited the statements by Brandt Jean and the Charleston church survivors as examples of an endemic pattern of forgiveness gone wrong in caste-based societies: Subordinated people give forgiveness out of coercion, as a condition of survival. In the system of race, Wilkerson writes, forgiveness has been made into "a silent clause in a one-sided contract between the subordinate and the dominant."[7] In that "contract," White people can have their responsibility cleared if they find someone to speak their absolution. Like swiping a credit card for groceries, tearing off the receipt, and walking away, they use apology statements to close off future obligations and relationships. Apologies leave nothing left to anticipate and nothing left to hope.

In a 2022 journal issue dedicated to the anthropology of grace, Black theologian Vincent Lloyd returned to Obama's Charleston speech as an example of something else that goes askew with grace. Lloyd points out

---

[5] Barack Obama, "President Obama Delivers Eulogy," C-SPAN, June 26, 2015, www.youtube.com/watch?v=x9IGyidtfGI.

[6] Roxane Gay, "Why I Can't Forgive Dylann Roof," *New York Times*, June 23, 2015, www.nytimes.com/2015/06/24/opinion/why-i-cant-forgive-dylann-roof.html.

[7] Isabel Wilkerson, *Caste: The Origins of Our Discontents* (Random House, 2020), 288.

that the presidential speech implied that a representative of the state could declare grace on behalf of shooting victims and their families. Is grace something that can be "willed into being by a politician"? If a politician declares grace without anticipation of a transformative response, is it truly grace? In Lloyd's assessment,

> Obama's performance of grace, like his rhetoric of hope, pacifies. It turns attention away from the depths of white supremacy, as not just an individual vice or a subculture but a pathology of the United States as a whole, infecting everything from laws and policies to ways of seeing, knowing, and feeling. And it distracts from the grassroots organizing work that would be required to rightly address racial injustice. Grace promises unity in transformation, but from a position of power.[8]

Was this just another instance of enabling White people to absolve their consciences so they could settle back into comfortable indifference? Lloyd goes so far as to call the grace in that speech not real grace at all. "False copies of grace pin us to the status quo, securing the interests of the wealthy and powerful. The real thing, ever elusive, promises transformation."[9]

Finally, a third complicated story of grace and race.

From time to time, White individuals hear about my research and want to help. These conversations often go like something this.

"That sounds like a great topic," they tell me. Then comes an offer. "I know somebody who would be a great fit for that research." They suggest a friend, a relative, or themselves.

"Tell me more about why you recommend that person," I ask.

They expound on the merits of this person. "They're so generous and they give so much. They started a program at our church/workplace/city.

---

[8] Vincent Lloyd, "Afterword: Amazing Grace," *The Cambridge Journal of Anthropology* 40, no. 1 (2022): 122.
[9] Lloyd, "Afterword: Amazing Grace," 124.

They're making a real difference. So many people of color must be so grateful for what they've done."

They mean well. Occasionally they even name individuals who have already been included in the study. But as these kinds of conversations piled up, I noticed something about the picture they painted, and it had something to do with grace. The directionality of grace that White people often used to qualify racial justice experts moved in one direction: They assumed White people would qualify by *giving* grace, not by *receiving* it or *responding* to it.

These sorts of "let me recommend somebody" conversations reminded me of an article I read by anthropologist Omri Elisha. He studied the ways that White evangelicals in suburban Knoxville, Tennessee, attempted to provide faith-based social welfare across class and race divides. Unlike White participants in my study, Elisha's were not selected by those affected by their service, and he thus observed many troubles in their activism. Elisha's interviewees also talked a lot about grace. They imagined grace flowing unilaterally from rich to poor, which often meant White to Black. With that vision of grace, they bumped into a predicament when it came to living out the results of grace. At one level, they wanted to give charity unconditionally, just as they imagined God's grace as unconditional. At the same time, they became frustrated when their acts of compassion did not result in conversion or life change on the part of the aid recipients. They were "frequently troubled when charity recipients do not respond with proper gratitude or some comparable demonstration of personal reformation."[10] In their view, grace was a gift of the middle class, bound to a hidden logic that the poor should be accountable to rich donors.

Each of these three stories points to some false form of grace that does not meet the criteria of Christian grace outlined in the previous chapter—it is not given from creditor to debtor, not given freely, not ultimately

---

[10]Omri Elisha, "Moral Ambitions of Grace: The Paradox of Compassion and Accountability in Evangelical Faith-Based Activism," *Cultural Anthropology*, no. 23 (2008): 171.

sourced from God, or not anticipating free response. These stories offer insights into legitimate reasons that people of color are often skeptical of teachings about grace in the context of racism. Grace goes wrong. A lot. So let's review.

Grace can flow to and from people of all social locations. Everybody needs it.

Grace is not a warm feeling.

Grace is not a charitable handout from wealthy to poor.

Grace is not the sole duty of those harmed by injustice. It must not be squeezed from them as a condition of survival.

Grace is not a politician's benevolent declaration over the heads of those harmed.

Grace, in its ideal form, is given with free agency, though it is impossible to trace all the influential factors leading to any individual's actions.

Grace expands the freedom of the giver. Rather than fueling compassion fatigue, it lessens the fatigue of having no power over repeated offenses.

Grace is not the only way people of color respond to racism, nor is it everything White people need to become advocates for justice. The struggle against racism is long and multifaceted.

The history of racism produces a prior condition of indebtedness for White people. Many White people do not see their indebtedness. Others, upon seeing it, do not care. Learning the history of racism brings that indebtedness to light. This prior indebtedness is a setup for grace.

People of color do give grace in that context of racial indebtedness, frequently and freely. Christians of color see God as their source for such grace, and teachings on grace and race abound in many predominantly non-White churches.

Grace does not deny wrongs—it begins with a clear naming of wrongs.

Grace is not a one-sided clause of a contract. It anticipates response. Responses might include gratitude, restitution, reparations, repentance, future relationship, or paying forward. Grace givers cannot demand response, and grace does not expire when it doesn't elicit a certain response within a limited timeline. But grace does set in motion anticipation for more to happen.

The fact that grace goes wrong doesn't mean it can't go right. People in this research often explicitly named differences between fake grace and a kind of real grace that works for long-term racial justice. They knew grace at an experiential level. They could point to moments in their own lives when they'd seen it happen, and they understood it as a principle that mattered in the wider context of justice and injustice. And because grace opens relationships, rather than closing off relationships, it becomes central to long-term perseverance and irrepressible hope. Let's return to the four defining features of grace covered in the previous chapter to see how people applied grace to race. Recall that grace is a gift that (1) occurs within a prior condition of indebtedness, (2) is given rather than demanded or deserved, (3) traces ultimately to God, and (4) anticipates response.

||||||||

As people gain understanding of the history and ongoing patterns of racism, they begin to realize that a certain indebtedness arises from racism. The directionality of power and racial privilege has, on the whole, taken from people of color and given to White people. Resources have not always flowed directly from one set of hands to another, and tracing those flows is rarely simple. Sometimes the culpability can be traced to an individual; other times blame occurs through vast systems that are difficult to pinpoint. But the net result is clear: White people have gained resources, people of color have had resources taken, and the two are interconnected. White individuals have accrued and inherited wealth and privileges through land theft, enslavement, Jim Crow laws, segregation, inequitable health care and education, immigration laws, and discriminatory everyday interactions. The list does not end. Where does one begin to pay this back? Where does one begin to ask forgiveness? As one Black woman in my study repeated several times during our conversation, "Everyone is complicit." More lives have been fractured than could ever be counted. Repayment to zero would take lifetimes.

In this context of indebtedness, even ordinary acts of kindness from people of color toward White people can seem utterly absurd. Why would Mark take time to stay at the table telling Hannah what she did wrong? Why would a Black caregiver attend the funeral of Candice's bigoted grandmother? Why would Latina strangers pray for Jenna? How could it make sense to give more undeserved goodness to those who already received more than they gave back? How could that be fair?

In the context of the racial caste system, ordinary acts of grace from people of color toward White people can signal a reworking of what makes sense. Everyone involved knows that the account will never be zero. As one Black man put it, the only real alternative to grace is "we can mimic countries who have been fighting wars for hundreds and hundreds of years. Because then, where does it stop? Where does the pain stop?" The debtor can't make things even, and neither can the one who is indebted. If they wait until the accounts reach zero to begin a relationship, that relationship will never happen. Grace doesn't bring the account to zero—it shatters the account to smithereens.

The three elements of collision, asking why, and responding to grace did not necessarily occur in that order in people's lives. Sometimes, as in Candice's story of her grandmother, the experience of grace happened long before she had a robust understanding of racial injustice. The order of occurrence wasn't important, but here's what was important: Grace experiences had to be interpreted through the lens of collisions and why questions. With grace stories earlier in life, White people used what they learned later to look back and reinterpret acts of grace. Those stories took on new meaning when they realized that people of color had many reasons to treat them far worse.

This was the case with Ameerah and Ian, a Black woman and a White man whom I interviewed separately. Both were leaders in Christian organizations—Ian in a predominantly White ministry and Ameerah in a predominantly Black one. They met regularly in a prayer gathering with a dozen other ministry leaders, nearly all of whom were White and male. The first real conversation they had together was a train wreck.

Ameerah explained that for months leading up to the day of that conversation, her frustration had been building. Several significant racist incidents had affected Black people in their city during those months, and each time she came to prayer meetings eager to pray for these pressing concerns. Each month, other group members were both uninformed and dismissive when she tried to share what Black people were experiencing.

Finally, Ameerah made a plan to explain to the group how their disinterest and denial affected her. She asked another woman of color to join her at an upcoming meeting and wrote down ahead of time what she planned to say. She could have just stopped coming to the meetings, but she cared enough to try for change. Her hands were shaking as she read from her prepared statement. "I'm frustrated with being in this group because I love prayer. I know the importance of prayer, but no one ever talks about people of color and what they're going through. This city is in national news about the experiences of people of color. And no one says nothing."

Ian was at the prayer meeting that day.

I interviewed Ian outside of his home on a warm morning as construction vehicles rolled noisily down the street, regularly interrupting our conversation with enforced silences that allowed Ian to pause and choose his words. He recalled feeling shocked when Ameerah spoke up. Ian assumed at the time that he was different from the rest. When the meeting ended, he went straight to Ameerah to chat. Looking back, he could see what went wrong. "Here's this White savior," he said of his past self, "rubbing his hands together, ready to roll up his sleeves, thinking, *I'm not part of the problem here. I'm ready and willing and able to do whatever it takes. I'm going to eradicate racism in my community. All these other people are sinners, but I'm not. What do I need to do?* And I thought she was going to give me a list of things to do."

Ameerah saw straight through his self-deflecting tactics and flippant apology. "By that point when he came up to me, I was like, 'I'm done.'" During the meeting, she felt overwhelming pushback. "They shut down. They didn't give me eye contact. They stopped talking. They didn't really engage in prayer or anything." One man responded by telling her, "Sometimes what looks like racism isn't really racism." Later she would uncover the full extent of the pushback. One man contacted her to ask her to apologize for offending him that day, and someone would prevent a donor from supporting her work. Already by the time Ian approached her, she had made up her mind. "I can't get burned out trying to teach White people when the work I'm called to do, the work I'm paid for, is reaching Black people with the gospel. So I shifted and started saying, 'Hey, here's some resources.'"

Ian recalled hearing her say, "It's not my job to educate you. You have Google, just educate yourself about racism and then come back and talk to me. But you do the work that you need to do and then talk to me about partnering." He was stunned. "At the time it seemed to me like anger. Now I think it was probably more like just the exasperation of having had the question asked perhaps hundreds of times. My initial response to that was I was really angry. WTF, I just asked you what I could do to help, and you told me to go get lost?" He thought he was on the good side. How dare she call out him? It shook him to the core.

That collision unsettled Ian enough to take some next steps. "Afterwards I thought, I have a relationship with her, so I know I can't write her off as just some kind of socially maladjusted person who's angry, another angry Black woman or whatever. There's got to be something to what she said. So I did start educating myself about how White people behave and how big a problem racism is. At first I just showed up to credential myself as a good person. But I did start to do the work, and I did learn." He learned not to expect Black people to educate him on lessons he wouldn't put effort into. And he learned not to expect an easy justification—a soft, conscience-absolving "you're off the hook for being better than some other White folks." He learned better responses—accompaniment, lament, repentance, reparations.

But this season of learning wasn't the end of the story Ian told. "The blessing that really came out of all that was that Ameerah wasn't just being rhetorical when she said, 'Go do the work and then come back and talk to me.' When she saw that I was doing the work, she stayed in conversation with me."

He saw their ongoing relationship as a gift, and he did not take it lightly, especially when things got difficult. Recently, due to an administrative glitch, his church had stopped sending ministry support to her Black-led ministry, and she asked him hard questions about what happened. "How did you not notice? Does this indicate a deeper problem? Do you actually care less about supporting this ministry than other White-led ministries?" He took this feedback to heart and brought it up at church leadership meetings. "I've learned so much from her alone as a human being."

Admitting his own faults didn't come easy for Ian. Perhaps it doesn't for anyone. For ministry leaders who see themselves as guides to others, admitting failures can be especially difficult. Ian made clear from the start of his interview that he considered his own failures to be crucial to the story of his transformation. Even as I asked Ian permission to begin recording the interview, Ian mused on repentance. "I totally give you permission to say anything from my life. I've definitely had my moments when I realized I am racist. I welcome the opportunity to confess my racism and to talk about moments where I've suddenly caught a glimpse of myself in the mirror and said, 'Oh, my goodness, I didn't think I was like that, but I am like that.' I'll tell you about some of those things and certainly feel free to put them out there, edited or unedited, as long as it tells the true story."

Ian had learned about grace not only from the grace it took for Ameerah to speak truth but through a series of seemingly small events.

He began regularly visiting a church led by a Black pastor, and one day that pastor unexpectedly texted him, "Hey, I'm missing you, man. I really appreciate you." It was a simple gesture, probably insignificant to the pastor, but to Ian, it pointed to something bigger. He said it was part of a cultural pattern that impressed him in African American churches—something he referred to as "Black love," a phrase I heard from two other participants as well. Others use the term *enwrapment* to describe similar experiences.[11] Black church members demonstrated love to each other in ways Ian didn't expect to witness, much less receive. "They express appreciation of one another, gratitude for one another. The spontaneity and depth and genuineness of it really impressed me. There's a warmth and an openness and a lack of inhibition in expressing emotion."

In messages as subtle as the text from this pastor, Ian found himself welcomed into interracial friendships of a different sort than he had previously experienced. Ian and the Black pastor both acknowledged that a history of racism surrounded them. They knew that between Ian's people and this pastor's people, immeasurable debts of harm had accrued across history and were still accruing. And in this context, Ian was invited into coconspiratorial work against racism and into friendship. That did not compute. As Ian put it, "It's wonderful to be loved by people that have every reason to hate you, but they don't."

|||||||||

If grace must be given freely rather than demanded or deserved, that means people of color must be free to choose when and how to give grace. That doesn't mean it will be an easy choice. For Ian, receiving Ameerah's bold condemnation became a starting point for transformation. But what about Ameerah's side of the story?

"I have not been to that prayer gathering since that time. That was traumatizing to me." We were meeting online because she had moved

---

[11]Term used in a White interviewee in research by Mark R. Warren, *Fire in the Heart: How White Activists Embrace Racial Justice* (Oxford University Press, 2010), 75.

away from the city where the prayer meeting took place. Now she lived in a predominantly Black neighborhood. "I realized after moving—about a month after—how traumatizing it was to live there as a Black Christian woman. I just woke up one day here and I was like, 'Why does it feel easier to breathe?'"

Does grace always emotionally drain the people who extend it? Certainly it does at times. Kevin, an Asian American pastor at a multiracial church, explained how he counsels Christians of color as they navigate questions of how much energy to expend working with White people. "We ask them to be able to share their story and be open. For some, we're asking you to be bridge persons. We're asking you to be able to answer questions, to be able to step out of your culture and go, 'Okay, I see what you're experiencing, let me help you.' Not everybody's called to that. Not everybody can. Not everybody is actually equipped to, but some of us are. But of course, we as a church are also helping to curate those and make sure that you're not going to get hurt—or at least we hope you're not going to get hurt." He actively sought ways to avoid creating situations where people of color would be pressured into sacrificing themselves.[12] Like Ameerah, he recognized that there are times when the most important step for people of color is to find communities where they can heal from trauma and breathe.

But giving grace is not necessarily draining. In fact, there's something in the very structure of grace that can make these experiences as beneficial

---

[12] Hahrie Han's study of one megachurch's race education program includes a story that further corroborates what I heard—that White people find moments of grace from people of color deeply moving, and people of color do at times voluntarily offer such grace, but attempts to structure grace into programmatic curricula risk overriding the qualities of grace that it be uncoerced and anticipating a response. In the original roll-out of the curriculum she studied, the church included an exercise in which participants publicly repented of race-related sins. After one White woman confessed making excuses for a racist relative, a Black woman looked her in the eyes and said, "You are forgiven." The White woman said later that it was "one of the holiest experiences of my entire life." Han notes that the "leaders dropped this exercise from subsequent iterations of the program because they worried it created a sense of false absolution for white people." Han, *Undivided: The Quest for Racial Solidarity in an American Church* (Knopf, 2024), 93.

to the giver as to the recipient, especially in the context of racism.[13] Grace, by definition, comes from a free giver. That means enacting grace can have the effect of enhancing the giver's own freedom. Latino scholar Patrick Reyes makes the argument that the ability to give or not give is central to the process of achieving full freedom as people of color.

> We cannot achieve freedom until we are free to give a gift without obligation or expectation. When the demand of solidarity is made, it maintains the logic of power over. . . . It is, however, only in our complete freedom, on our terms, and the gift of our love on our terms, that freedom exists. The oppressed, in achieving freedom, will not do what was done to us to others. We will offer the gift, but we must be free to give it. We must be able to define liberation on our terms, reclaiming the purposes that were stolen from our ancestors.[14]

Free gifts can make free givers.

Grace goes wrong when it constricts rather than expands the freedom of those harmed. It's difficult to determine, though, whether an act stems from coercion or freedom. In Amber Guyger's trial and Obama's "Amazing Grace" speech, public opinion split over this question. Is uncoerced grace possible in the legal atmosphere of a courtroom? Is freedom stolen from survivors when a politician speaks grace on their behalf? One thing that came through in my research was this: that coerced grace *can* happen does not mean that freely given grace *can't* happen.

A White man named Ryan explained the undemandable nature of grace this way: "Christianity regularly invites us to step away from the

---

[13]Sociologist Angel Adams Parham suggests that a "disposition toward grace" appears in the Black intellectual tradition. She contrasts three ways in which people cope with the troubled racial history of the West, advocating for the approach she calls the "integrative blues mode." This mode enables people to critique social harms while also co-creating a hope-filled reimagining of society through a disposition of grace. Parham, "Stories in the Land: Race, Place, and Memory in American Life," Wheaton College, Wheaton, IL, March 6, 2025.

[14]Reyes credits Frantz Fanon and Nelson Maldonado-Torres for influencing his thinking on this topic. Patrick B. Reyes, *The Purpose Gap: Empowering Communities of Color to Find Meaning and Thrive* (Westminster John Knox, 2021), 46.

question of what's deserved or this list of shoulds. And I think for a person of color to offer insights or vulnerability, it's just an act of grace. It's a gift that is not—should never be—demanded of them. It's not a should. And in fact, there's good reason why they would say, 'No. Hard pass.'" Like Ian, Ryan recalled ordinary times when people of color "encouraged or challenged or even just spent time with me." Of those, he said, "I count it a gift. You don't have to. Hopefully, it's not like we're hanging out because you're Black and I'm White and this is the foundation of our whole relationship, but in a really broad sense, any relationship is an act of generosity and grace towards one another." He emphasized the freedom that must surround grace. "You don't get to demand grace. If you do, you've missed the whole point! As soon as you say, 'Hey, I deserve grace,' that's not grace anymore. You're taking something. And that breaks relationships. I think that's a gross perversion of grace that really, at the heart of it, reveals that you've put yourself at the center of the story again."

Free grace from people of color to White people is a system that runs counter to established patterns of race relations. Grace reverses the hierarchy of White control over non-White others. It's a decolonial process that repels attempts to own the will of others. It's a noncapitalist kind of exchange—parties are not weighing what they might gain in various alternatives and choosing the action that wins them the greatest profit. Instead they are giving and receiving without seeking equivalence. Grace is offensive both to the conservative and to the liberal. White conservatives tend to want grace to be easier, as in, "Get over this already, the damage is past, so stop bothering me." White progressives tend to think grace should be harder. They expect that working through racism should be a constant struggle in which they do not ask anything of people of color. "I am going to be working on this until the day I die, and to ask one more iota of kindness from people of color is to burden them further." Once, when I gave a talk about this research, a White listener commented, "That doesn't seem fair." She was right—grace is not fair. Grace isn't meant to be fair, and it challenges everyone to stop thinking in terms of fairness but to think instead in terms of relationship.

∎∣∎∣∎∣∎∣∎

"It's hard for me to answer these questions without going back to Jesus," a Black man named Quentin observed midway through our interview. He had brought up the concept of grace, and his explanation emphasized why it matters to him as a person of color that the ultimate source of grace is God.

Quentin said he saw a direct tie between receiving grace from Christ and his ability to give grace as a Black person. "We have to give grace. If our thing is reconciliation to Jesus and reconciliation to the Father, and that's through unity, that's through love, the only way we can do that is by giving grace. Grace has to be the core of what we're doing. Everything Jesus talked about was always a spiritual level. So when Jesus talks about grace, of course grace isn't easy. If it was, everyone would do it. It's a higher standard. Jesus asks of us a higher standard. Grace is costly, but ultimately the cost is paid by Christ, who initiates grace into humanity and also enables humans to give grace through Christ's example and empowerment."

By tracing back to God the ability to give grace, Quentin and several other people of color I spoke with found strength to extend grace even when, as in Ameerah's case, grace was painful. A Black man named Nathaniel who had worked for several years in a challenging church setting told me he had chosen to continue working at the church only because he felt God had personally led him there. He believed God enabled him to work with people who would not necessarily understand racism. "God has just kind of worked with me and brought me to a spot where I can say, 'You're going to have to hang with people knowing their loyalty will not be as yours. You're going to have to hang with them.' And that's scary for me. That's intimately scary for me." Similarly, an Asian American woman named Eunice who worked in a predominantly White workplace told me several stories of confronting White leaders about decisions that negatively affected people of color. "I hate doing this over and over again," Eunice said. "I feel like the bad guy. I think giving constructive feedback is just a hard life skill to have overall. But it's important."

In the midst of recounting frustrating experiences with entrenched racism, both Nathaniel and Eunice spoke of drawing on God's guidance and power. Nathaniel said that recently God had opened doors to join two different groups addressing racism in organizations. Previously he would have seen these as "just not my thing." Now, as he considered those invitations, he was asking himself, "Am I committed to my journey with God or not? Am I going to say, 'No, God, you're taking too much from me?' God wants to do a work in me. So I walked through." Eunice spoke of God providing surprising encouragement and support through racially charged confrontations. "Every time I really needed to hear it, God put someone in a conversation or even just an offhand comment to remind me that yes, there is loneliness in being the first or the only person to say something, but it *is* possible to embody both grace and truth in that role."

Several people pointed out that grace may be a distinguishing difference between the ways Christians and non-Christians deal with racism. Some inferred that grace might never make sense outside the context of a loving God who initiates grace. Christians believe that God is the source of all gifts, and those gifts backfill all the other gifts given by humans. God is, in the metaphor of the previous chapter, the first one to push the pendulum. Several Christians of color pointed out that God has enabled Christians of color to uniquely demonstrate grace. One Black woman put it this way: "We have to understand that the Black faith is built upon those two things—extending grace and love. The fact that we as Black people are even still Christians in the numbers that we are is a miracle. And that is a product of extending so much love and grace. We've had the unfortunate opportunity to exercise love and grace in ways that, for instance, White Christians have not."

Another Black man said, "The Black church is the core of our society, the moral fabric of the community. That's all because of our faith. Our faith has led us, and encouraged us, and strengthened us to leave slavery, to become the better part of who we are, to love others, to forgive others, to turn the other cheek. We've done this from a faith perspective." These individuals did not mean that only people of color can extend grace or that Christians of color do not also live out every other aspect of Christian life, including receiving grace themselves. But they saw in the overarching story of American racism a meta-level narrative of Black people extending grace as a witness to God's original grace.

In Christian understandings of forgiveness, absolution comes ultimately from God, demonstrated through the focal act of grace: the death of God's Son Jesus at the hands of humans, followed by his resurrection to life. This event marks God's extension of grace for all wrongdoing across all time. It anticipates a freely given response by humans of acceptance, repentance, and gratitude.[15] In the context of racism, that means White people can work through their forgiveness with God rather than requiring individuals of color to forgive sins. People of color I interviewed did not want to be in the position of absolving White people's guilt like priests in confessional boxes. One Black man named Jonathan described his annoyance when White people attempted to ask him forgiveness for White guilt in general. "I don't care about your guilt," he said. "That's between you and Jesus. I'm here about your actions. That's what I'm going to address."

Jonathan had developed a friendship with a White man named Oliver, who made a similar point in his interview. "It's not every person of color's responsibility to correct every White person or to educate," Oliver said. At the same time, he was grateful that God enabled people such as Jonathan to give grace. "I think that there are some who have that calling, like God is using them to further the conversation. And you know, that's

---

[15]For more on Christian theology of grace, see John M. G. Barclay, *Paul and the Gift* (Eerdmans, 2015).

between them and God. That's not me putting that on them. But there's no doubt that God is using Jonathan to do this. I mean Jonathan could have been like, 'You know what, my week doesn't need a sit-down with a bunch of White guys as they're sorting through this.' But he says yes. And I know that he does it because of his faith. He references that all the time. He's like, 'I'm here because of God. I'm here because God wants me to do this.'" Oliver summarized the role of grace in Jonathan's friendship, "It's a real Jesus-y type of love, because it's like, I love you despite you."

|||||||||

As we saw in the last chapter, grace anticipates response. Just as the gift of grace cannot be demanded, neither can the response be demanded. Grace doesn't substitute for reparations—it clears a space in which conversations about reparations can happen with generosity, care, lament, and acknowledgment. It does not purchase a response or withdraw what was given if that response doesn't come. It simply opens a door for response, bidding someone in.

Grace is meant to be a beginning, not an end. Navajo Christian activist Mark Charles uses the following story as a metaphor for how White people might respond to their deep indebtedness to Indigenous people:

> It feels like our indigenous people share an old grandmother who lives in a very large house. It is a beautiful place with plenty of rooms and comfortable furniture. But years ago, some people came into her house and locked her upstairs in the bedroom. Today her home is full of people. They are sitting on her furniture. They are eating her food. They are having a party in her house. They have since come upstairs and unlocked the door to her bedroom, but now it is much later, and she is tired, old, weak, and sick; so she can't or doesn't want to come out. But what is the most hurtful and what causes her the most pain is that virtually no one from this party ever comes upstairs to find the grandmother in the bedroom.

> No one sits down next to her on the bed, takes her hand, and simply says, "Thank you. Thank you for letting us be in your house." On the surface, this metaphor seems to suggest an easy answer. "Is that it? All we need to do is say thank you?" But that's the beauty of this metaphor. Because that's not it at all. Saying thank you requires a fundamental shift in thinking. Saying thank you reverses the roles. . . . Saying thank you is not the end, but merely a step into the beginning.[16]

This parable points to a seemingly contradictory aspect of grace: The anticipated response is both as simple as saying thank you and as complicated as a lifetime of action. The response anticipated by grace is not cheap. "Cheap grace," a term several interviewees used, occurs when recipients drop their response. As an example of cheap grace, one Black man said White people often quote the biblical phrase, "Do justice, love mercy" (Micah 6:8). Speaking as if to a White Christian, he said, "Don't tell me how much you want to love mercy and do justice. White people want the mercy part without the doing-justice part."

As we saw in the previous chapter, there are many ways to respond to grace, including reparation, restoration, and apology. "We have to ask for forgiveness," one White man told me. "How do you receive grace from someone if you can't ever ask for it? Yes, you can't *demand* it. And yes, there are plenty of people of color who are not ready to give forgiveness. I meet them in my neighborhood. And I get it. But we still have to ask for it." Genuine apologies for racist incidents are rare, and when they happen, they stand out. A Black man named Bryce described a time when an Asian American man deeply offended him, and the conversation they had in a car ride home afterward. "He humbled himself. I've never seen a man humble himself like that. He be like, 'I'm sorry. You know that I love you and I wouldn't put you in a situation that would

---

[16]Mark Charles and Soong-Chan Rah, *Unsettling Truths: The Ongoing, Dehumanizing Legacy of the Doctrine of Discovery* (InterVarsity Press, 2019), 194–95.

harm you.' And that meant a lot to me because he was able to swallow his pride. And that was something that I'd never seen before."

Just as those harmed cannot be forced to forgive, perpetrators of harm cannot be forced into repentance. Grace doesn't shame or cancel. In the years following George Floyd's death, many viral social media topics involved calling out public figures for racist incidents. The term "cancel culture" came to describe this trend, which some interpreted as necessary accountability and others as bloodthirsty shaming.[17] At its best, accountability through public discourse can produce institutional change, but problems arise when public call-outs attempt to force repentance. If public shame is used as a crowbar to coerce repentance, the result is rarely satisfactory to either party. No one wants a nongenuine apology. Grace takes a different approach from cancel culture. It names harm for what it is, seeing the wide context of that harm, and then it opens a space for repentance without shoving or threatening.

For grace to work, it must be a relational process. As we've seen, asking why requires agentic intentionality from White people, whereas collisions require the opposite—releasing agency. Grace fits somewhere in between. Recipients of grace choose certain behaviors. But grace can never happen alone. It depends on a giver carrying out their own motivations and behaviors. Racism at its core is not just an individual problem; it is a social problem—a rupture in social fabric. This makes grace uniquely suited to begin mending the social process of racism.

Grace sets the pendulum of generosity in motion. In doing so, grace can be a starting point for *covenant communities*—give-and-receive relationships in which people share a level of long-term commitment to each other. But grace does not have to occur within long-term

---

[17]See Greg Lukianoff and Jonathan Haidt, *The Coddling of the American Mind: How Good Intentions and Bad Ideas Are Setting Up a Generation for Failure* (Penguin, 2018); Emily A. Vogels et al., "Americans and 'Cancel Culture': Where Some See Calls for Accountability, Others See Censorship, Punishment," Pew Research Center, May 19, 2021, www.pewresearch.org/internet/2021/05/19/americans-and-cancel-culture-where-some-see-calls-for-accountability-others-see-censorship-punishment/.

friendships. Several stories of grace I heard involved one-time connections between people who would never meet again—the man on the corner saying hello, the book written so that many could understand, the woman giving hugs at church. These instances of grace prompted White individuals to respond, but they responded in the context of other settings and relationships.

By noticing past incidents of grace in their lives, White people also worked through a problem that often arises among White advocates for racial justice: the desire for approval. As White people looked back at moments when they received undeserved kindness from people of color, they recognized they need not always be treated in this way. That realization can have the powerful effect of freeing White people from the constant need for approval from people of color.[18] It also frees people of color from the obligation to demonstrate grace to every last White person, as if ending racism depends on it. Transformation happens as White people realize they are already surrounded by grace.

For Ian, an abiding recognition of grace freed him to take risks in addressing racism. He went on to support Ameerah's ministry financially and initiate connections between his church and her ministry. He made it a priority to attend events in the city focused on addressing racism and encouraged his congregation to do the same. He built relationships with several individuals of color and regularly attended a Black-led church. "My relationship with Ameerah is not perfect," he said, "but it's a relationship where I think we could say we genuinely are allies. I think we still have a lot of work to do."

Ameerah attested that Ian had changed. "I can tell he's bought in and actually doing something." She smiled as she described open

---

[18]bell hooks describes the importance of White people developing a combination of steady assurance and humility. "Ongoing resistance to white supremacism is genuine [among White people] when it is not determined in any way by the approval or disapproval of people of color. This does not mean that they do not listen and learn from critique, but rather that they understand fully that their choice to be anti-racist must be constant and sustained." hooks, *Teaching Community: A Pedagogy of Hope* (Routledge, 2003), 64-65.

conversations she has with him. "Over time, shoot, now he can call me and be like, 'Hey, I got this idea, what you think?' And I'll tell him, 'Hey Ian, that's good!' or 'Ian, don't do that.'" She playfully rolled her eyes in mock scolding. "That's because we built that relational capital. And I know he's serious. I know he does care and he does desire to see real change."

When I told one friend about this research, she said grace sounds like the "special sauce." I told her I don't see grace as the special sauce at all. A special sauce gets squirted on when a burger is already complete. You can eat a burger without the special sauce and it's still a burger. But through this research, I've come to believe that long-term commitments to racial justice don't happen without grace. Grace is not the special sauce. Grace is the burger.

Receiving grace is not a substitute for collisions or asking why.[19] None of the three elements I have described waves a magic wand over an individual or an institution to immediately erase their racist socialization. But together, these three form a trifecta that carries people through the time and training required for lasting change.

To see how these three elements fit together, let's look at one more story. Vicky, a White church pastor I interviewed, said one of her first experiences leading her to care about racism began when she joined a Black gospel choir in college. "So I was one of like five White people in an all-Black gospel choir, at a college that was mostly White. We would go to places all around the nearby states. And because I was part of this

---

[19]Some readers may be wondering, Do both Christian and non-Christian White people need to experience grace in order to become long-term advocates for racial justice? The answer is complicated. I can't verify the ways that non-Christians interpret grace-like interactions, because they were not the focus of this research. But other research on White activists of diverse religious backgrounds suggests that the question of how to move beyond guilt is unavoidable for White people dealing with race. "Whites need to get beyond guilt to do something constructive," researcher Mark Warren writes. White activists he studied tended to deal with self-blame by focusing instead on the historical and structural forces, careful self-monitoring, proving their commitment over time, and open communication. He did not use the word *grace* or trace its source to God, but he quotes interviewees who spoke of the need to acknowledge the imbalance between those harming and those harmed, and to forge trusting relationships to address those harms (Warren, *Fire in the Heart*, 121).

choir and we traveled, I spent at least two out of four Sundays in a Black church." Black congregants hosted choir members as they traveled. "We'd stay at people's houses. And just to see that constant love—like they just wanted to feed you all the time. And the acceptance of me. There was never a feeling that they didn't want me there. As one of the White students, we were just accepted right along with the Black students." In other words, she felt grace before she had words for it.

She found herself enjoying culturally diverse settings. "I think that's where I really started to understand the difference in culture and wanted to know more. Because these people I'm singing with, I'm enjoying. And these people I'm meeting, I'm enjoying. But their life is not like my church service. And I *loved* it."

Over time, she stumbled into important why questions about injustice and culpability. In a college course on social injustice and global politics, she recalls discovering, "Oh, wait a minute, this is a mess." She spent time in the Middle East studying Israeli and Palestinian history, and she started relating the systemic violence there to racial history in the United States. "I started applying that back and thinking, 'Well, it's not that much different here.' So I think that's when really my eyes were opened. I don't know that I completely understood how, but I started with a lot more reading, a lot more listening to people." Through her twenties and thirties, she actively sought opportunities to hang out with people who were culturally and racially different from herself. Through asking why questions, she reinterpreted her experiences of welcome from Black families not just as isolated acts of kindness but as radical resistance against an oppressive system.

Vicky also learned about marginalization through approximating experiences stemming from her own subordinated social location as a woman. "When I decided to become a pastor, I had the experience of being a young, White, single female in a male-driven world, and I learned a lot about inequality firsthand." When she took her oral exam to become licensed as a pastor, another male pastor from her church was in the room taking his exam at the same time. The examiners interrogated her harshly, doubting her qualifications at every turn. Then they whisked the White male colleague through with few follow-up questions and high accolades. The male colleague noticed what happened. In future meetings, he stood up for her. She had been laughing as she began telling the story, but now her voice became sober. "That's when I was like, 'You know, I can only fight for myself so much. I have to have someone else fight for me.' That's when I realized I needed White men who were already established in the church to fight for me as a young single woman, who would say it was okay for me to speak." She briskly wiped away a tear. "That's when I really started to think, 'Okay, if I need people to stand up for me and fight for me, I need to be standing up for the people I can stand up for.' And that's when I really got more active." She attended advocacy events led by Black churches in town and joined a team working to create more racially and culturally inclusive systems at her church. "And that just became a way of living."

We have seen how the three elements of collision, asking why, and responding to grace fit together in the context of racism. Through these experiences, White people learn to recognize, question, and replace the White social imaginary. They find an answer to the question of what to do about culpability for wrongs that can never be undone. And they find themselves within a pendulum of giving and receiving that sets ongoing relationships in motion. Grace is primarily an interpersonal experience, but it enables and sets a pattern for purposeful action across society.

This combination of collision, asking why, and responding to grace produces a new kind of hope, and that hope sustains a new way of living. It's time to return to the question left unanswered: How do advocates for racial justice hope? What basis do they have for an enduring hope, and how do they live out that hope? In part six, we'll see how lasting pursuits of racial justice grow from a unique kind of hope that is rooted in grace.

PART 6

Abiding Hope

TWELVE

Why Hope

WHEN MARK AND Hannah sat face-to-face over dinner in the wake of her confession of wearing a blackface Halloween costume, she read in his face a question: If you've been disappointed so many times before, how do you dare hope for change? We return now to that question.

To approach this question, we've walked through a journey. I implore you not to skip your way to this part of the book. Each of the three elements described in the preceding chapters contributes to forming a kind of hope that can replace White delusional hope. Transformation is a process and, more often than not, a slow one. It's a process that happens through external forces pressing against individuals in ways they don't control, as well as through intentional choices made by individuals and groups. Much of that process happens without obvious external evidence. That does not mean people should wait to act until after they have everything right, nor does it mean that the process hits an endpoint when all change is complete. What it does mean is that if you want lasting change, you need to do the preparatory work and ongoing maintenance work, not just the flashy work that makes a good Instagram post.

The three transformative elements I've discussed so far—collisions, asking why, and responding to grace—repeat in cycles of deepening growth throughout a person's lifetime. Now it's time to consider, what do White people committed to racial justice actually *do*? And what keeps them from giving up? When they encounter perseverance pitfalls, what keeps White people from taking the easy route back to a White enclave lifestyle?

As we saw in part two, not all hopes are equal. Hopes are dispositions built around shared social imaginaries we are constantly learning and teaching. Delusional White hopes cause real harm, and they do not offer the endurance needed to confront entrenched racist systems. I characterized those hopes as optimistic (avoiding the bad) and conventional (anticipating that the good future will extend from the pattern of past to present). Collisions and asking why can alert people to the deficiencies of those hopes, but people will need something to replace old hopes. The question we face is not whether to hope—if we look toward the future at all, we do so with some version of hope, however tenuous, cynical, or despairing that hope may be. The real questions we face are how we hope and what world we make out of those hopes.

As we have seen, hope is multidimensional. To render a well-rounded picture of the hope that sustains racial justice for the long haul, I will focus on three questions: why hope, what to hope for, and what to do along the way. The coming chapters cover each one in turn.

This chapter begins with the question, Why hope? For Christians with a deep and lasting commitment to racial justice, I found that hope begins where our last chapter left off: with grace. Hope is founded on the abiding knowledge that despite the reality and pervasiveness of the bad, *goodness interrupts.*

To see what hope founded on interrupting goodness looks like in practice, we'll consider the account of a White couple in South Africa named Carl and Adele. While their experience in postapartheid South Africa differs in some ways from the United States, the contours of their transformative journeys overlap with what I found elsewhere. They too experienced collisions, asking why, and responding to grace. They were some of the first people to convince me that if this research would be about addressing racism, it also must be about hope.

When I asked around among my longtime friends in South Africa for recommendations of White people pursuing racial justice, one friend insisted I meet Carl and Adele. I was hesitant to travel the long journey it would take to visit this couple, but my friend kept persuading. She said Carl and Adele had moved to South Africa more than twenty years earlier from Europe, and since then they had lived as the only White family in a Black township. It's hard to explain to Americans just how unimaginable that choice is to most South Africans. Since the dismantling of apartheid in the mid-nineties, many Black South Africans have moved into areas that were formerly restricted for Whites only, but the reverse almost never happens. Over my five years living in the country, I met only a dozen White people who lived in Black townships. Finally I agreed to call Adele, and she quickly invited me to stay with them for a few days.

Arriving at the address Adele provided, I parked alongside a barbed-wire gate resembling any other gate along the dirt road. A passerby spotted me checking my phone and introduced himself as a neighbor. As he went in search of Carl or Adele, I studied their residence. Like other homesteads in the township, it included several small buildings made of cement with corrugated tin roofs. A sturdy fence protected their large garden from roaming chickens and goats. Fruit trees dotted the yard. The neighbor returned, chatting amiably with Adele, and she welcomed me inside.

That night as Adele prepared dinner, I sat talking with her for some time before Carl arrived home from work. He shook my hand and settled into a kitchen chair as Adele brought him up to speed in the conversation. I had just asked her why they continued living there.

"Oh, we still don't know that," Carl said with a shrug and a playful grin. Then suddenly he held up his hand as if to pause and turned to face me. "Wait, are you a Christian?"

I nodded yes.

"Good, because unless you're a believer, it just won't make sense."

That first conversation lingered long after dinner, then picked up again the next morning as we sipped steaming cups of a coffee substitute made of barley and chicory. Adele and Carl had first moved there with a plan to stay for one year. They tried the sorts of things they imagined missionaries should do—children's programs, church programs, charity. "We were so naive," Carl said. "Everything just falls apart. That one year was so full of confusion and disappointment. I was so angry with God. I am not a very fat guy, but I think I lost half of my weight, that year, poof!" Carl had a way of juxtaposing humor with heaviness.

After one year, they returned to Europe defeated. There they realized, though, that they were no longer the same people. The year of rough collisions in South Africa had shattered their White imaginary. The world no longer made sense. Carl recalled opening boxes of decorative dishes they had left in storage, wondering now why anyone owned such things. "I looked with different eyes on our European lifestyle. People were running every morning out of the house to the workplace, being very important, and coming back in the evening, and you never see your children, but you have to keep going because your flat costs 1.8 million and you need a car and insurance. Everything spins in a circle. And being here was my first opportunity to look at that with different eyes."

Adele added that they remembered their South African neighbors with fondness. "Somehow this place stayed in our hearts."

Falling back on their familiar framework for White-Black interactions, they started praying that some other Europeans would move to the South African township as missionaries. "Of course no one would," Carl mused. "Why would they?" Eventually they realized they might be praying for the wrong people. What if *they* moved back to that South African township?

And so they returned. The time in Europe had renewed their optimism, and they arrived expecting to fix their surroundings. They planted fruit trees. Carl built a workshop to train young men for employment. Adele started a preschool. A woman recovering from a violent relationship moved in with them. They hosted volunteers. Wealthy White donors from cities came to hand out day-old baked goods to their neighbors.

The destructive legacy of colonialism, apartheid, and poverty would not be lightly mended by this well-meaning university-educated family of White foreigners. Burglars stole Carl's tools. Electricity and water cut out unexpectedly almost daily. They watched with shame as White visitors urged Black children to smile for photos while they lined up for handouts. The woman staying with them died of AIDS. One night a man broke into their home. Carl woke to the sound of Adele's scream. His voice boomed across the township as he forcefully wrangled the intruder off the property, earning a reputation as a force not to be trifled with. Afterward he felt horrified by his own capacity for violence.

"You give much, much, much, and the outcome is nothing," Adele said mournfully. Their fruit trees became a kind of symbol of their frustration. When the trees bore fruit, people would linger by the gate asking for an orange. "And we would just pick one and give them, thinking 'Oh, how good we are.' But the tree is empty after half a week, and nothing changed." One thing was becoming clear—the hope they brought was not going to sustain them.

"We are people used to giving 120 percent for everyone, so we found ourselves—" Carl paused to find the word, since English was not his first language.

"Depressed?" I suggested.

Carl nodded. "I had completely overdone it. I cried nonstop. I couldn't work anymore. I was just done. I had no glue." A few years later, Adele hit her own dark season. "I had a near burnout. I was really, really, really, really, really finished," she recalled.

"Why did you stay, then?" I had returned to that first question I had asked Carl.

Their shift toward perseverance came gradually, they said. They started spending less time trying to fit into White communities and let this place be their true home. "Everybody thinks we are weird," Adele said. "We don't fit in the White South African society, we will never fit in the Black society, and we don't fit in the European society anymore either. We see different things now." Instead of giving in to the pitfall of loneliness, Carl embraced that strangeness as strength. "We've had to make a system which does not conform to anybody's system—it just fits for us. I am convinced God especially uses the strange people. The majority of people have their only focus on being uniform with society. But God uses us for this work because he knows we are crazy enough to do it. But craziness is nothing you can multiply or publish or make a new standard."

At the same time, they were rearranging their hopes. "I think we learned to be open to how God leads. That was our main focus." They stopped expecting that their neighborhood's problems would be solved—not in their lifetime, maybe ever. Beneath layers of false hope, they found a bare hope that God might do something or might not. Either way, God would still be God and still be good.

They also peeled away goals. They saw how their original goals had been shaped by a colonialist expectation to control, a savior-ist expectation to be heroes, and an individualist expectation to forge their path alone. Carl said they were done acting like they could earn medals on a jacket. "That's not what God wants."

"What is the goal?" Carl mused aloud. He paused long before attempting to answer. "To change Zulu people? Rubbish! You can't change Zulu people. God does not send the two of us to change the Zulu nation."

Adele chimed in, "I think for the first time I learned to really ask God, 'What shall I do here?'"

Carl agreed. "God knows the people, he sends us, and he knows the outcome already, so we must listen to that more, but that's a difficult one. God wants us to be here, to stand by, to ask him daily what he would like for that day, and whom to help and whom not. Most of the time I have no clue what we are actually doing. I trust the Lord, I trust my wife, I trust my neighbors, and everyone has to find his part in the whole game."

Finding their "part in the whole game" included learning to be receivers as much as givers. Over the years they had discovered that receiving was not just about politeness; it was the only way to survive. "If I need help, *always*"—she emphasized the word—"everybody comes and helps," Adele said. "They give to us as they can. With information, with house-sitting, with whatever. They bake us cakes. They gave us these glasses." Carl held up his glass and clinked it with mine. When they accidentally left their gate open one night, neighbors woke them in the middle of the night to make sure it was safely locked. "People *care* about us," Adele said with a tone of awe. "We get much from whatever they can give. Much, much, much." Her eyes twinkled with delight as she said a group of young boys had pooled their money to buy her a dress. It didn't fit—not even close. "It was very long! And I asked them, am I allowed to cut it as a T-shirt, because I can't wear a dress like that?" We all laughed. "I wear it often, that T-shirt."

That evening I met the group of boys at a Bible study Adele led in a one-room community center that she had worked with neighbors to build. I'd never seen anything like their group. She spoke in their own language, diligently learned over many years. In the dim light of a bare bulb, she and eight boys read a passage from the book of Malachi about trusting God. Often they laughed freely. Other times, such as when a boy asked why bad things happen to good people, they grew serious. The camaraderie of the group held a kind of sacredness. I marveled that these guys came back every single week to hang out with a fifty-year-old White woman, whom they treated with such candor and respect. Adele occasionally instructed, but mostly she invited them to talk. Everyone contributed. They told Adele about school subjects they struggled in and made plans to meet together soon. "Each one of us can help each other with whatever subjects they knew best," one boy explained the plan.

They asked me questions—what I write, where I had traveled, my hobbies. I returned with questions for them—their nicknames, hobbies, and what they think about having White people as neighbors. One of the more confident boys grew somber as he told me about Adele and Carl. He said all the boys loved them deeply.

The next day we returned to the same building, this time for an after-school time for younger kids. Adele handed me a stack of books and directed me to a tiny plastic chair where for the next hour children eagerly took turns reading to me. Meanwhile Adele taught youngsters to match numbers at a table full of dominoes. Other children spread Legos across the floor, spun hula hoops, sorted plastic nuts and bolts, or colored outlined words on papers she prepared for them. When the time was finished, everyone helped tidy up. As they finished, some danced on tables, while others rocked joyously on a rocking horse or talked eagerly together, before they gathered to close with a song about Jesus' love. A few girls offered to carry Adele's things home beside us. She said they often get the keys to open up before she arrives, or to watch movies on weekends, and she has no problem trusting them. This is our place together, she said, not hers.

The trust with which she handed keys to teenagers and children stood in stark contrast to the walls, security cameras, and private security companies that protect nearly every White and upper-class home in South Africa. "It's all fear, fear, fear, fear," Carl told me later. "Fear is such a dominating thing." For him, he said it's the reverse—he would fear for his soul if he returned to that mindset.

One could get the idea from watching Adele sort dominoes and laugh with teenage neighbors that their life was all peace and joy. Back in their kitchen, Adele handed me a bowl full of homemade yogurt sprinkled with diced mangoes from the tree outside the window. As we ate, they reminded me that peace and joy was only part of the story. They said even now, they always have to check their racist tendencies. "It needs *all* this correction," Carl said with a sigh. "Always I'm telling myself, shut your mouth, think a second, and put it in the right relation."

Adele agreed. "Yeah, our awareness to race changed 100 percent. We were not aware of race issues before we came, and now we are very aware of it."

Carl smiled. "I am not the naive European anymore. And I am not the racist White guy either. I'm somewhere in between. And what it needs is a permanent correction in myself."

They had come to understand why life would not be easy in this underresourced postapartheid township. "We understand the disaster of racism. We see it." Adele had a graduate degree in education, and she knew that her efforts to keep a few children engaged in school were tiny compared to the chronic underfunding of Black schools in South Africa. She listed recent changes in government education policies and shrugged, not convinced that there would be any long-term improvement. "I have hope," she said with a tentative tone. Then she paused and gave a wry smile. "Carl, now, he has no hope."

I stared into my yogurt, giving Carl time to choose his words.

He shrugged and smiled nonchalantly at Adele's statement without denying it. "I don't believe—how do I say it? I don't believe the whole thing we're doing here is based on the outcome that society changes, or culture changes, or any *things* change. As long as I'm here, the more I battle to believe in those big changes. If you put your hope in those things you need some reason for it. And I don't see it. From time to time, I'm successful, but that is actually not what I believe in. I'm pretty convinced we have an impact on a few people, to a certain extent. I don't know. And we do change things, and what impact it had we might see when we stand in front of Jesus and look back. But to name something which gives our nation hope or whatever? I have no clue. I don't know where to put my hope in, if I think long about it." He went back to listing failures they had witnessed in churches and the government. "There aren't many arguments left if you want to talk people into hope."

The follow-up question was already on my mind again—*so why stay?* Why live and work there? They could have returned to the predominantly White world where racism is tucked out of sight and mind. Carl anticipated the question before I voiced it. "Now you could say, well, why are we here then? Pack your stuff and go! What pulls me out is the handful of people who are different. And here's the point: I know God thinks differently. For him, just five people are worth doing something for. And that's how I try to think." His words brought to my mind the first disclaimer he'd given me—*unless you're a believer, it just won't make sense.*

When I returned home and compiled my recordings and notes from the days with Adele and Carl, I labeled each file with the name of their township. When the apartheid government forcefully relocated African people into townships, they often chose township names that glossed over the injustice. South African maps are dotted with place names meaning "new home," "beautiful place," and "our place." Following that model, some aspiring township founder had dubbed this place with a name meaning "good hope."

How fitting, I thought. The township was founded out of a horrific delusional hope, but as Carl and Adele lived there, deepening their understanding of society, absorbing the hope modeled by their neighbors, and clinging to promises of God, they were slowly cultivating a better way of hoping.

▌▌▌▌▌▌▌▌

When I asked Carl and Adele why they hoped, their responses used the words *God* and *Jesus* a lot. So did other interviewees. A Latina woman named Milena told me succinctly, "Jesus is at like the center of my hope." Such a response might seem like a trite and unexamined Sunday school answer. If their warrant for hope were as simple as "in Jesus," there might not be any discernible difference between the hopes of people selected for this study and other Christians. But as we saw with grace, concepts that are held in common across Christianity can be applied to the issue of racism in very different ways. Adherents to delusional hope also use Scripture to justify their conventional and optimistic hopes through "Jesus." But when people in this study named Jesus as their source of hope, they were referencing a particular context and story line that did not lead to conventionality and optimism.

When people like Carl, Adele, and Milena said they hoped in Jesus, they referenced not just a person but a story line. Jesus had a context. That context was a very messy social situation. And into that context came a repeating narrative: Goodness interrupts the bad. Milena, who began her reason for hope with the brief statement, "Jesus is the center of my hope," then took a breath and launched into the rolling rhythm of a preacher at the culmination of a vibrant sermon. "My hope is in knowing the promises that come afterwards, that we live by faith and not by sight. And we claim things that even though we don't see them yet, we're trusting. We're trusting that he's going to call people from every tribe, tongue, and nation. That this *will* happen. My hope can't be on the leadership of my church, my hope can't be on the people at my church, my hope can't be on the politicians, my hope can't even be on myself. Because we are all so fallen. My hope has to remain consistently on Jesus who is the author, the finisher of *all* this. He will perfect us. We are in progress." The story line of the ultimate good entering into the bad was what shows Milena and other Christians why to hope in the tangle of racism.

The story line of Jesus that people referenced begins with Jesus present at the creation of the universe, bringing into existence all goodness where previously there was nothing. It is the story of a God who walked with humans through the history recorded in Hebrew Scriptures, including betrayals, wars, rapes, enslavement, and corruption. Scattered between all of that, God rescues, forgives, and restores. And then, for thirty-some years, God lives on earth as a human named Jesus. Before Jesus' birth he is called by the angel foretelling his birth *Emmanuel*, meaning "God with us." Jesus experiences all the human struggles—temptation, pain, sorrow, discrimination, and exploitation—and he meets these with both the power to heal and the restraint to remain amid the struggle, even to the point of his own wrongful execution. It's a story of God-as-human fully dying and then fully coming to life again three days later, to the surprise of everybody. It's a story that Christians interpret as the centerpiece to all of history—the evidence that God, being perfectly loving, perfectly powerful, and perfectly good, draws near to people. When Christians hope in Jesus, they hope in a God who shows up as goodness in the midst of the bad.[1] It's a story of an unruly, untamed God, who is always good but vexingly unpredictable in the outworking of that goodness.

Christians believe this story has a good ending. In the final and forthcoming chapter of history, God makes a new earth and heals society itself. In the words of the apostle John, quoting a voice from heaven in his dream of that future, "God's dwelling place is now among the people, and he will dwell with them. They will be his people, and God himself will be with them and be their God. 'He will wipe every tear from their eyes. There will be no more death' or mourning or crying or pain, for the old order of things has passed away" (Revelation 21:3-4). In his vision, John sees a tree of life planted at the center of the new society with leaves "for the healing of the nations," and the people in that society are together from "every nation, tribe, people and language" (Revelation 22:2; 7:9). Believing in an end in which goodness will be perfected doesn't mean Christians have nothing worth struggling for in the present; it just means, in the words attributed to another John—John Lennon—that everything will be okay in the end, so if it's not okay, it's not the end. This ending is the final and permanent interruption of the bad by goodness.

In the story line of the Christian God, where there is nothingness, God interrupts with creation. Where there is ruin, God interrupts with power to rebuild. Where there is death, God interrupts with life. Where there is debt, God interrupts with the offer of forgiveness by grace. There is no prior deserving of goodness; it comes because goodness is what God does, full stop. Goodness from God is undeserved, surprising, radical, incongruous. In other words, God's goodness comes of grace.

---

[1] As theologian Josef Pieper writes, Christian hope "has its source in a truly divine substance in man, in grace." Pieper, *On Hope*, trans. Mary Frances McCarthy (Ignatius, 1986), 99.

As we have seen, Christians believe God initiated a story line and pattern of grace toward humans, and this pattern is the ordering principle for all of humanity and creation. A Christian social imagination, then, centers on a belief that however bad things get, God's goodness interrupts, sometimes *ex nihilo*, sometimes through humans following God's ways, but always there is a possibility of bold, defiant goodness breaking through. As Carl said, "Here's the point: I know God thinks differently."

Some people noted that this sort of hope is where Christian approaches to racial justice diverge from secular and other faith traditions. Even before I mentioned the word *hope* in an interview with a White man named Pete, he said that what sets apart non-Christians and Christians in racial justice work is how they hope. "It makes all the difference that I can lean on my faith. That shows itself mostly around hopefulness. I know that on my own, my energy, my love, my compassion, has such limits. To be reminded that God's justice, compassion, mercy—all those things—are limitless, it matters greatly." I asked him to explain his hopefulness further, and he said, "I realize how patient and long-suffering God is. I think about the God of history, what he has witnessed of all of humanity, and I realize that my hope can't be then determined on a timeline that I choose. Am I willing to have hope regardless of seeing certain successes in my lifetime? What if it happens in twenty years? Will I be faithful now to pray for something that I may not be a part of?"

One Black man described Jesus' story as the reason not only for his own hope but for the hope of African American Christians across history. "People see hope in the Black church, but that's all because of our faith. Our faith has led us, and encouraged us, and strengthened us to leave slavery, to become the better part of who we are, to love others, to forgive others, to turn the other cheek. We've done this from a faith perspective. I believe there's a power in working with Jesus, a spiritual power, a transformational power that walks with you."

Theologians have argued that this sort of hope in the interrupting power of God is not just one of many possible Christian interpretations of hope; it is *the* Christian hope. Jürgen Moltmann writes, "Genuine hope is not blind optimism. It is hope with open eyes, which sees the suffering and yet believes in the future."[2] Miroslav Volf builds on Moltmann's argument, saying optimism merely discerns that "the future to be born out of the present will be good." Real Christian hope "is not based on accurate extrapolation about future from the character of the present. The hope for future is not born out of the present. The future good that is the object of hope is a new thing." Drawing on Romans 8:24, Volf writes, "Hope that is seen is not hope." In every instance of true Christian hope, "we always hope against reasonable expectation."[3] Theologian Walter Brueggemann refers to the spiritual work of determining how to hope as *prophetic imagination*. To practice the discipline of prophetic imagination is to bring hopes in line with God's character and then publicly express "*those very hopes and yearnings* that have been denied so long and suppressed so deeply that we no longer know they are there."[4]

|||||||||

People in this study clearly drew on Christian teachings to form their hope, but there was a second key influence to the way they hoped: traditions of people of color. When I asked one Black woman what she wanted White people to know about hope, she said, "That they need to have some friends that have real struggles and watch how they hope." White people I talked with were doing that. One White woman said about people of color she spent time with, "Their way of hoping is so literally against any imagination that I have ever had. I haven't figured it out yet, but I feel like there's a nugget in there."

---

[2] Jürgen Moltmann, *Experiences of God* (Fortress, 2007), 14; see also Moltmann, *The Spirit of Hope: Theology for a World in Peril* (Westminster John Knox, 2019).
[3] Miroslav Volf, "Hope Pt. 1, The Thing with Feathers," Yale Center for Faith & Culture, May 9, 2020, https://faith.yale.edu/media/hope-pt-1-the-thing-with-feathers.
[4] Walter Brueggemann, *The Prophetic Imagination*, 2nd ed. (Fortress, 2001), 67, italics original.

She was noticing something: that people of color in White-dominated societies learn resilient ways of hoping forged through the disappointments of inequity and injustice. They do not optimistically flee from the bad, nor do they expect goodness to be the conventional norm. They anticipate goodness, but as an interruption. Pete, the White man quoted earlier who said the differences between secular and Christian approaches to racial justice are most evident in hopefulness, went on to explain how he learned that hope. "I think that comes with age and experience, and I would also say I'm learning that from other cultures. The first thought that comes to my mind of what I've learned from my Black brothers and sisters in the faith is lament. How to move toward lament and not move quickly out of it."

Nearly every Black-led church service I attended included teaching about how to hope. Sometimes the theme came up subtly, as in the corporately repeated phrase, "Lord, do it again." Other times pastors offered entire sermons on hope. "The topic of today's sermon is holy resilience," one Black pastor began, "and holy resilience must be rooted in Christ." He focused on Romans 5:3-5: "We also glory in our sufferings, because we know that suffering produces perseverance; perseverance, character; and character, hope. And hope does not put us to shame, because God's love has been poured out into our hearts through the Holy Spirit, who has been given to us." His emphasis was threefold: Hope comes through suffering, because Christ endured suffering, and with regular reassurance given by the Holy Spirit. The pastor normalized suffering, saying, "There are only three types of people—those in trouble, those coming out of trouble, and those on the way to trouble." His examples of sufferings turned specifically to those of Black people, who were in the majority in the congregation. "When I think of resilience, my first thought is African American people." He launched into a litany of suffering and resilience across African American history from enslavement, to Jim Crow, to the Supreme Court's recent decision to reverse affirmative action, wrapping up with reassurance that hope across all of this history is based on Christ.

Philosopher Jonathan Lear explores the contours of a kind of hope evidenced through a letter written by Plenty Coups, the last great chief of the Crow Nation, at a time when the cultural devastation of his people seemed inevitable. "When the buffalo went away the hearts of my people fell to the ground," Plenty Coups writes, "and they could not lift them up again. After this nothing happened." Lear draws from the Crow Nation's history to describe a kind of hope that he calls "radical hope"—a hope "directed toward a future goodness that transcends the current ability to understand what it is."[5]

Examples of scholars of color who convey radical hope in the face of racism abound. Legal scholar Derrick Bell, in *Faces at the Bottom of the Well*, refers to a kind of "forward motion without hope." He calls for new narratives that offer hope rather than despair by sourcing hope from "oppressed people who defied social death." He finds a certain freedom in Black practices that replace trite optimism with realism and strategic activism: "Freed of the stifling rigidity of relying unthinkingly on the slogan 'we shall overcome,' we are impelled both to live each day more fully and to examine critically the actual effectiveness of traditional civil rights remedies."[6] Philosopher and public intellectual Cornel West writes poetically, "I am in no way optimistic, but I remain a prisoner of hope."[7] He says marginalized people—particularly African Americans—have shown the world how to maintain "hope on a tightrope," a "kind of blues-inflected hope rather than a cheap American optimism."[8] In a book titled *Freedom Dreams: The Black Radical Imagination*, Robin Kelley traces hoped-for dreams of Black Americans across history. He argues that such dreams must be noticed and named, because "unless we have the space to imagine and a vision of what it means fully to realize

---

[5] Jonathan Lear, *Radical Hope: Ethics in the Face of Cultural Devastation* (Harvard University Press, 2008), 103.
[6] Derrick Bell, *Faces at the Bottom of the Well: The Permanence of Racism*, repr. ed. (Basic Books, 1992), 197, 199.
[7] Cornel West, *Hope on a Tightrope: Words and Wisdom* (Smiley Books, 2008), 41.
[8] West, *Hope on a Tightrope*, 41.

our humanity, all the protests and demonstrations in the world won't bring about our liberation."[9]

White people learned ways of hoping from people of color, but they had to do the work of figuring out how their own lives fit into those visions of hope. For those who grounded their hope on the interruptions of goodness into the long history of racism, often this mean embracing their own rarity. Several spoke of recognizing that by becoming Christians who cared about racial justice, they became their own kind of numerical minority among the wider body of White Christians. Like Martin Luther King Jr., their hope was based on a marginal portion of those who call themselves Christians, "the inner spiritual church, the church within the church, as the true ecclesia and the hope of the world," who "have broken loose from the paralyzing chains of conformity and joined us as active partners in the struggle for freedom."[10]

Several expressed a view that marginality is strength, not weakness. I heard people describe their hopes as "small," "micro," "marginal," "not to scale," "not on my timeline," and "tidbit, tidbit." They understood that most White people would not voluntarily fight for racial justice, but those numerical odds were not cause for despair. Some went so far as to imply that struggles for racial justice might be better off not going mainstream, as those efforts might become watered down or manipulated toward other ends. Several pointed out that people of color have been marginal in society, so leadership for racial justice has always come from the margins. They saw this not as accidental but as a broader template for movements for justice—change regularly initiates from the margins, from people capable of seeing from another angle, who have more to gain from change than from consistency. Some saw the same narrative modeled in Jesus' life—a man born in a stable to an unwed mother of a politically subordinated and nationless ethnic group, growing up to

---

[9]Robin D. G. Kelley, *Freedom Dreams: The Black Radical Imagination* (Beacon, 2003), 198.
[10]Martin Luther King Jr., "Letter from a Birmingham Jail," African Studies Center—University of Pennsylvania, April 16, 1963, 17, www.africa.upenn.edu/Articles_Gen/Letter_Birmingham.html.

initiate change from outside formal political and religious power structures. They saw marginality as the place goodness could—and perhaps most likely would—interrupt.

Two hours into a conversation with one Asian American man named James, I could sense that he had been testing how I would respond to increasingly bolder statements about his disappointments with White Christians. When I asked about his hopes, he looked at me with a quirky smile, as if deliberating, and then dropped this: "Honestly, I think I hope that the White North American church will become less."

I told James I wasn't surprised, and he wasn't alone. His words reminded me of Lynn's half-joking advice that the White North American church "take a bye this round." Another White man had told me, "Most of my hope for the American church is grounded in a non-White church. It feels like there's like a vibrancy and a life there. The spirit seems to be living and active in ways that are beautiful and profound and seem to point to the biblical story line into the heart of Jesus. It seems more alive and well in those spaces. That is like a great gift from the non-White communities to the broader community—I get to discover and learn about who Jesus really is, thanks to my Black and Brown brothers and sisters." These people weren't hoping that fewer White people would follow God but rather that more would do just that—follow God, not put themselves first. In so doing, they could make space for the influence of people of color to become comparatively greater.

When I asked one Black woman about what gives her hope, she said, "This research. That people will sit down and honestly talk about ways in which they could do better." Often during or after an interview, someone would let out a kind of sigh and tell me they were grateful for reminding them and the world that there are in fact White people working for racial justice long term, even if they are few. These moments often restored my own hope to continue researching and writing. As bell hooks writes, "There are so many individuals I could name whose lives bear witness to the power of anti-racist White people, folks like longtime activist Grace

Lee Boggs, that it would take pages and pages to share their stories. These pages should be written. Everyone should hear their testimony."[11] These people may be few, but we do well to remember that they do exist and to find out why.[12]

As we saw in this chapter, the foundation for hope among those in this research did not tend to be an expectation that the positive events they had seen would automatically multiply to become a dominant social pattern. In contrast to conventionalist hope, people did not believe they could settle into colorblindness while the wheels of progress worked out the little unpleasantries of the present. Rather, they saw small victories as evidence that in this world, injustice remains, but goodness interrupts. As Carl said, "Just five people are worth doing something for." Moments that fueled their hope might be as small as a smile on their way to work or as weighty as a new legislative act. Just as grace experiences pointed to possibility despite impossibilities, their hopes were founded on interruptions of goodness amid the bad. Having explored the *why* of resilient Christian hope for justice, we turn next to a second question: what to hope for.

---

[11]bell hooks, *Teaching Community: A Pedagogy of Hope* (Routledge, 2003), 65.
[12]hooks explores a historical split that occurred between Black justice advocates who chose to reject the possibility of White people contributing to that movement, and others—herself included—who insist on the role of "rare White folks who had the courage to choose against racism." She advocates strongly for practices that acknowledge positive motion. "There have been many quiet moments of incredible shifts in thought and action that are radical and revolutionary. To honor and value these moments rightly we must name them even as we continue rigorous critique. Both exercises in recognition, naming the problem but also fully and deeply articulating what we do that works to address and resolve issues, are needed to generate anew and inspire a spirit of ongoing resistance. When we only name the problem, when we state complaint without a constructive focus on resolution, we take away hope. In this way critique can become merely an expression of profound cynicism, which then works to sustain dominator culture" (hooks, *Teaching Community*, 52, xiii-xiv).

THIRTEEN

What to Hope For

"The more I learn about history and the more I learn about what was done to Indigenous people, the more I despair." Renee let out a sigh as she began to talk about hope. The very story that led to our introduction carried the sting of that history. In present-day Madison, Wisconsin, my primary research site, people self-identifying as Native American in the 2020 census made up only 0.02 percent of the population—a total of 756 people. Because I struggled to find Indigenous Christians from the area to interview, I reached out to Renee Kylestewa Begay—whose real name I have used with her permission to honor her expertise and specific life experiences—to discuss my research in the context of her expertise as a national leader in Indigenous Christian ministry.

Stories of Indigenous people have often been told as narratives of despair. But this was not the intent of Renee's story, nor the complete story of Indigenous people in Madison or anywhere.[1] Indigenous people including the Ho-Chunk, Fox (Meskwaki), Sauk, and other tribes have lived continuously in the area where I now live for more than ten thousand years. They gave names to this place, including Teejop and Taychopera, long before European Americans built a city and called it

---

[1]David Treuer, an anthropologist and Ojibwe tribal member, devotes his book *The Heartbeat of Wounded Knee* to disputing the common narrative that Native American ways of life died with the massacre of more than 150 Sioux people at Wounded Knee in 1890. The book traces how Indigenous people have struggled and succeeded in preserving their identity and culture through centuries of resistance and resourcefulness. Treuer, *The Heartbeat of Wounded Knee: Native America from 1890 to the Present* (Riverhead Books, 2019).

Madison, Wisconsin. Since European American settlers arrived, the history of Indigenous people passed through disease, warfare, genocide, forced treaties, relocation, assimilation, and allotment. Especially during the latter decades of the twentieth century, however, the ongoing resourcefulness and persistence of Indigenous people has resulted in federal and state policies that have tended to shift toward self-governance for Indigenous people. This resurgence of self-determination has coincided with economic growth, population growth, and mounting evidence of cultural flourishing among Indigenous people.[2]

Renee credits those shifts to the work of Creator God. Renee is of the Pueblo of Zuni of southwest New Mexico, from the Sandhill Crane clan of her mother and the Eagle clan of her father. She grew up active in Zuni cultural life and deeply grounded in her Indigenous identity. During high school she became a Christian, but at first that religious faith and her Indigenous culture didn't seem to fit neatly together. In college, she joined a predominantly White student ministry. There too, leaders seemed unable to answer her questions about how to live with both Indigenous and Christian identities. Then she visited a Latino and Latina student ministry, and something clicked. She saw Christianity contextualized for a cultural group that had been ignored by larger ministries, and she felt a surge of spiritual energy. "The meeting was at a house, there was music, there was food, there was conversation, there was dancing at the end. I was like, I want that for our Indigenous community!" She and a fellow student named Donnie, whom she later married, started a Bible study for Indigenous students. That group grew to become Nations, an Indigenous student Christian ministry affiliated with the organization Cru, which she directed for many years. She and Donnie later founded the Talking Circle, an

---

[2]Ana I. Sánchez-Rivera, Paul Jacobs, and Cody Spence, "A Look at the Largest American Indian and Alaska Native Tribes and Villages in the Nation, Tribal Areas and States," Census.gov, October 3, 2023, www.census.gov/library/stories/2023/10/2020-census-dhc-a-aian-population .html; National Congress of American Indians, *Tribal Nations and the United States: An Introduction*, 2020.

online resource dedicated to building good relationships with and among Indigenous people.

When Renee talked about her own and her people's stories, the narrative didn't end with despair. "It's easy for me to go into despair, but the hope for me is in partnering with other Indigenous folks in this work, and it's really exciting what Creator is doing right now." She listed some of the signs of Creator's work through those partnerships between Indigenous Christian thought leaders, speakers, authors, and organizations. She summed up her way of hoping using phrases Indigenous elders had taught her: "relating to one another in a good way, relating to God in a good way, relating to ourselves in a good way."

As I asked people in this research what they hoped for, the list of their answers grew long. People mentioned churches where everyone belongs, education systems where all children learn, housing systems where everyone has a home, and an end to discrimination. Their responses reminded me that even people with long-term commitments to racial justice genuinely differ on some core beliefs about what racial justice should look like. If they had been in one room to discuss goals together, we certainly would have had a robust conversation. Should the goal focus on top-level structures or bottom-up evidence at the grassroots level? To what extent should White people become a part of predominantly non-White groups? How important are interracial relationships in racial justice? Should churches aim for multiracial congregations or affinity spaces where people of minoritized groups can experience a respite from minority experiences endured during the rest of their week? People held differing views on these topics.

But such differences do not overshadow the great degree of agreement in the ways people spoke of their hopes for racial justice. There are goals of racial justice that are flexible enough to incorporate differing contexts and circumstances while still pointing us to something of substance. And of all the ways people described these hoped-for goals, Renee's seemed to best encompass the rest. In this chapter, we'll see how people in this research hoped for "relating in a good way," which included seeking mutuality, righted systems, and everyday love. To see how people pursue these goals together, we'll focus on a conversation between four friends.

| | | | | | | | |

When I invited Anna to participate in this research, she didn't suggest an interview alone in a coffee shop or living room. She invited me and three good friends to a pub on a Friday night.

Anna and I walked to the pub together from her home. On the way, she told stories about places we passed. Here was the park where she joined neighbors painting a mural to honor the first Indigenous inhabitants of this place. Here was the public elementary school her children attended, with the new playground she and the staff had raised money to build where once there was a cracked asphalt parking lot. Here across from the school was the corner where young men used to sell drugs, until one of the friends we were able to meet helped her ask them to leave. Here, waving from a porch, was Miss Edwards, an older Black friend who, decades earlier, had been among the first Black residents to move into this neighborhood during a dramatic swing from White segregation to White flight. Next door, Anna pointed out a newly arrived White family. When Anna's family moved into the neighborhood, only a handful of other White people lived on the block, all of whom sent their children to private schools outside the neighborhood. In the two decades since, housing prices had doubled, driven by a perception that this neighborhood was "up and coming." Now more White neighbors were sending their kids to the local public school, and a recent news article held up the school as a positive example. Anna worried that the very changes she and her neighbors had fought to implement would drive out the people who worked for those changes. Black long-term residents such as Miss Edwards would benefit from a rise in the value of their homes, but would her grandchildren want to pay property taxes in the neighborhood, and would they feel at home here? "Gentrification is so complicated." Anna said. "Sometimes everything just feels so complicated and tough. That's why I need these people you're going to meet."

When we arrived at the pub, her friends Ezra and Ed were already waiting. As a Black leader in their multigenerational and multiracial church, Ezra spoke with an unwavering calm, as if he had seen and weathered all things. Ezra introduced me to a White man named Ed, his partner. Some time later, amid jokes of his perpetual lateness, came Noah, a White man whose mixed-race children I had met earlier in the day when they came to play at Anna's house. I was finding it difficult to remember which kids belonged in which house, so fluidly did they mingle from family to family.

The four friends were thick in conversation well before the waitress returned with a tray of cider, ale, and lemonade. Early in the conversation, before I raised questions about their hopes, Noah brought up the topic of this chapter: the importance of knowing the goals beyond racial justice. "You have to ask, 'What is the community you envision?'" He answered his own question with another rhetorical question, "How do you not see forgiveness and grace being a part of it?" Grace was what made gatherings like this one and churches like theirs possible, but it was a part of not only the means to an end but the end itself. "How do we get anywhere without forgiveness and grace being fundamental to what we're doing?"

Ezra was also eager to pick up the thread of forgiveness. "Forgiveness is letting go of the hope that the past will be different," he said. "Let go of the coulda-woulda-shouldas. The past might be helpful for *informing* what you do moving forward. But you gotta let go of the hope that it *was* different." He said that the longer he works in the church, the more convinced he is that forgiveness needs to be central to everything they do. "It used to be that the norm was, when people got hurt, they would slingshot away from the community. And then if they came back, the hurt is never really addressed. So what we're trying to be intentional about doing is creating the kind of conditions where people who are in silos can interact with each other." He said he used to feel like preaching about "the cross thing" was used in a showy way, trying to get people to an emotion-driven altar call. "But what I recognize now is it's the ultimate truth-speaking moment to be able to receive grace and forgiveness for yourself in a way that prayerfully will enable you to share that with others. Because there is no way of doing this right! If you're intending on doing this by making sure that you get the road map right, that you never say the wrong thing, you never hurt yourself in the process, then you might as well not be involved in it. Because that's going to be a part of it. But if you recognize, 'Hey, I'm going to mess up, but I hope and trust that folks know my heart,' and you offer that back and receive it when it's done to you, then you can make some progress. It's scratchy, bleedy work."

"You know, living this close in community means we've all seen each other's shadow side," Anna said. "And that is so rare. We all know all of each other's foibles and stuff! And we love each other in that. These families here are like family in every sense of the word. They're like lifers. We've been *in it*. These families are a significant reason we stayed where we are." They exchanged stories of hard times weathered together, peppered with inside jokes and the gentle ribbing of longtime friends.

Noah expanded on how their friendship through hard times exemplified something at the end goal of racial justice. "If you want to bang the drum and hold people accountable, that still doesn't get us all the way to the place of the community we want. That gets us a sense of justice, but not the empathy and compassion that's a deep resource we can draw from. If you want to be engaged in racial justice, if you want to create a community where this genuinely happens, yes, there needs to be that accountability and anger. There also needs to be a way to circumvent that in order to get everyone still around the table and working in this harmonious community. Otherwise, what's the end you're getting to? We're going to have just an imbalance of power the other way. And maybe that's justice, too, but it's not the justice that we're trying to seek out. We're seeking out a justice that moves us *to* community rather than a justice that just says, 'All right. We're all even now.' We don't want to get to the point where we're even! We want to get to where we're working together."

Noah had named an important contrast—the difference between making the world "even" versus an ultimate end of mutuality. As we saw in the discussion of grace in part five, when people exchange goods or services in amounts that they determine to be equal, they can walk away from that exchange as an over-and-done event. In contrast, when people give with the expectation that the recipient will give back some willingly chosen gift another time, the relationship can begin to swing back and forth in a pendulum of giving and receiving. The word *reciprocity* describes this sort of back and forth, which sometimes balances out and sometimes leans to one side or another. Reciprocity means living within ongoing indebtedness of exchanges. Sometimes one person's tab of indebtedness runs a little higher, sometimes another's. The relationship is such that the tab does not need to be counted, and yet if the account grows conspicuously lopsided, the relationship will struggle. Sometimes grace—free giving from creditor to debtor—is a part of that reciprocity.

I use the word *mutuality* here to describe one step further—relationships in which people reciprocate in exchanging some goods and *also* hold certain goods, sentiments, or experiences in common. Mutuality is a necessary condition of all living things—the full flourishing of any creature depends on the flourishing of someone else. Thus, as Potowatami scholar Robin Wall Kimmerer writes, "All flourishing is mutual."[3] Sometimes mutuality happens through interactions directly related to racism, such as supporting each other through a racially charged incident, but it also stretches into the mundane. In subsequent visits to the homes, church, and neighborhood of Anna, Noah, Ezra, and Ed, I witnessed these friends' and their neighbors' lives intertwining through rides to school, birthday parties, takeout pizza nights, shared

---

[3] Robin Wall Kimmerer, *The Serviceberry: Abundance and Reciprocity in the Natural World* (Simon & Schuster Audio, 2024), 33.

lawnmowers, snack donations for church coffee hour, and jamming together around a piano. "We've shared Thanksgivings. We've shared family crises. We've shared a lot of laughing and goofy things," Anna said.

Mutuality cannot happen unless all parties have the freedom to both give and receive, to hold and to let go. Racism interrupts all these. Often conversations about justice focus on the ways racism inhibits receiving human rights and necessities. When people relate in a good way, society can allocate resources so that people receive access to water, food, shelter, companionship, mobility, education, health care, and other essentials with some degree of agency. But supplying their own needs is not all that humans ultimately desire. Humans are not exclusively *receiving* beings; they are also *giving* beings. When capacities to give are blocked, people feel stymied no less than when their capacities to receive are blocked. Often the most painful sting of unemployment is not the lack of a paycheck; it's the feeling that the world doesn't need what you have to offer. When a person's gifts are treated as irrelevant and valueless, society communicates a message that a person is also, by extension, irrelevant and valueless. Similarly, relating in a good way means having freedom to choose emotions, stories, and experiences to share, and also those that might not be shared.

Racism interrupts mutuality in multiple ways. The historical design of the racial caste system causes White people to extract resources from people of color, often indirectly and unknowingly. And yet the racist ideology paints White people as the net givers—good, generous White saviors who are the philanthropists and donors of the world. Thus racist societies train White people to envision themselves as givers while in actuality allowing them to be net receivers. At other times, mutuality is interrupted when White people become aware of racial injustice and desire to "do something," but, in not knowing how to approach the problem, their efforts are misguided and unwelcome.

People of color experience another set of interruptions to mutual giving and receiving. Historically, the net flow of resources has flowed away from their ownership. At the same time, the dominant racial ideology paradoxically communicates that their gifts are not wanted. They are turned down for job applications, rejected for promotions, channeled into the least dignified jobs.

In another research conversation, I sat at the kitchen table of a White married couple named John and Sarah. We were already two hours into the conversation when I finally arrived at the question, "What do you think the goal of racial justice is?"

Sarah looked stunned. "What *is* the goal? I have no idea what the goal is!"

John also seemed caught off-guard by the question, and he mused that it's a question too rarely answered. "If you listen to some people, there is no right way to be a White person. No matter what you do in the arena of race, it's wrong. I don't know what the right answer is, but I can definitely say *that* is the wrong answer."

Sarah had been formulating a response as John spoke, and she suddenly interjected with confidence. "Just being able to live in God's community. To have connections with others who are different from yourself. That's a real blessing. And I think for us, it's never been about what we can give. Just being a part of this community is its own blessing. Some people are hard-wired for activism, and that's good, and they're probably not going to see it that way, but—" She took a deep breath. "It's good to love and be loved, and try to do good for your neighbors." They pointed out that many White people new to racial justice awareness try to position themselves as generous givers. In mutuality, race does not dictate who is a giver and who is a receiver—everybody becomes knitted together by being both.

Sarah turned to John. "What's that verse you really like about bringing treasures . . . ?"

John paraphrased Revelation 21:24: "The kings of the earth bring their treasures into the new Jerusalem."[4] He explained how he relates this to

---

[4] "The nations will walk by its light, and the kings of the earth will bring their splendor into it" (Revelation 21:24 NIV).

the goal of racial justice. "In the new Jerusalem that Jesus creates, we'll all be able to bring our treasures there." He paused long, letting an image take shape in my mind of a place where everyone freely gives and freely receives without shame or lacking. "I think that there are some treasures that people have to offer that are just not in demand here," he lamented.

"Maybe that is the goal." Sarah picked up the train of thought. "To be able to live interconnected. And celebrate our God-given gifts of each culture. But of course, we have some work to do first because of the power imbalance."

Mutuality is inhibited by power imbalances, but the opposite is also true—practices of mutuality break down power imbalances. As one Black woman put it in an interview, "What I ask White people to do is to see if they can be in some kind of equal-status relationship. Go for a cup of coffee, go to a movie. Have lunch with a person of color in your workplace. Because you're in the same exact place. You need to hear how they got there." bell hooks advises similarly: "Striving to be mutual is the principle that best mediates situations where there is unequal status."[5] Sociological research has shown that mere contact between White people and people of color is not likely to produce change among White people, but when White people regularly interact with people of color with equal or higher socioeconomic status than themselves, they are more likely to develop lasting commitments to racial justice.[6] Having pastors, teachers, managers, and mentors of color can interrupt White people's deeply engrained habits of broken mutuality.

Sarah and John had made active choices to break down power imbalances by giving and receiving what people in their social position don't usually give or receive. Much like Carl and Adele giving mangoes and receiving T-shirts and neighborly protection, John and Sarah sprinkled stories of mutuality throughout their interview—parents who prayed for

---

[5]bell hooks, *Teaching Community: A Pedagogy of Hope* (Routledge, 2003), 63.
[6]Mary R. Jackman and Marie Crane, "'Some of My Best Friends Are Black . . .': Interracial Friendship and Whites' Racial Attitudes," *The Public Opinion Quarterly* 50, no. 4 (1986): 459-86.

each other's children, music ensembles, friends they would bump into at school meetings. When their predominantly Black church asked for volunteers to teach Sunday school, John volunteered. As a White highly educated man, teaching Black third-grade girls in the basement of a church was not his comfort zone. "I spent a lot of years in the basement. Literally," he said. The arrangement was both symbolically and experientially transformative. "The third graders eat me for lunch," he said with a laugh. Young Black women taught him about hair, friendships, and their experiences in public school. "In the conversations about hair—you listen," he said. "I think just listening is indispensable." He recognized that this was a setting in which he and these Black youngsters were forging a new power dynamic by giving and receiving in ways that rarely happened in the surrounding society. This thickly woven fabric of mutuality was one mark of relating in a good way.

||||||||

When people described their hopes in interviews, they talked a lot about relationships. As my research assistant and I reviewed and coded responses, we were surprised not only by how often people spoke of relationships but that people of color spoke even more frequently than White people did about the importance of interracial relationships. We cautiously considered what to make of this trend. Research done even within Madison has shown that interracial relationships alone are not enough to solve racism, and poorly designed attempts to bring together interracial connections can even cause more harm than good to people of color.[7] White people often unconsciously benefit from the appearance of being "good White people" when they have diverse relationships, whether or not those relationships benefit people of color.[8] When

---

[7] Katherine J. Cramer, *Talking About Race: Community Dialogues and the Politics of Difference* (University of Chicago Press, 2007); Jackman and Crane, "'Some of My Best Friends.'"
[8] The term *racial capital*, coined by Nancy Leong, describes this privilege of good standing afforded to White people in relationships and institutions due to the presence of people of color in those settings. Leong, "Racial Capitalism," *Harvard Law Review* 126, no. 8 (2008): 2153-2226.

White individuals are steeped in racist imaginations, they inflict microaggressions on others unknowingly, even against people they think of as friends. For people of color, spending time in closer proximity to White people can mean putting themselves at greater risk of experiencing the effects of racism. For all these reasons, we hesitated to suggest that relationships were a goal, or necessarily even a means, to racial justice.

As we looked more closely at the ways that people brought up relationships, though, it became clear that people were not just talking about any kind of relationship between diverse people. They were talking about specific modes of relating in a good way. They were building social institutions and structures that enable people to relate in a good way far beyond the interpersonal level. A second marker of relating in a good way is *making social systems right.*

Creating functional social systems does not happen without intentional effort. It requires addressing inequalities and actively empowering people whose power has been curtailed. It involves changing how certain institutions work. In the short run, that will probably cause some discomfort.

Ezra said that when he started working at their interracial church, another Black pastor warned him, "I've seen White churches with Black members and Black churches with White members, but I have yet to see an integrated church where power is all integrated." Ezra went on, "That's what we're trying to do now. There's been a change in really empowering the congregation to tackle issues of power. That's where the stronghold is. I've been the most encouraged in the last few years that we've started to really to address that." He said he has noticed that their church has started taking longer to make decisions, and that's a good thing. He sees it as a sign that those in power are learning to make space for those with less power to be heard. "The culture has changed among the leaders to actually be able to create room for difference. We can mull on things. If you have an issue, we don't have to jump on it immediately." Changing the dynamics of institutions such as churches, schools, workplaces, and health-care systems is complicated work, and it requires actively creating ways to incorporate the perspectives of those who have been disappointed by these institutions.

To create righted systems, people need to evaluate social systems not just according to whether those systems benefit them as individuals but according to whether the systems allow the wider society to thrive. Potawatomi philosopher Kyle Powys Whyte offers a useful concept for evaluating the quality of social systems: *collective continuance*, which he defines as "a society's overall adaptive capacity to maintain its members' cultural integrity, health, economic vitality, and political order into the future and avoid having its members experience preventable harms."[9] Righted social systems are not just useful for the present; they allow for the flourishing of communities into the future. Whyte explores collective continuance using the example of food sovereignty among Indigenous people. He shows how colonialism interrupted the abilities of Indigenous people to access food resources and make decisions for the good of their own people. Doing so dismantled long-standing social and ecological systems that had protected the collective continuance of Indigenous peoples. Once destroyed, such systems were exceedingly difficult to replace. One cannot quickly rebuild ecological diversity, decision-making protocols, or trust between disparate groups. Broken systems have a tendency to spiral outward, breaking other systems.

Beverly Daniel Tatum, a psychologist who has researched racism for over three decades, uses the analogy of a moving walkway to describe the process of righting systems.[10] Racism is like a moving walkway that carries people in one direction whether they contribute their own energy in that direction or not. That walkway directs everyone toward racist outcomes—inequalities in hiring, incomes, belonging, health,

---

[9] Kyle Powys Whyte, "Food Sovereignty, Justice, and Indigenous Peoples: An Essay on Settler Colonialism and Collective Continuance," in *The Oxford Handbook of Food Ethics*, ed. Anne Barnhill, Mark Budolfson, and Tyler Doggett (Oxford University Press, 2018), 355.
[10] Beverly Daniel Tatum, *Why Are All the Black Kids Sitting Together in the Cafeteria? And Other Conversations About Race* (Basic Books, 1997), 91.

and more. But people on the walkway have several options. Some walk in the direction of the walkway, speeding their movement in the wrong direction. Tatum refers to this as *active* racist behavior. Others merely ride along at the speed of the walkway—what Tatum calls *passive* racist behavior. Those who recognize that the walkway leads in the wrong direction might make other choices. They might turn around and start walking in the opposite direction, or they might jump off the walkway altogether. Those options—which begin to fit into the category Tatum calls *actively antiracist* behavior—begin to change the surroundings. But people on the walkway might do still more. They could urge others on the walkway to turn around, or shut down the walkway, or dismantle it and rebuild something that supports people in a better direction. In other words, a complete solution to injustice involves changing the system itself.

Repairing systems requires people to observe what goes wrong in the current system, reimagine something better, and then boldly implement it. Rather than a conventionalist hope that trusts the automatic movement of society, people in this research hoped for a future in which they would dismantle and rebuild some walkways.

In recent years, public conversations about racism have increasingly focused on the goal of righting social systems. The word *systemic* more often appears in conjunction with the word *racism*, highlighting that racism is not simply a problem of a few cruel individuals but a combination of countless institutional and cultural norms established through centuries of intentional and unintentional decisions. Righted systems play a necessary part in establishing a hoped-for society. And yet righted systems are not an ultimate end—they are means to other ends. People who succeed in passing a new law or changing a company's hiring practices might feel some satisfaction at their achievement, but what they ultimately desire is the *results* of righted systems. This brings us to the third marker of relating in a good way—everyday love.

"My hope," Anna said as we were finishing up our drinks, "is that we can normalize this kind of thing so racial justice isn't like 'Oh gosh, this again!'" Noah's hearty laughter boomed across the bustling pub, and Anna continued. "This should be normal, so it's not like we have to literally get off the couch before we can run. It can just be a natural part of life that we corporately build muscles for. And when we're exercising those muscles, we're finding joy in it."

Ed had been quiet through much of the conversation. At times Ed's eyes twinkled with curiosity, but he seemed hesitant to interject, allowing instead for most of the talking to come from Noah and Anna, each at least a decade younger than Ed, and the sage-like pastor Ezra. Ed told me he didn't grow up attending church much; he had worked in blue-collar jobs all his life. "I'm not one of those NPR types," he said with a playful smile. I was grateful when Ezra turned to him and asked, "Is there any perspective on this whole racial thing that you want to throw in, something you see that hasn't been said yet?"

Ed thought for a moment. "I've lived through the fifties, sixties, seventies. Every decade seems to have a different issue. Sometimes it seems like it's moving so fast and I'm just trying to keep up. But in doing that, sometimes I just step back and just live in it. Not try to fix it, just learn what's happening. And sometimes the best way to fix it is just *live* it."

The insightfulness of Ed's comment slipped past me at the moment, but Noah noticed. "To segue off Ed's comment," he said, "you have to live in it. And that's important. You have to look for where there's life within a hopeless situation. You can always look to where there's death. Death is around us all the time. If you fix your eyes only there, things can seem really bleak. You can always drift into hopelessness. But if you craft a life that incorporates this—this living with people who are different from you, and not just as a passing thing—then there's always places to find life. I always come back to that. There's *life* in this. How can you lose hope when there's life in this work, and there's life in this way of living? Our work is about dealing with and confronting death. But we see death from a place of remembering that there's life in this. You have to dwell where the life is."

"Dwelling where the life is" aptly described these friends at the pub. They were a living picture of something worth hoping for, people in a system of good relationships with each other, God, and themselves. Much of what I witnessed in the time I spent with them and their neighbors might seem to have little to do with racial justice: walks through the neighborhood, advising each other on the best bus routes, showing up at each other's kids' schools, and laughing around a big table with people who aren't going anywhere else. When systems are set right and mutuality becomes habit, relating in a good way does not—and indeed should not—include thinking or talking about race in every interaction. By most appearances, these friends were just living life together with people they loved. And that had everything to do with racial justice.

Everyday love means tethering racial justice to ordinary life. White people in this research were not just addressing racism in special events; they were weaving it into whatever sphere of influence they found themselves in. They were not trying to match the culture or experiences of people of color. They were manifesting their own culture in ways that related well to others. As one Black woman said she advises White people, "Just be cool. Let it be natural. Let it be as you would anybody else. Don't make it weird."

An elderly White man named Robert spoke of everyday love as the centerpiece of his hopes. "The opposite of hopelessness, I'd say, is not optimism. It's not, 'Oh, yeah, everything's going to turn out just fine.' No. It is excitement about doing what I think Jesus taught us to do, and that is to go put our love into action, to act on that love, and make a difference for as many people as you can." He started listing global statistics that could leave a person hopeless—the number of displaced persons, hungry children, and unhoused people in the world. "But I'm not hopeless!" he went on. "I feel that it just makes it clearer and clearer that our efforts should be directed toward encouraging and persuading people to put their faith into action and go out and love people of all types and act on that love." He recalled a phrase he heard from Christian theologian Walter Wink: "Relentless love is the most powerful force in the universe." Robert paused to let the words sink in. "And I think that's true. I think relentless love can overcome. You know, you may get chopped to pieces. And you might get executed or shot or die in hurricanes or whatever. But if there's enough relentless love out there, it pushes the darkness back. Over, and over, and over again. I've seen it."

When I asked one White man what's unique about White people who stay committed to racial justice long term, he said, "They end up long-term friends with people who are a different complexion than they are. They eat with them, they spend time with children and families, they worship together. It's not an event—it's a lifestyle. I'm not taking selfies of myself while I'm doing this." The Latina woman who had recommended Anna for this research gave a similar description of what she sees in Anna's mindset. "For her, it's not just this one thing that I do. It's almost like trying to be healthier—it has to become ingrained in my lifestyle for there to be a long-term impact. It can't just be one more thing I add, like I'm going to add this book club, or I'm going to add this activity, or I'm going to go to a Juneteenth event. It has to be part of my everyday life that the things I read, the people I associate with, my whole life is committed to this. And then when I see something of injustice, it hurts me just as much. I feel that. It's not just this distant thing."

When I explained to my son what this book was about, he asked, "Is this a book for people who are like superstars who make their whole life about racial justice, or is it for everybody?" I considered the question carefully. Certainly, the people of color I interviewed were selective about the White individuals they chose to recommend—they did not choose just anybody. This is a book about a transformative process that continues across a lifetime of perseverance and intentionality, and not every person will take that journey. And yet, that doesn't rule anyone out from taking the journey. Of those people in this study who mentioned their parents' views, the number of those raised in liberal-leaning and conservative-leaning families were not significantly different. Nor did the factors leading them to be selected seem to stem from growing up in homogeneous or diverse settings, attaining certain levels of education, or working in particular sectors. The process of developing a commitment to racial justice is a remarkably flexible process that molds itself to many life circumstances.

The White people in this research were not superstars accomplishing extraordinary feats, and several asked me directly to be careful not to portray them as such. Few worked in organizations designed solely to address racism, and few had racial justice written into their job descriptions. Their careers included educators and educational support staff; health-care providers; pastors, parachurch ministers, and church administrators; writers; researchers; civil servants; computer programmers; artists; construction workers; and military. Some had chosen these career paths with the intent to apply their unique skills to racial justice, while others found ways to make changes from within the career paths they were already in when they began learning about racial justice. They made the big decisions—where to live, whom to treat as family, whom to spend time with on ordinary weekdays—in ways that made racial justice the default. Rather than squeezing racial justice into special events or volunteer hours, they tethered it to the nonnegotiable routines of life. For some, that meant placing themselves in a neighborhood or faith community where they would be in regular contact with people pursuing racial justice. They were more likely than the broader population of White people to be immersed in diverse churches, neighborhoods, or workplaces. At least 57 percent of White interviewees had made intentional decisions to live in neighborhoods with non-White neighbors, and at least 67 percent had been a part of a predominantly non-White church.

But more importantly, racial justice was not a fancy coat they put on for a part of their day and took off afterward. It was a part of them.

Much research on racial justice has focused on the *scale* of change. As the moving walkway metaphor demonstrates, changes in society need to happen not just at the level of individuals but at the scale of systems that change the direction of movement for hundreds or thousands of people at a time. In the scholarly emphasis on scale, however, sometimes the factor that gets overlooked is *longevity*. As we saw in the previous chapter, many people in this research did not expect change to happen at a wide scale. What they did expect was tenacity. Racial justice was woven into their lives like a thick web, through relationships of grace and mutuality and an established habitus of practices.

Everyday love was not just a goal for White people. The phrase also points to a freedom and authenticity experienced by people of color. A Black woman named Kayla highlighted this goal. Early in the interview, Kayla said, "Look, I love my identity. I love that God made me a Black woman. But with that comes a fight. Every day. I fight sometimes even to show up. I long for a day when Black people don't have to struggle against racism anymore, when we wouldn't have to do anything but *be*. We wish we could just be. But we can't." I hadn't yet asked my usual questions about hope, so I followed up by asking Kayla to talk about what she sees as the goal of racial justice. "Good question," she said, then paused and spoke slowly. "What I hope for is that *all* people can live anywhere and *just be*." She finished the sentence and stopped to consider whether she had more to add. She nodded. "I'm gonna leave it at that."

When people can "just be," they can manifest their own culture. For people of color, that means not being tolerated or assimilated into White-dominated spaces but having an abiding freedom to express the gifts of their own cultural heritage. One Black man pointed out that his city was good at being "tolerant" but not good at "including people of color into the fabric." Tolerating is not the same as relating in a good way.

Sometimes the word *welcoming*, for all its positive, hospitable connotations, can become a cover for tolerating. As one Black woman mused, "What does it look like to not only say, 'You're welcome in *our* space,' but to create a space where people of color will actually develop that sense of belonging, and stay?" An Asian American pastor at a multiethnic church similarly said he advises White people not to "invite" people of color into the church but rather to "empower them to manifest their culture." He explained, "That's a different thing. It's quite often that churches say, 'Oh, well, we welcome everybody,' and it's absolutely true. If you're a person of color, you walk into those churches, you're very, very, welcome. But the problem is not that they're welcomed, the problem is that *guests* are welcomed. That means they are permanent guests. Family members don't welcome. I don't welcome my daughter when she comes home. She plops down on the sofa and dominates and grabs control of the room. That's what family does. Guests don't do that. And so there's an important distinction between welcoming people versus allowing people to say, 'This is my home.'"[11]

Having the freedom to authentically manifest one's own culture doesn't mean culture remains static. When people freely bring their own cultural and socioeconomic backgrounds into their interactions, new cultural forms can emerge out of the collective. Black theologian Willie James Jennings writes that as he considers his Native American, Korean, Ghanaian, Maori, and Khoisan students, he hopes for something more than restoring Indigenous worlds that have been broken into pieces. "I wanted a drawing of those pieces together, a throwing of them into the air, an allowing of the Spirit of the living God to take those pieces and fit them together in new and life-giving ways that would be familiar, singing familiar songs, remembering people and lands, struggles and hopes, but

---

[11]Another Asian American man described a youth program he had been a part of at a diverse church that lived this out. "It was never about a church program. It was never about a youth mentorship program. It was really just about doing life with them. We gave them our life and invited them into ours. They welcome us into theirs and allowed them to just stay authentically who they were."

also new, with new songs, new futures that would mark a path toward what Christianity could be at the site of fragments. The work of joining fragments aligned with the work of loving and learning together: this was the fragment work I wanted to see."[12] He offers a compelling image of just living in a good way—fragments old and new being fit together by God in new and life-giving ways. The repairing of those fragments happens through everyday love.

Scholars and activists have often focused on love as both the telos, or ultimate aim, of racial justice and a means to that end. Martin Luther King Jr. made an effort to preach on loving enemies at least once a year, and bell hooks names a book chapter "Love Is Our Hope."[13] Love enables the solidarity required for many comprehensive changes in institutions, laws, and culture. Love enables people to practice what Carl Boggs calls *prefigurative politics*: "the embodiment, within the ongoing political practice of a movement, of those forms of social relations, decision-making, culture, and human experience that are the ultimate goal."[14] When people love each other while pursuing racial justice, they embody a way of being that is also the end goal.

Anna described how loving relationships among friends have been both a crucial means and a crucial end. "There have been times when we've felt like we literally cannot be here in this church—it was too painful." She didn't offer details, but by the nods around the table, it was clear the friends knew and had weathered together the situations she remembered. "The thing that kept us coming back was the relationships that we have with people here. Sometimes I get mixed up and start thinking, *This church is not doing it for me*. But then I'm like, *Wait a*

---

[12]Willie James Jennings, *After Whiteness: An Education in Belonging*, Theological Education Between the Times (Eerdmans, 2020), 39.

[13]Martin Luther King Jr., "Loving Your Enemies," sermon, November 17, 1957, Dexter Avenue Baptist Church, Montgomery, AL, https://kinginstitute.stanford.edu/king-papers/documents/loving-your-enemies-sermon-delivered-dexter-avenue-baptist-church; bell hooks, *Salvation: Black People and Love* (Harper Perennial, 2001).

[14]Carl Boggs, "Marxism, Prefigurative Communism, and the Problem of Workers' Control," *Radical America* 11, no. 1 (1977): 100.

minute. The people that we are sharing life with, who are making me a better person and giving me an opportunity to put love into the world and to be loved, that is what's important."

The apostle Paul explains love in this way: "Love is patient, love is kind. It does not envy, it does not boast, it is not proud. It does not dishonor others, it is not self-seeking, it is not easily angered, it keeps no record of wrongs. Love does not delight in evil but rejoices with the truth. It always protects, always trusts, always hopes, always perseveres. Love never fails" (1 Corinthians 13:4-8). Much of that passage matches what people said about racial justice throughout interviews and observations. Grace offers a way to enact the difficult challenge to "keep no record of wrongs." Through asking why, people "rejoice in the truth" and learn how to actively work to end evil. Throughout, they grow in their ability to "always hope, always trust, always persevere."

In contexts of racism, love also takes into account the effects of racial and generational trauma. People with lesser power in society, including people of color, are more likely to bear the psychological aftereffects of traumatic histories, and that affects relationships. A Black woman named Alicia put it this way: "Black folks have this history that's in their minds and their bodies. And White people have to take the initiative with them, because they actually don't know that you care about them. They don't know that. Even if you do, they don't know that. We doubt that. We wonder that all the time, everywhere we go. We're not trying to, it's just there. It's imprinted in us traumatically, and most of us have experienced so many microaggressions that it just informs how we feel, how we think. I'm sure we're sometimes unnecessarily suspicious of White folks' intentions. But I don't think we necessarily want to be, it's just that stuff has marked us. So take the initiative."

Alicia offered a metaphor to describe the need for people of differing histories to love each other by appropriately adapting to each other according to those histories. "If a woman's mother, and her mother's mother, and her mother's mother were all in terrible abusive relationships with men, even if it's hundreds of years later, would you blame a daughter in that family if she has no trust for men? Or she has terrible relationships with men? Or she doesn't have any peace in relating to men? Or she's guarded and angry? I'm not saying that any of those things are good for her or that she doesn't need to deal with those things because they're hurting her. But wouldn't everybody just understand that? And wouldn't it be incumbent on men if they're in relationship with that particular woman to say, 'Gosh, I know I need to deal very gently with this person, and I need to help her know that not all men are like that, even though that's been her family's experience for hundreds, maybe thousands of years'?" Love means learning how to adjust one's own behavior to support people affected by generational trauma.

Christians believe that love is worth pursuing, not only for an instrumental means to some other end but because love is the essence of God. Christianity's primary answer to the question of what to hope for is, in Renee's words, *relating to God in a good way*. For Christians, all other good relationships flow from and circle back to that relationship. As one Black woman put it, "The goal is to be with Jesus. So what does it look like to be with Jesus right now? I think the kingdom of God is the goal—to bring God's kingdom on earth. Which will result in *all* people being treated with the dignity that God gave them. And it will also result in more people coming to Jesus." She and many Christians I met with pointed out that racial justice is not a tacked-on, optional activity for Christians—it is what happens when people know God and live in God's ways throughout their lifetime.

Anna pointed out that Christians have a different perspective from other faith traditions when it comes to trying to love. Rather than believing they produce love from themselves, they believe love is a response to having been loved by God. "Something that Christianity offers is the sense that it's not actually about *us*," Anna explained. "Growing up I used to think we make things happen for God. And now I see it's like, nope, that's not how it works. It's a pivot to see that actually *we* respond to God's goodness and movement in the world. Everything we do is a response to something that's already happening that's bigger than us. People have been living in my neighborhood a long time before I ever got there and will continue a long time after, and I am a part of something larger that's not actually about me. I mean, I am responsible for my actions and for reflecting the goodness of God in the world, but ultimately, at the end of the day, it's not about me. I think that's a helpful recalibration because some of the discourse about racial justice is apocalyptic, like, 'If we don't do this it will all end.' And that's a lot of pressure. Look, the track record isn't good! If I have to trust in humanity to do good things, I'm not voting on humanity! But Christianity is saying you can respond out of God's goodness and work in the world—you're part of the bucket brigade, so get in line, and it is important. But we're not *that* important."

In this chapter we've seen how mutuality, righted systems, and everyday love are markers of the hoped-for telos of relating in a good way. In the final chapter, we'll consider what it means to actively live out that hope. What do Christians committed to racial justice do in the middle space, when the good way has not yet interrupted, when there's still a long way to go toward living in a good way?

FOURTEEN

What to Do with Hope

As I was sketching the outline of this book, I reached out to several experts to talk through what I was learning and check for feedback. One of those experts was Gloria Ladson-Billings, an influential scholar of race studies and education at the University of Wisconsin–Madison and an active church member. As we reflected on my research, she also told stories from her own life.

Her ancestors, she said, never would have imagined that a Black woman would achieve what she had in her lifetime. "I'm four generations out of slavery," she recounted. "My grandparents were sharecroppers on both sides. My parents grew up in legal apartheid, state-sponsored segregation. My mother could not try on a hat in a downtown department store." For those ancestors, ending systems of slavery, sharecropping, or segregation seemed impossible, much less becoming a distinguished professor at a top research institution in the nation. "But just because something is impossible doesn't mean it's not worth doing," Gloria said, paraphrasing author Derrick Bell. "Slavery was impossible. But it didn't mean that my ancestors didn't fight against it. You could never get ahead in sharecropping, but that didn't mean they didn't fight against it. Those folks who were enslaved didn't see what my life would be today, but they didn't have to see it. They just knew where they were in the struggle. And to presume that the struggle will not continue today is really folly."

If interrupting goodness describes the foundational reason for hope among Christians in this study, and relating in a good way describes what they hoped for, what does the journey from one to the other look like? To Gloria and others in this research, it was clear that the way forward would be heavy, hard, or even impossible. They met those challenges with a hope that was rugged, enduring, and even startlingly joyful—*a struggling hope.*

Gloria went on to explain the way she hopes. "The ethos among White Americans is this idea that the world has to be about winners and losers. But the African American ethos is not about winning; it's about participation in the struggle. We are not called to win; we're called to struggle. Your testimony is always going to be what you did as a part of the struggle."

To Gloria, that struggle would assuredly be heavy, but heaviness did not produce despair. As a metaphor to explain why, she referenced the Greek myth of Sisyphus, a man condemned forever to repeatedly roll a boulder up a steep hill, only to see it roll back down. "You *know* that boulder is coming back down that hill!" Gloria exclaimed. "But the idea is this: White Americans focus on the boulder. But the African American struggle is focused on Sisyphus. Sculptural renderings and paintings of Sisyphus will show you a person with these incredible biceps, amazing quadriceps and deltoids. It's about the strength that Sisyphus has developed from pushing this daggone boulder. It is *going* to come back down the hill. But listen, your job is not about getting the boulder up the hill. Your job is that you're gonna get up there and push it. And as you're pushing it, you're going to get stronger."

Just as Gloria listed the physical muscles that grew strong in Sisyphus's body by pushing "that daggone boulder," people develop muscles of soul, mind, and body when they continually pursue racial justice with a struggling hope. The intent of this book has been to examine how people come to treat racial justice not just as a passing interest but as the shape of their very posture. It's worth pausing to consider this word *posture*. A posture is a habitual way of carrying one's body, formed through years of repeated actions within a context of external pressures, constraints, and influences. You cannot develop an enduring posture simply by contorting yourself to match a diagram on a website. To carry that posture continuously through your daily activities requires stretching, repetition, and building core strength. If you start from a place of poor alignment, you might also need a chiropractor to help with some readjustments.

When it comes to developing an enduring posture for racial justice work, our surrounding society misaligns every one of us. We each need the equivalent of regular chiropractic work. It might involve a lot of joint popping, muscle stretching, and maybe some years wearing a brace. We can't do this alone—we need experts, mentors, grace givers, challengers, encouragers, and companions. That posture-development work happens through repeating cycles of the three elements we have seen—collisions, asking why, and responding to grace. It also happens as people exercise an abiding hope—a hope rooted in interrupting goodness, aimed for a good way of relating, and struggling along the way. In this chapter we'll consider four postures that White people learn as they practice a struggling hope: lamenting, mending, risking, and leaning into joy.

―――――――

Recall Lynn, Anna's neighbor who described herself as having "more than one foot in agnosticism." When she heard the organ of her Christian college chapel belting out triumphant battle hymns after the attack on the World Trade Center, she longed for something she didn't yet know a word for. The professor who stood up and said, "We need to lament" introduced her to that word. Since that time, teaching on lament has become more common in the American church, spurred especially by the book *Prophetic Lament* by theologian Soong-Chan Rah. He defines lament as honesty before God and other people, through which we recognize the struggles of life and cry out for justice.[1] Rah argues that

---

[1] Soong-Chan Rah, *Prophetic Lament: A Call for Justice in Troubled Times* (InterVarsity Press, 2015), 47, 23.

American evangelical Christians who benefit from injustice tend to overemphasize praise in their communal practices and underemphasize lament. This stems, he argues, both from a dearth of theological training and from a fear of losing their grip on privilege.

Lament names the bad. It acknowledges specific hurts and harms. Participating in lament is an act of resistance against dominant ways of responding to harm, both for sufferers and those who cause suffering. Among those who suffer, lament resists the tendency to stuff down painful emotions, only to have these resurface unabated in the future. For those responsible for suffering, lament resists the self-protective silencing around culpability. Lament does not necessarily fix what's wrong, but it brings people together to acknowledge the ways people are affected by harm.

For Christians, lament also includes acknowledging that the character of God offers a reason for hope. The many biblical psalms of lament nearly all include a declaration of the Lord's character or a request of God in addition to a naming of the sorrow. As one of many examples, Psalm 61 packs these into the space of two verses: "From the ends of the earth I call to you, I call as my heart grows faint; lead me to the rock that is higher than I. For you have been my refuge, a strong tower against the foe" (Psalm 61:2-3). This lament juxtaposes a direct complaint about human evil with a reminder that God is still good. Christians who lament are remembering that God does not ignore evil but suffers through it, and ultimately, in God's own surprising timing, interrupts and conquers it.

Many of the rituals popularized by the Black Lives Matter movement and other justice movements are rituals of lament. Speaking the names of Black individuals killed by police. Kneeling for eight minutes and forty-six seconds in acknowledgment of the time police officer Derek Chauvin knelt on George Floyd's neck.[2] Lying motionless in public

---

[2]The actual time was later revised to nine minutes and twenty-nine seconds upon review of body camera footage.

die-in protests. Many people I interviewed had participated in rituals such as these. To these they also added experiences of laments built into church life. Laments in churches could include prayers and liturgical readings woven into ordinary Sunday worship services, gatherings in response to current events, and annual rhythms around events such as Juneteenth, Indigenous Peoples' Day, Martin Luther King Jr. Day, and ethnic heritage months. Lament is a posture that acknowledges that the boulder of racism is heavy, and pressing against it will be a struggle.

When I asked the Black woman named Ameerah at the end of her interview what she would like me to be sure to include in this book, she said, "The first thing that comes to mind—which you might already have—is that it's *hard*." She was right—I did already have those words from her. When I reviewed the interview transcript, I counted sixteen times when she said the words "it's hard." Recall that Ameerah had confronted a group of mostly White male pastors and ministry leaders to implore them to pray for people of color in their midst. Through her whole description of that process, she reiterated how hard it was. "I knew what I wrote was going to be hard," she recalled of her preparations for that confrontational prayer meeting. When she asked a friend to review what she planned, the friend told her the same thing: "Yeah, it'll be hard. But it's needed." At the start of the conversation with the ministry leaders, she warned the people in the room: "I begged them, hold back offense, because it's going to be heavy and it's going to be hard and it's going to be uncomfortable." When she talked to Ian immediately after the meeting, it was hard, and sometimes even years later their conversations were still hard. Raising money to support a Black-led ministry was hard. Leaving to find a more supportive community was hard. Her work among other Black people who experienced discrimination continued to be heavy and hard. Ameerah saw struggle as integral to life as a Christian. "It's super hard to do this work, but it's also super hard to reflect Jesus. And most believers in Jesus are not reflecting Jesus. If they were, they would be doing this type of work."

Lamenting the difficulty of the struggle is not the opposite of hoping; it is a way of hoping. Ameerah unknowingly echoed something I would later read from theologian Walter Brueggemann: "The hope Jesus announces here is heavy and hard. . . . Hope is easy and flimsy for those who already have richness, fullness, and laughter now, but hope is hard for those who are denied the riches, prevented from fullness, and have no reason to laugh."[3] Through collisions and asking why, White people lose their flimsy and easy ways of hoping. Like Carl and Adele, sometimes they feel they have no hope at all. Hoping will at times feel nearly impossible, like hauling a boulder up a mountain only to watch it roll back down again and again. Lament is a posture of sharing the heaviness of that hope with God and others.

⁞⁞⁞⁞⁞⁞⁞

As we saw in the previous chapter, one aspect of the hoped-for outcome of racial justice work is *righted systems*. But righted systems never remain stable forever. In the same way that Gloria Ladson-Billings knew Sisyphus's boulder would come back down the hill, people committed to racial justice know that social systems need perpetual righting.

In chapter seven I defined racism using an analogy of a rupture in the social fabric. To extend that metaphor, one posture of addressing racial injustice, then, is *mending the social fabric*. A social fabric is never a completed project, like an embroidery to hang on the wall. It is a living artwork that people contribute to throughout their lives. Human systems always require maintenance and adaptability. As people cycle through institutions, as new needs arise, and as the world changes, social systems need capacities for continual assessment and improvement. As one White man put it, "It's not an event—it's a lifestyle." Pursuing the goal of a mended social fabric requires, then, that people within those systems *become* menders.

---

[3]Walter Brueggemann, *The Prophetic Imagination*, 2nd ed. (Fortress, 2001), 104.

Because racism is a problem with social causes, it requires solutions at the social level. Mending the social fabric is not just about one or two individuals feeling better, or becoming friends, or showing up at an event, or learning new information. It's about finding the ways that those micro events fit together with a multiplicity of events that will reshape the contours of institutions and culture. Menders find ways to patch society together in new ways. They hold the shredded fabric in their hands, trace the sources and extent of the tear, and get to work weaving and stitching.

Having raised two kids with a fervor for life that often results in ripped clothing, and often doing so on a tight budget, I have spent many hours with my children through the years mending their clothes. Sometimes we iron a patch on the underside of the cloth or restitch a seam in a way that the result will be nearly invisible. Other times we choose colorful fabrics to stitch boldly on the surface so that the patch itself contributes to the character of the garment. Likewise, in addressing racial injustice, mending the social fabric is sometimes only visible to those most closely involved or to those trained to notice. Other times the mending is brightly visible, as in the Japanese art called *sashiko*, which reinforces everyday fabrics with decorative patterns of tiny stitches. The public nature of the story can become part of the goal in the mending even as the result becomes a focal point to the beauty of the whole. Whether the mending happens in more covert ways or more public, mending restores a fabric to functionality.

At the same time, mending creates a shared story that adds another layer of value. When I sit with my children teaching them to press the pedal of the sewing machine or slide the iron across a patch, our relationship deepens. The memory of that relationship comes to mind when we see the patch again. Mending not only fixes a problem; it becomes a part of the meanings shared by communities. The memory of the tear as well as the memory of its mending add a value that extends beyond functionality. Mending has both a functional value in restoring the systems that distribute resources and enable individuals to live, and a psychosocial value in fostering purpose, joy, and love.

People who become menders struggle together to improve the institutions of which they are a part. I met with several pastors who had created partnerships among churches of differing ethnic and racial compositions. They knew that such partnerships could easily settle into power hierarchies matching the surrounding society, so they intentionally designed systems to counter that tendency. In one example, three congregations—a predominantly Asian American one, a predominantly Black one, and a predominantly White one—had begun working together. Pastors took turns preaching, and they also agreed to meet every week to preview each other's sermons. The practice sharpened the preaching skills of each, particularly by creating a consistent setting in which pastors of color could speak up about cultural and socioeconomic references that were normalized in White settings but less relevant for people of color. Together they chose topics and examples that would allow all congregants to relate.

Other examples of mending institutions included setting a budget and a regular rhythm for race-related trainings for leaders, creating affinity groups where people of color within larger predominantly White spaces could meet, and advocating for policies affecting racial inclusivity at administrative, denominational, or governmental levels. People in this study did not expect to live in a world in which no one ever makes a racist mistake again. They anticipated that the work of mending would be ongoing but that the mending itself could be prefigurative of the world they hoped for. As one White woman told me, "It feels like the only hope left to us is that of solidarity, however flawed and fragile and fractured and stuck together again and again with spit and duct tape and good will." People with a struggling hope become menders, and as menders, they take risks.

People who know in advance that a task will be difficult can respond in two opposing ways: They may freeze out of fear of failing, or they may relax into a brave or even playful freedom. Whether a person responds with frozenness or freedom depends largely on what they believe will happen if they fail. Do their past experiences cause them to expect to be shamed, punished, and cast out of community? If so, they likely will tiptoe in fear. Do past circumstances lead them to expect to receive honest correction, grace, and reincorporation into a communal struggle? In such healthy social contexts, they can experience a freedom that enables a posture of risk taking.

A White man named Oliver described risk-taking freedom that he experienced in a small multiracial group of friends. In an earlier chapter, I quoted his description of that group as a place where he experienced "a real Jesus-y type of love, because it's like, I love you despite you." Oliver went on to describe how the group created an environment that fostered freedom and courage. "As time has gone on, the trust level and the vulnerability has gone up with me and the other participants. And we do take risks. For me, I might start to say something, and wonder, 'Am I going to sound like the typical middle-aged White guy?' I don't want my peers to think of me like that. But I can take that risk. I can say, 'Well, this is what I think about something,' and I get feedback. People are just trying to listen. And when you always get that trust and vulnerability, you realize, nobody's here to pounce on you. If you were going to write some of the things people have said there on social media, you would be canceled and hung out to dry. But in this small group, it's not like that. It's really an iron-sharpens-iron situation in which people are just saying, 'Hey, maybe you're missing this or that.' It's high challenge, but it's high support."

One advantage Christians have for addressing racial injustice is that the institution of the church, when operating according to its own stated intent, offers a setting uniquely suited for that combination of "high challenge and high support." Ezra, the Black man at the pub conversation, used the term *covenant community* to describe the commitment to unity among Christians. "By definition, a church is a covenant community. It's folks who have a commitment to one another for living life together and exploring things at a deeper level than just a book club." Unlike book clubs, work committees, and volunteer organizations that come together over shared interests or discrete tasks, churches come together for the shared purpose of following a God who desires unity among people. The church is an institution founded on the principle that grace—not a perfect track record—justifies each person's belonging in a group. As Naomi, an Asian American leader in a church, said, "At the end of the day, I'm not going to throw you off the island, because that's not an option." She went on to describe the importance of being in communities that take the risk of staying together, even when disagreements arise. "The commitment to still love one another is not just a fuzzy feeling. We have to figure it out. We have to stick to the hot mess. And sometimes it's not going to be fun. Not only not fun, but there's something at stake. Look, it's a sign of the kingdom when it is hot and messy. I'm not saying that toxic abusive behavior should happen, but if we're really engaging with each other, how could it be anything but a hot mess? Too often that's when people leave. But that's the moment right before when you might actually experience transformation. You've got to stick with it."

As one Black man said, "You can't microwave trust." At another church, people used a metaphor of a simmering crock pot to describe the kind of "hot mess" of risk taking that characterizes a flourishing diverse church.[4] If there are no bubbles in a crock pot, the heat is too low and nothing's happening. If the pot is boiling over, it's time to turn down the heat. Being part of a diverse group of people pursuing racial

---

[4]The interviewee learned of this metaphor from Brian McCormack, who writes, "A leader's job is to function like the thermostat on a crock pot, keeping enough heat among their people so things begin to change, but not so much that individual parts get scorched." McCormack credits Tod Bolsinger for the metaphor. Brian Robert McCormack, "The Possible Church: Stories of Those Who Have Led White Congregations into a Multiethnic Reality" (DMin thesis, Divinity School of Duke University, 2022), 48; Tod E. Bolsinger, *Canoeing the Mountains: Christian Leadership in Uncharted Territory*, expanded ed. (InterVarsity Press, 2018), 140.

justice together requires discerning when to turn down the heat in order to slowly work through certain conflicts and questions, and when to turn up the heat by taking new risks. A pastor of the church explained, "We need to move through conflicts with grace, and good listening, and patience with one another. And we need to be having honest conversations."

Covenantal community is a core value in the institution of the church, but churches are not the only institutions in which people can establish practices of unconditional acceptance to foster risk taking. One Black woman summarized how the four pillars of the YWCA—humanity, community, growth, and restoration—enable people to pursue the organization's mission to "empower women, eliminate racism, and promote justice, peace, freedom, and dignity for all." She explained the importance of each pillar. "I need to see you as a human being. That's number one. I also need to be a community with you. But while we're in community, sometimes I'm going to make a mistake. So that's where that growth comes in. But then I also need to be restored back into community. That's what this whole thing is about. Those four things." She said these pillars enable people to take risks. "Guess what—you're going to make a mistake! This work is messy, okay? It's messy. This work is hard. But any relationship is. So if you are really serious about relationship building and being in a relationship specifically with communities of color, yeah, you're gonna mess up! That's part of the growing journey."

I commonly heard two seemingly opposed types of advice from people of color for White people: Learn to follow the leaders of color, and don't wait for the approval of people of color. Both have their place. People of color learn about racism by experiencing the brunt of it, and they tap into decades and centuries of experiencing and resisting racism. White people need to follow and learn from that ongoing struggle. But there are also White people who develop a kind of addiction to hand holding. They worry constantly about offending someone, and when they show up to help in the struggle, they expect to be recognized and thanked. For White people, sometimes risking means learning how *not* to need approval or expressions of grace from people of color at every turn. That comes of having a thick network of experiences among people of color, and also a self-awareness of one's own limitations. One White man described what that feels like. "Crosscultural courage is like, I'm terrified. I'm afraid. I don't really know what I'm doing, and I'm trying, but I know that I could really cause some damage. I know that I'm scared. I know that. I am scared that someday someone's going to ask me to do something to prove that I'm antiracist enough and I'm going to feel like I don't want to do that. But I'm still going to show up. I'm still going to be here. I'm still going to trust God even if I don't understand all the time or I'm still working through it."

Risking is not just a posture individuals practice on their own; it is a capacity enabled by communities that foster trust.[5] To trust is, by definition, to take a risk, relying on someone or something even when you cannot fully prove its reliability. Another metaphor I heard used to describe the process of building trust is a communal water reservoir. Imagine a community of people who get their water from a reservoir that everyone also helps refill from time to time. People draw from their communal trust reservoirs in times of change, trauma, conflict, and personal need, and when taking creative risks. If the water level is low or inconsistent, people will limit the risks they take, and the group will be worse off as a whole. In flourishing groups, people make more deposits into the trust reservoir than they remove, and the reservoir grows deeper with passing time. With a reservoir that has grown deep over time, each individual does not need to perfectly match their deposits and withdrawals. Grace comes easier when the trust reservoir is full. With an assurance of sufficiency, both withdrawals and deposits can become sources of joy as they reinforce group belonging.

---

[5] Rob Scapp states that the most important lesson in racial justice work is "the need to establish a genuine sense of community based on trust." Quoted in bell hooks, *Teaching Community: A Pedagogy of Hope* (Routledge, 2003), 109.

Ideally, people take risks in communities where the trust reservoir is deep. But sometimes people living with a struggling hope will practice a posture of risking even when the trust reservoir is nearly empty. Anita, a Latina woman, told a story in which people of differing ethnic backgrounds came together with an unexpected trust in each other. When Anita's parents were new to the United States, her younger brother began acting out in school, and their parents were unsure what to do. They spoke little English and were afraid of the legal consequences of the situation. A White social worker came to their home to talk with them. Anita, who worked now in a school herself, pointed out that this scenario could easily have gone poorly. "I've definitely been in situations later on in my professional career where White people think they know best. I've seen examples that still upset me sometimes to think about it. That social worker could have played them. She could have betrayed them for sure. She could have just gone back to her office thinking, 'These Mexican parents, they just need to get with the program.' Thank God it didn't happen, because they were vulnerable. They were tired. Tired of dealing with this stuff. And they were scared, too, because the law was involved." They were "talking to a strange White lady about what's going on with their son." From Anita's parents' side, the relationship with the social worker was risky.

But something in the relationship between Anita's parents and the social worker worked. When I asked Anita to describe what she saw working in that interaction, she said, "The social worker was not telling my parents what to do, and I think that that felt safe to them. She was not pushing her agenda. She was also not judging their parenting style. I think she wanted to come alongside them. She was going to value the fact that they were good people and they just wanted the best for their son. She was not just going to come in to tell them what to do or to correct them. She valued them. She saw that they loved their son, and she believed them."

The White social worker believed and trusted Anita's parents, and her parents also chose to trust the social worker. "They took her at her word, and they believed that she was for them. My parents opened up about how they were feeling. And it wasn't that she necessarily had answers for them; it's just that they knew that they could talk to her. There was this sense of transparency."

Risk taking is a posture learned in community, through extending and responding to grace, through building a reservoir of trust, and through making the choice to see the value and humanity in others. Risking enables the creative innovation necessary to relate in a good way and mend the social fabric.

|||||||||

The three postures of a struggling hope that I've described so far—lamenting, mending, and risking—might sound arduous, and indeed, they often are. But living with a struggling hope is not all about sorrow. To struggle in hope also involves joy.

Again and again, people I interviewed insisted that pursuing racial justice for the long haul involves joy. Not only do people need snatches of joy when things go right, but even amid the struggle they need to *lean into* joy—noticing, naming, savoring, sharing, and celebrating joy.

Two different people used the phrase "lean into joy." One was Anna during the pub conversation. The more time I spent among her, Ezra, Noah, and Ed, the more I noticed their joy. "I don't care what background you come from," Anna said, "if this racial justice work is not fun at any level, it's not sustainable! You can only do hard things for so long. That's part of what we as a church have to offer, because there's a lot of joy in knowing each other and spending time with each other." The friends listed activities they organized on a regular basis with the explicit purpose of leaning into the joy: meals together, events with kids and youth, and casually stopping to visit each other. "And that's actually part of the work!" Anna reiterated. "I think we need to frame it that way, like sometimes actually the work of growth in this area of racial justice is just leaning into our joy."

Joy might seem a strange topic to fit into a chapter on struggling, but without struggle, joy can become superficial. Anna pointed out that often instead of fostering real joy, churches foster a "fake, false joy. Every week, we smile! But it's very shallow. So how do you actually have *authentic* joy?"

Noah added, "How do you stay in the space where you see where you want to go, and you see where we are, and it's a long way? How do you stay in that liminal space? I think part of it is having fun."

"A sense of humor goes so far," Ezra contributed. "You've got to not take yourself too seriously."

The other person who used the phrase "leaning into joy" was Naomi, the Asian American leader introduced in chapter two who originally hesitated to recommend any White Christians for my research. We were already well past the time we had planned to finish her interview, but the topic of hope struck a nerve. She began to speak with a growing energy and a rhythm akin to spoken word poetry. "I would probably describe myself as either a really hopeful pessimist or a crabby optimist," she said. "I find no hope in not naming what really is happening. We have to be really honest about what is really happening and the shit show that we are in, and that has been going on for a long time." She recalled recent national events that had revealed racist systems still woven into the systems and beliefs of America. "Look, here's the reality. Things will get worse. People are going to die. And if we can't be honest about those really hard places, it's very hard for me to find hope.

"I think we need to do a lot more lamenting," she went on. "I think that's part of the problem. We don't *acknowledge*. We haven't metabolized all the crap, so we're just hoping it'll go away. Like if we just don't talk about it, it'll go away. And that's proven to be deadly. I think we have to have wisdom to learn from people who have actually gone through stuff. Learn what it means to hold on to hope. Not a foolish or naive hope."

She called her hope a "Romans 8 hope," referencing the words of the apostle Paul in Romans 8:35-39:

> Who shall separate us from the love of Christ? Shall trouble or hardship or persecution or famine or nakedness or danger or sword? As it is written:
>
>> "For your sake we face death all day long;
>> we are considered as sheep to be slaughtered."
>
> No, in all these things we are more than conquerors through him who loved us. For I am convinced that neither death nor life, neither angels nor demons, neither the present nor the future, nor any powers, neither height nor depth, nor anything else in all creation, will be able to separate us from the love of God that is in Christ Jesus our Lord.

Naomi went on to explain her Romans 8 hope. "I think my hope is the Spirit intercedes, so I don't need to be the only one who watches what's going wrong. The truth may be that I witness a lot of destruction in my lifetime, but ultimately if nothing can separate us from the love of God, then I will hold on to that. I can sit in a mystery of holding on to that hope. I can say, 'Even *that*, everything I'm seeing go wrong, will not be so powerful to separate us from the love of God.' I am fundamentally a person of hope, not because of me personally but because I live in these faith traditions. My hope is not shiny or happy at all. It's totally bruised and bloodied and it's scraping by my fingernails. On days you may not be able to see it. But there's maybe a scrap of it hanging on and pressing on."

She paused and chuckled quietly. "I'm not a miserable person, I promise. But I do value naming things for what they are, like the prophets, and if you read the prophets in the Bible, they're a mess! They're like the most miserable people in the Bible. So I am leaning into joy. I think it's an act of resistance to play, to practice joyful things in the midst of it. That's exactly what we need to do in the midst of all the horrible things—joyfully gather. And not in denial, but as an act of resistance. We play, we eat, we celebrate, we do all those things. But it's only hopeful to me if we can actually be honest about what is also really happening: both/and. I think they both need to coexist."

Naomi's words tied together much of what we have seen in this book. Struggling hope is built on the warrant of a God who interrupts—the Spirit interceding so humans don't have to be the only ones watching what's going wrong. A struggling hope is not optimistic. It laments and refuses to deny what has gone wrong. And precisely because of all that is horrible, it leans into joy.

||||||||

One question remains: *What will you do with hope?*

You might have been expecting to get to the end of this book and find an action plan—how to go fix things in a few easy steps. If you've arrived at this page asking whether there is something you can do next, my answer is *yes, but it will never be just one thing*. I encourage you to talk through the questions in appendix B with a group. Pay attention to your own life narrative and especially to the ways you might discover new meanings and interpretations to past life events. Remembering can point you to areas you would like to grow and also to the ways you have already been shaped by collisions and grace. Anthropologists, therapists, and race scholars have often used the term *re-membering* to highlight the ways that recollecting life memories and finding new meanings to those events can lead us to create and re-create bonds that have been lost.[6]

As you re-member, know that others have gone before you on this journey. In the book *Braiding Sweetgrass,* Potawatomi biologist Robin Wall Kimmerer uses an ecological metaphor to describe White people

---

[6]Eileen O'Brien also points out that White people become activists not just through experiencing isolated turning points but through recognizing "narrative linkages across events." O'Brien, *Whites Confront Racism: Antiracists and Their Paths to Action* (Rowman & Littlefield, 2001), 30. See also Cynthia B. Dillard, "Re-membering Culture: Bearing Witness to the Spirit of Identity in Research," *Race Ethnicity and Education* 11, no. 1 (2008): 87-93; Barbara Myerhoff, "Life History Among the Elderly: Performance, Visibility and Remembering," in *A Crack in the Mirror: Reflective Perspectives in Anthropology*, ed. J. Ruby (University of Pennsylvania Press, 1982); Michael White, *Narratives of Therapists' Lives* (Dulwich Centre, 1997).

willing to live in the strange pursuit of racial justice. The plant *plantago* came to the Americas with European immigrants. Because the plant tended to thrive in trampled pathways that Europeans traveled as they invaded the land, Indigenous North Americans referred to the plant as "White man's footprints." But unlike many invasive European plants, plantago joined local ecosystems in ways that benefited people and landscape alike. It mingled with the surrounding ecosystem in ways that received and gave. Indigenous people came to recognize the healing properties of plantago for both soil and humans. "Plantain is not indigenous but 'naturalized,'" Kimmerer writes.[7] She raises the question of what sorts of footsteps White people might learn to leave. How do White people enter into human ecologies in ways that bring mutual healing rather than destruction?

The answer this book offers is not a proof that things will get better. It is, rather, a set of possibilities, a testimony of what can happen when people become something they were not before. It is also an exploration of hope in the space of that uncertain possibility.

Recall Hannah, the White woman whose story at the table with Mark began this book. When we met, she had been attending a Black-led church for several years. When I asked about how she hopes, Hannah began with a story about a Black friend from that church. "She bursts into these mini sermons sometimes unplanned because she's just marvelous," Hannah said. "And the other day she was testifying about Black joy." Hannah described the context—the friend was recovering from a serious medical condition and at the same time addressing a grievous case of racial discrimination at work. "And she was imploring us to be thankful for the miracle of joy. Wow. I mean, that's the epitome of hope for me. This woman who has every reason to be beaten down, you know? The things that were done to her were just beyond my imagination. So for her to have that experience and still just be able to attest to the miracle

---

[7]Robin Wall Kimmerer, *Braiding Sweetgrass: Indigenous Wisdom, Scientific Knowledge and the Teachings of Plants* (Milkweed Editions, 2015), 269.

of joy, I mean, how can that not be hopeful? That's the most hopeful thing I've ever heard in my life. And her passion and faith is so strong. How can it not be real? That's why I'm so hopeful. I'm so hopeful because I see I see so many African Americans who are still so passionate about their faith. I come into church being like, 'I'll have what she's having.'"

In this book we've traced how White Christians come to say to their brothers and sisters of color, "I'll have what they're having." They do not pretend to take on the experience of being a person of color themselves, but they step into what can come out of those experiences—the collisions, the questions, the grace, the faith, the solidarity, the struggle, and ultimately the joy. Together, they step into abiding hope.

AFTERWORD

Kindred

IN WRITING THIS BOOK as a researcher, I did not want my own story to outweigh the carefully analyzed stories of seventy other people. My life has as many idiosyncrasies as any human life, and this book is not designed to present myself as an example of what others can or should do. It is a single story among the hundreds I learned of in this research. At the same time, every researcher's own context and experience do matter. Surrounding circumstances shape the questions a researcher asks, the ways they listen, and the analyses they settle into. Revealing that context as honestly as possible is one way to allow readers a fuller picture of the research itself. As I considered what to include in this book, I felt that in the context of all of the stories I have received as gifts, it was only appropriate to give you my own as well.

As with anyone's story, this story has no definitive beginning. But let us begin here: In the mid-nineteenth century, two sisters were growing up in a red farmhouse in rural Wisconsin. Their father drove a truck every day from one dairy farm to the next, loading up heavy cans of milk, while their mother went to town to style people's hair in a beauty salon. The older sister walked along the country road to a one-room schoolhouse. By the time the younger sister began school, the little farm school was closing, and the sisters began riding the bus together to the bigger school in town.

These two sisters were White, and mostly they didn't think about that or the people who were otherwise. In town they met a few kids from

Mexico, whose parents came to pick peas in the same fields where the sisters' parents fell in love decades earlier. Indigenous people floated through their imaginations through the cowboy movies on TV, the yodeling cowboy songs their dad sang, and the mysterious arrowheads he pulled from their fields. Black people were dangerous, or far away, or absent altogether.

These sisters were the first generation in their family to attend college. Both went to the big state school nearby, the University of Wisconsin–Madison. There they each fell in love with the men who would become their husbands. At the older sister's wedding, their father stood straight and serious, afraid to eat from the banquet because he feared their meager savings had not purchased enough for all the guests. When the younger sister married, a different fear gripped him. He refused to attend the wedding at all. He vowed that his new son-in-law would never set foot in his house, and he held to that decision all his life. The older sister's husband was White. The younger sister's husband was Black.

Both husbands would go on to become professors. The older sister's husband would get a job and buy a home halfway between Madison and the farm where the sisters grew up.

The younger sister's husband would get a job in Nigeria, where he was born, and the couple would eventually decide on a divorce. This sister would buy a home in Madison and fall in love with another Black man.

But before that, the older sister had a baby girl, Christine—and that's me.

Two years later the younger sister had a daughter—my cousin.

In my first memory of this cousin, we are sitting on the floor at our grandparents' home. From behind us each of our mothers is combing our hair. My grandmother sits in a chair nearby, and, as a retired beautician, talks with our mothers about hair. They say that my hair is smooth, my cousin's unruly. My aunt tugs the comb through her daughter's curls, and my cousin whimpers. My mother and grandmother say they don't know what to do about this hair. I am confused—what makes this

AFTERWORD

cousin's hair so unsuited for combs? I do not know to ask what made this comb and this way of combing so unsuited for her hair. The elders' conversation teaches me that something is wrong. It is not wrong with me; it is wrong with this other one, her hair, her body.

In most of my memories with my cousin, she and I are playing happily with my brother and an older cousin. We spend weeks together in the summer and weekends throughout the year. We wander in fields, climb trees, throw our shoes in rivers, hit wiffle balls through our grandfather's apple orchard, explore their haymow, laugh and learn in the brave adventures of children. We are a troop of cousins all within four years of age, and sometimes we fight as families do, leaving each other out of games and bickering over the best dress-up costumes or the first turn on the swing.

One day this cousin leaves some game we are playing and runs to a bedroom, closing the door behind her. Her mother calls the other three of us and our mothers to the kitchen for a serious talk.

"What did you say to her?" My aunt's face is angry, and we don't know why.

"Nothing." We look to each other, confused. We don't want to be in trouble and we want our cousin to come back so we can keep playing. We try to recount what happened, but nobody remembers anything unusual.

"You kids are mean to her," our aunt says. "Stop it. You need to be nice to her."

I don't remember whether she gave a reason for needing to be nice, but I know that my mind filled in a reason—*because she is youngest cousin*. Surely that was it. When she sent us on our way to return to our play, the three of us talked about it together in whispers, wanting to get this right. "She's youngest. Be nice." What I don't remember anyone saying is, *because she is Black and everyone else in this family is White*. It was the 1980s, and nice White people didn't talk about race, but it remained a silent signifying signifier between us.

Only years later would I talk with this cousin about our childhoods and learn that she remembered that day, too. She remembered her mother coming into the bedroom and finding her in tears. She had asked her mom, "Why do I look different than the rest of the family?" She remembers the pain of that day, but she also remembers how her mother comforted her, offering a reassuring and steady love that would continue throughout their lives.

Her childhood was shaped by hurts from people who had no idea they were hurting her. Mine was shaped by hurting people I had no idea I was hurting. I was not taught words to name those hurts, much less ways to stop the hurting—only "be nice." I would go on trying to be nice year after year. My family went to a Methodist church where nearly everyone was White. Once a year a Black gospel choir came to sing alongside our choir, and the White members giggled as they learned to sway and clap awkwardly along with the Black visitors. A few songs in the hymnal were listed as "African American spirituals," and when occasionally we sang "We Shall Overcome," I imagined White Christians in northern towns like ours always on the good side of history. We were not like those southern White Christians who appeared in my imagination as caricatures whipping their slaves and preaching silly things about the descendants of Ham. We were normal, nice Christian people.

In time, my cousin began spending more time with school friends who talked and dressed and did their hair like her. Her life and mine became busier, and we saw less of each other. In high school both my cousin and I developed crushes on boys who happened to share the same name. Mine was a White boy, hers Black. I shyly avoided my crush and never so much as held his hand. My cousin and her crush dated, and in her junior year, she discovered she was pregnant. She gave birth to a daughter and pressed on to finish high school.

I was attending the University of Wisconsin–Madison when she graduated from a high school in the same city, and I came to her graduation ceremony. I sat next to her partner. We passed their baby daughter back and forth, laughing at the pudgy hands reaching up for our faces. Afterward we found the cousin in the lobby to share congratulations,

AFTERWORD

then said goodbye. I went home to my college dorm. My cousin went home with her daughter and mother. Her child's father went to a party.

That night, someone at the party shot and killed him.

I remember standing in my dorm room holding the phone as my mother told me the news. I remember thinking, *This feels like a movie. Do people get shot in real life?* And then some part of me desperate to make sense scrounged up an explanation. *This happens in real life for Black people. Black people get shot in real life. Not White people.* This was what I'd been given to make sense of this horror, like a box in which to place the pieces of a puzzle. Maybe I could have left it there—sealed up the pieces in their box and put the box on a shelf to tuck it out of the way, where White people place such things. But I could see that the puzzle, when assembled, still made no sense. I didn't know why the pieces in the box were the only ones we'd been given or why no one else seemed to care what they depicted. And I knew something important was at stake here. This was not a movie—this was real. This happened to real people. My people. Dead people. Mourning people. Widowed and fatherless people. This. Was. Not. Okay.

The answers I'd been given did not answer the questions that needed answers. If this is real life for Black people, why? Why had my own life and that of my cousin, daughters of blood sisters, turned out so differently? Surely the answer was beyond our individual preferences and personalities. I had known her since childhood, and the similarities and differences we shared were no greater or less than those between me and my other family members. Surely something in the world around us factored into this outcome. How was it that no one else seemed curious or concerned about this mystery that seemed to have something to do with a young man's death?

I was like a child carrying around that box of mismatched puzzle pieces through college, taking it out from time to time with people I thought should know better, searching for help. *Have you seen this, too? Have you noticed? Do you know how to solve it?* Surely there must be a solution, if only I could find the right smart person. I told White people, because I hardly knew anyone who was not White. I asked a White friend who was dating a Black woman, a White professor teaching a class about Africa, and White people three times my age who I expected to have figured this out through longevity. They all seemed to know even less than the little I knew about what to do with these pieces. If I told my cousin's story, the shock and sympathy people offered made me feel awkward, so I stopped talking about it.

I worked during my junior and senior years in college as a residence hall assistant. One year I put together an event for my floor called "Let's Talk About Race." Four people came, all of them White. They sat politely with somber faces and said very little. I don't know what I thought we'd discuss, but I expected that somehow, by pooling what we knew, we might get somewhere. Instead we sat uncomfortably admitting what we didn't know.

In the months that followed it became glaringly obvious that the little we knew was too little. In several rooms on our floor, White and Black roommates had been paired together as first-year students. My first hint that something wasn't working came from a Black first-year student knocking quietly on my door late one evening. She sat on my couch and asked with gentle kindness, "Why do all the White girls on the floor assume I'm not interested in being their friend?" She said she'd come from a high school in a city where 99 percent of students were Black, and now at this school where more than 90 percent were White, she simply didn't understand what was happening. Her White roommate left each night for dinner with the White girls from next door and never invited her, as if it never occurred to her that a Black roommate could join them. Tears leaked from the corners of her eyes as she asked my advice. She too was holding out a box of mismatched pieces, expecting surely someone could put them back together.

But I could not put the pieces together in a way that took away her pain. My training had not come close to preparing me to lead a floor of

Black and White residents through their first interracial interactions. Midway through the year, a thin whisp of a White girl told me in timid mumbles that she was intimidated by her roommate, a tall Black girl with a joyfully confident personality. She didn't know how to speak to her roommate about their shared space—when to open the curtains, where to place their belongings, how loudly to play their music. I gave her phrases I'd learned in my job training to help roommates communicate and sent her on her way. Later that month her parents came to visit. They took a roll of masking tape, knelt on the floor, and taped a line down the middle of the dorm room. Students told me later they'd heard a slamming door and the parents screaming at the Black roommate, "You won't cross over that line onto our daughter's side." The hall director stepped in to assign new roommates, and I was grateful but troubled by my inability to handle the situation. Before the dust had settled from that move, the tension between another pair of White and Black roommates rose to a boil. In the middle of an argument, the White student picked up the heavy 1990s-era box television of the Black student and threw it across the room. It was, quite literally, a collision for us all.

I was majoring in English and music, and for one music theory class I began writing a song. I called it "Cellophane Wall," a metaphor meant to convey the invisible but consequential separations between racial groups. I knew that our society taught us to erect these walls, protecting some from trauma and others from truth. The music was filled with dissonant chords and crashing rhythms. I repeated the few lines I'd written, rewriting and erasing again and again, but could not figure out how to end the song. I did not know how to take down walls or whether anyone could.

Like the story of Hannah and her blackface Halloween costume, this portion of my story happened at the University of Wisconsin–Madison in the 1990s. There were not many people there talking about racial justice at the time, but there were some, and my life shifted course because I found at least a few of them. I took a class about Africa because it fulfilled my "diversity requirement," and for the first time in college I read books that wrestled with racism and colonialism—Zora Neale Hurston's *Their Eyes Were Watching God* and Chinua Achebe's *Things Fall Apart*. I heard a talk by Richard Davis, a Black professor of music who would become influential advocate for racial justice, and he concluded with an offer to meet with anyone interested in talking more about racism. I remember walking past his office door multiple times before I summoned the courage to knock and ask about that offer. Not only did he honor his offer to talk, but he invited me to lunch later that week. I can still picture the garbanzo beans and blue cheese on the salad he bought for us as we talked. Mostly I remember how he listened to my story and I listened to his, and how he assured me that I must keep learning, keep asking why questions, keep noticing when the pieces don't fit, and call it as it is.

Around this time a White friend told me about a Spanish-speaking church she wanted to visit and convinced me to come along. The pastor's family invited us to their home, ignored our fumbling Spanish, fed us, laughed with us, and kept inviting us back. Soon I was playing piano for the church, and my friend was volunteering in the youth group, and families from the church were feeding one or both of us nearly every week.

I took more classes about African history, malnutrition and inequality, and Latin American economics. I was writing a final paper in the Latin American economics class when somehow I got it into my head that in those fifteen pages I could solve some great problem of injustice in the world. I battered my professor with questions during office hours and came home from the library with a backpack full of books, many more than the assignment required. I took copious notes, reading with a hungry expectation that every subsequent page surely would bring the solution. I hoped with an optimism that there were answers to be found if only I checked the right book out of the library. I was running on the fumes of the full tank of delusional hopes I'd been given as a kid, the child of a professor and a grade school teacher in White America.

The more I read, the less I felt certain of any possible thesis for my paper. The more I learned, the bigger the problems appeared. I saw that the problems were too big to solve in a college research paper, too big to solve in my lifetime or a thousand lifetimes. I lay on my dorm room floor surrounded by piles of books and dropped the notebook where I'd been scribbling notes. I pressed my forehead into my scratchy green carpet and began to sob. I cried out to God, repeating again and again, "These problems are so, so big."

In the silence of that dorm room, words came to my mind as clearly as I have ever felt anything like the voice of God: "Yes. I know. These problems are so, so big. I know. But remember, I am always bigger."

Looking back, I see how that conversation with God was a first turning point toward responding to injustice with a hope grounded in God's interrupting grace. When I graduated, my husband and I began moving to places where we would be proximate to people working out God's promise that "blessed are you who are poor, for yours is the kingdom of God" (Luke 6:20). We lived among war refugees in the United States and in rural communities in Nicaragua and South Africa. We made a lot of mistakes. People kept giving us grace. That grace tethered me to these communities, to God, and to the struggle of joining a better way.

During the years that I've been working on this book, two other things have happened that remind me of God's incongruous grace. The first was a conversation with my cousin. We walked through a botanical garden halfway between our homes, talking together about our childhood memories and the ways race shaped us each. In the years since her first daughter's father was killed, difficulties had continued to mar the lives of many people in her life, but there was a power and wisdom in her voice as she told how God given her strength through all circumstances.

I told her a story that I realized she had never heard about our shared grandfather, the man who refused to let her own father enter the family home.

I was in middle school when our grandfather died, and I watched his final breath. My parents had purchased tickets to a professional baseball game as a Father's Day present for this grandfather, and my parents and brother and I joined our grandparents for a tailgate lunch before the game. We were walking from our minivan to the stadium when I turned around to say something to my brother, who was walking beside my grandfather. I remember with all of the drama of a slow-motion camera how I saw my grandfather's expression suddenly shift from surprise to blankness, how his body tipped forward, hands pinned to his side, crashing face-down into the blacktop.

In the chaos that followed—cries for help, people gathering, mother and grandmother trying to roll over his bulky body, those motionless eyes—I remember this: a stranger in suspenders and a plaid shirt appeared and knelt beside us. With elegant calmness, he helped roll my grandfather, took his pulse, and began CPR. I do not know the name of that man, but I know this detail: He was Black. The pounding rhythm of breaths and beats followed a rhythm that has pounded through centuries: "Is there hope? Is there hope?" This Black stranger trying to save my grandfather's life did not know the man's racist past, but surely he had known other White men of his sort. As my grandfather's gaze turned to glassy stillness, this Black man pumped his final heartbeats. Such grace.

As I was writing this book, my cousin and I considered together what elements to include from our shared story and how to make space for her to tell her life story as it extends far beyond what I include here from my perspective. "I'm learning the power in telling your testimony, your story," she wrote to me in a letter. "I'm grateful to have good memories with my White family and my God-sent Black family. Just because there was challenges does not mean there was not any great memories. I thank God for keeping me through life's troubles. God is why I'm still here today and

AFTERWORD

alright and blessed." As we talked through memories we had never discussed before, we noted how God was drawing us together even through this writing. "The story's not done," she reminded me on a phone call. "That's the best part—the story's not done!"

A second story. As I was finishing the final pages of this book, I joined a group of people coming together from the two churches I attend: a predominantly White church and a predominantly Black church. We were planning an event that would use art and a common table to foster a healing space for a neighborhood afflicted by violence and exploitation. As we took turns around a table introducing ourselves and telling how we chose to be there, a Black woman said that she had learned to allow Christ to give her the capacity to cover over the sins of racism. I listened wishing I had a pen in hand—here was yet another explanation of grace. She mentioned she had attended the University of Wisconsin–Madison, and suddenly a memory flickered through my mind. I knew this woman. Later I spoke with her and confirmed my hunch—she was a resident on my dorm floor in that year when I first witnessed an explosion of racial bigotry. When I asked her about it, she said for her it was far from the first or worst she had seen. But for me this chance re-encounter had meaning. Twenty-five years after those years of troubling collisions, grace had brought us back together in a struggle for a common hope.

A few weeks later, I sat in that friend's church. As the choir finished the opening song, a woman stepped forward to read the verse of that day: Psalm 133:1. "How very good and pleasant it is when kindred live together in unity" (NRSV). Later the pastor expounded on the verse, word by word. Unity is not only morally *good*; it is *pleasant* to experience. He pointed to the word *when* to remind us, "It's not like this all the time." He paused dramatically. "We do not normally have the mentality of unity." But unity also *is*—it is not impossible. "When people are unified they support each other. They bear one another's burdens. And they work together to make sure we accomplish a common goal." He gained momentum as he finished the sermon. "Unity among believers serves as a powerful witness to the world. That when they see the church working and walking together, they will wonder what type of God they serve, that Black people and White people can serve God together, that poor people and affluent people can serve God together, that educated and uneducated people can walk together and be in the same place and nobody is feeling as if they're being judged. Is there anybody in the church that can testify?"

Hands raised across the congregation. I raised mine.

My eyes lingered in the psalm on another word, because it was the word I had chosen to title this afterword: *kindred*. This is the story of my kindred—my cousins, my bloodline. It is also a story of all of us kindred, the human family—how we become instruments of each other's pain, how we become instruments of each other's healing, and how we carry that hope together.

Acknowledgments

MORE PEOPLE MAKE A BOOK possible than can ever be named, and in this sort of research some names are intentionally withheld. So first and foremost, I am grateful to all the people who formed the bedrock of this book by sharing time and insights during interviews and visits to your churches, workplaces, and homes. Your names are changed in this book, but you know who you are. Please know that I appreciate you and am a better person because of you.

I also have become increasingly grateful for scholars who poured their own life's work into research that came before mine, making my own work possible. Footnotes and bibliographies should be regarded with as much solemn gratitude as acknowledgments pages.

As to those whom I can thank by name, I am grateful especially to my research assistant, Princess Vaulx, for her partnership through the research phase. Two John Stott Faculty Grants in Human Needs and Global Resources supported hiring an assistant and other aspects of this research. My editors, Jon Boyd and Rebecca Carhart-Mader, and the whole team of editors and publicists at InterVarsity Press believed in this work, honed it, and ushered it to readers' hands. Early readers—Amy Murray, Sarah Pollasch, Carolyn Hui, Marcia Bosscher, and Christina Cappy—offered invaluable feedback, as did students in my classes who read and discussed early drafts. Teaching assistants through the years helped me find literature, check transcriptions, copyedit, and manage the endless deluge of work, including Anna Cole, Mikaela Dieter, Nathaniel DeSouza, Isabelle Griess, Zana Martinez, and Joe Saperstein. I'm awed and grateful for my daughter Phoebe's inventive support through the index writing tasks. And I could not have written this book without the love of family members mentioned in this book, along with my amazing kids, Phoebe and Zeke, and especially my husband, Adam. You supported me through this project with encouragement, idea soundboarding, patience, laughter, and unwavering hope. Finally and most of all, this project rests on the goodness of God, source of all grace and hope.

APPENDIX A

People Studying People

OFTEN WHEN WE READ NEWS STORIES about social issues, we're reading quantitative statistics derived from surveys or institutional records. Quantitative studies have the advantage of being able to achieve some level of statistical representation across large populations, and their results are relatively easy to communicate in bite-size pieces through graphs and numbers. There are some questions, though, that don't easily lend themselves to quantitative methodology. People who design multiple-choice surveys take a stab at what choices should be listed, but the results don't offer detail, and they don't tell us whether those surveyed wished they had some other options to choose from. Likewise, studying institutional records can often tell us what decisions people made at a point in time, but they don't necessarily tell us why they made those choices. When looking for a detailed exploration of *how* and *why* people behave as they do, researchers often turn to qualitative methods.

Qualitative studies generally aim for depth over breadth. For qualitative research, the intentionality in selecting, conducting, and analyzing those interviews is of utmost importance. Unlike journalists working on quick deadlines to create articles that sell, qualitative researchers typically spend years reading previous scholarship on a topic, getting feedback on their research methods, and sorting and coding their findings. I conducted the earliest interviews for this research in 2019 and finished editing the manuscript more than five years later, in 2025. Qualitative researchers select participants with intentionality. Whereas a Gallup poll might survey thousands of people, in this research, I interviewed seventy. The seventy people in this study included thirty-eight men and thirty-two women. Their ages ranged from twenties to eighties, with every decade represented in between. While I do not divulge precise numbers in order to protect privacy, the thirty who were people of color included Asian and Asian American people identifying as ethnically Korean, Chinese, Hmong, Bhutanese, and Indian; Indigenous North Americans of multiple tribes; African Americans and individuals raised in multiple African nations; Latino and Latina people of several national backgrounds; and several who identified with more than one of these categories. They attended church in a variety of denominations, lived in a variety of neighborhoods, and included people raised across a spectrum of conservative and progressive homes.

Rather than use multiple-choice questions, qualitative researchers pose open-ended questions that elicit stories and richly detailed explanations. My interviews lasted one to three hours. I came with a set of questions, but I also followed the threads of the stories and ideas people brought up, allowing them to define terms and bring up what seemed important to them. As an interviewer, one's own self becomes a part of the research, and one necessarily interprets data as an individual. To help notice what I might otherwise have missed, I worked with a research assistant, a young Black woman from Madison named Princess Vaulx, who also reviewed and coded every interview and talked me through what she noticed.

APPENDIX A: PEOPLE STUDYING PEOPLE

From the Research Assistant

BY PRINCESS VAULX

I grew up in poverty in inner-city Milwaukee, Wisconsin. It was my three brothers, mom, dad, and me. I can remember the constant routine of being displaced year after year. In and out and in and out. Moving was very normal, and it was never my choice.

In high school I had a meaningful experience with a White Christian committed to the work of racial justice. She was the executive director of a Christian ministry in Milwaukee that was committed to serving low-income individuals and families, and they had been serving our family since I was eight. In the midst of continuous displacement, they were our constant. It was also the place I was introduced to the Lord.

Right before the fall of my senior year of high school, my family was served with another eviction notice, requiring us to move out of the state. In order to attend college the following year with in-state tuition, I could not leave Wisconsin. She stepped up and invited me to live with her for one year. I hadn't had many interactions with her, and neither had she with me. However, she knew that it was integral that I stayed in Milwaukee for many reasons, so she invited me into her home.

And that was the work—to see a Black young female student so close to attending university facing the effects of generational poverty and to intervene. That will impact my future forever. Although she is no longer with me, she would often tell me that she did it because she was obeying the call of God on her life. When I had the opportunity to contribute to this research about what it meant for others to commit to that work and keep going, I knew Diane's reasons and the difference she made, and I wanted to know more.

Interviews reflect what one individual chooses to reveal, which can never be a complete picture. To learn more about how people live out their purported beliefs, anthropologists include participant observation as a complement to interviews. For this research, I spent over 120 hours as a participant-observer taking notes in churches, trainings, meetings, and other gatherings in which people dealt with racism.

Research comes of particular places. In this case, I chose four places, each for the contribution it could make to a well-rounded study of societies affected by white-supremacist racism. The main location, Madison, Wisconsin, I chose for several reasons. First, I already had a nuanced familiarity with it from living there for nearly two decades. Second, it has a sizable population of White Christians concerned with racial justice. And third, the city has well-documented profound racial disparities.

Many people in Madison know that the city was chosen for two years running as the "best place to live in the United States."[1] What many White people there don't know is that people of color often describe the city as precisely the opposite. In 2020, a study combining statistics on income, education, homeownership, and incarceration rated Wisconsin as having the highest racial disparities in the nation.[2] Few neighborhoods exist in Madison where middle- and upper-class people of diverse racial groups live together, and when I asked people to name settings where they experienced flourishing diversity, several were hard-pressed to think of any. Public schools could be the exception, having recently tipped to more non-White students than White, but even within schools, persistent patterns of neighborhood segregation and uneven resourcing leave everyday experiences of children and teachers more segregated than the district-wide numbers suggest. In 2023, only 10 percent of Black students in Madison's public schools achieved grade-level proficiency in reading, and Wisconsin overall had the widest disparities in the nation in both reading and math scores between Black and White students.[3]

---

[1] "Best Places to Live in the US in 2022," Livability.com, accessed June 16, 2023, https://livability.com/best-places/2022-top-100-best-places-to-live-in-the-us/top-100-2022-madison-wi/.
[2] Samuel Stebbins, "The Worst States for Black Americans," *24/7 Wall St.* (blog), February 15, 2022, https://247wallst.com/special-report/2022/02/15/the-worst-states-for-black-americans-2/.
[3] In 2024 Wisconsin implemented new testing standards, which meant literacy rates appeared to improve significantly across racial groups, but the results were not comparable to previous years' tests. Corrinne Hess, "State Tests Trending Up but Less Than 40 Percent of Wisconsin Students Are Proficient in Reading, Math," *Wisconsin Public Radio*, October 10, 2023, www.wpr.org

APPENDIX A: PEOPLE STUDYING PEOPLE

Madison's surrounding county incarcerates Black residents at eleven times the White incarceration rate and twice the national average rate for Black residents.[4]

Even as the city produces some of the sharpest racial inequalities in the nation, Madison has become a place where White people tend to think and talk a lot about racism. Many Christians in the city have participated in various nonprofit organizations that address racism. Two of the most prominent of these organizations are the local YWCA and an organization founded by a church in the 1990s to address racial inequalities, the Nehemiah Center for Urban Leadership. In 2013, founder and CEO of Nehemiah, Dr. Alex Gee, wrote a newspaper article titled "Justified Anger."[5] The article called for a concerted response to Madison's racial disparities, pointing to a report published earlier that year revealing that racial disparities in the surrounding county were among the highest in the nation.[6] The article went viral, catalyzing interest among people of color and White people in the city. The Nehemiah Center went on to develop a course titled Black History for a New Day, taught by Nehemiah staff and University of Wisconsin professors. During the Covid-19 pandemic and in the surge of national interest in racism after George Floyd's death, the course went online, and enrollment boomed to over one thousand participants. By the end of 2021, the course had trained over thirty-five hundred non-Black people from Madison

---

/education/state-tests-trending-less-40-percent-wisconsin-students-are-proficient-reading-math; Danielle Kaeding, "Wisconsin Has Widest Gap in the US for Math, Reading Scores Among White and Black Students," *Wisconsin Public Radio*, October 24, 2022, www.wpr.org/wisconsin-has-widest-gap-us-math-reading-scores-among-white-and-black-students.

[4]James Austin and Roger Ocker, "Dane County Jail Race and Ethnicity Disparity Analysis," Criminal Justice Council, April 2021, https://dane.legistar.com/View.ashx?M=F&ID=9431716&GUID=41F71825-0B83-4BA7-9CE9-A1DD314DE28E.

[5]Alex Gee, "Justified Anger: Rev. Alex Gee Says Madison Is Failing Its African-American Community," *The Cap Times*, January 13, 2013, https://captimes.com/news/local/city-life/justified-anger-rev-alex-gee-says-madison-is-failing-its-african-american-community/article_2556653d-4ac1-5a54-aee5-9619c94d36ff.html.

[6]"Race to Equity: A Baseline Report on the State of Racial Disparities in Dane County," Wisconsin Council on Children and Families, 2013, https://ncwwi.org/document/race-to-equity-a-baseline-report-on-the-state-of-racial-disparities-in-dane-county/.

and beyond. Madison is also home to the national offices of Christian organization InterVarsity Christian Fellowship, which works with university students across the country and which has at some key junctures made pivotal decisions to prioritize racial justice.[7] Current and former InterVarsity staff play leading roles in many local churches, and many are active proponents of racial justice.

As home to the state capital and the flagship state university, Madison leans politically liberal and highly educated. I heard a range of political views expressed as I observed church services across the city, but the most well-attended churches in the city tend to at least speak of themselves as supportive of racial justice. However, the people I interviewed came from across the state and nation, and their families of origin were fairly evenly distributed between conservative and liberal families.

I chose the other three research locations in order to check for consistency in my findings across contrasting settings. These locations included a predominantly Black neighborhood in an East Coast city, a small town in the post-Confederate South, and a predominantly Black community in South Africa. As a few examples of differences between these settings, in the rural South, the surrounding population leaned more conservative than in the other locations. Racial justice advocates there worked hard to create subcommunities sharing common values that were more noticeably set apart from their surrounding society than in the other research locations. Compared to other locations, these individuals tended to have more experience working closely with people who were highly skeptical of racial justice. In the East Coast city, I saw how a community deals with a longer history of White settlement than in the Midwest. The community bore the memory of successive waves of race demographics: Indigenous original caretakers of the land, European settlers of several ethnic groups, Black migrants of the Great Migration that prompted

---

[7] Anthea Butler, *White Evangelical Racism: The Politics of Morality in America* (University of North Carolina Press, 2021); John Schmalzbauer, "Whose Social Justice? Which Evangelicalism?," in *The New Evangelical Social Engagement*, ed. Brian Steensland and Philip Goff (Oxford University Press, 2013), 50-72.

White flight, and more recent signs of gentrification. People of a wide and complicated mix of class, race, ethnicity, and political persuasions coexisted. In that neighborhood and in South Africa, White people were in the minority. Residents noted that for Whites, minority status seemed to produce one of two extremes: fear or humility. While some of these dynamics were at play in Madison, they were outlined more starkly where White people could not take their own majority status for granted.

This research is, to some extent, an "insider ethnography"—a study of a cultural setting that I, as a researcher, identify with in certain significant ways.[8] In the late nineteenth century, when the discipline called anthropology was new, researchers most often chose to study groups they imagined to be very different from their own groups. Some of the earliest insider ethnographies were written by people from cultural settings considered "Other" to the predominantly White research community. These included Ella Cara Deloria, a linguist and anthropologist who wrote about her own Dakota people, and Zora Neale Hurston, a Black anthropologist and novelist who conducted fieldwork in her Florida hometown before going on to conduct research in Alabama, Jamaica, Haiti, Honduras, and Bermuda. In part because of the work of these and other anthropologists of color, anthropologists in the mid- to late twentieth century asked penetrating questions about the asymmetries or power and voice between the "we researchers" and the "they researched." Who gets to say who is studied and how? Who should have the power to watch another person's life and write about it in a published document backed by the authority of scholarly institutions? If the researcher can walk away afterward and ignore what happens to the "they" studied, who holds a researcher accountable, and to what standards?

Studying one's own group doesn't eliminate those challenges, but it does change the dynamics. Insider ethnography carries its own dangers of misrepresentation, as a researcher can be inclined to imagine that the

---

[8]Kirin Narayan, "How Native Is a 'Native' Anthropologist?," *American Anthropologist* 95, no. 3 (1993): 671-86.

people studied will think and behave as the researcher does. Sometimes in looking at people of our own group we're inclined to be more critical, sometimes less. The term *insider* itself is a complicated one. No definitive line exists between cultural groups, and thus every researcher navigates a complicated mix of insider and outsider qualities no matter how Indigenous they may seem to the community researched.[9] Anthropologists today stress that whoever is doing the studying or being studied, they always share some commonalities and some differences. Divisions of "we" and "they" are always our own constructions.

There is never such a thing as perfectly unbiased writing. No scholarly project ever achieves purely indifferent objectivity—always we work from the subjective place of who we are, asking the questions that matter to us and not some other questions. Even as we apply and analyze data, the very epistemologies that guide what we think we know reflect the culture that shapes us. As a researcher, I cannot erase myself altogether from the work. I can, however, write with awareness of the community that holds me to account. People in this book are my own community; many have become close friends. Some read early drafts of the manuscript, and several met with me multiple times to discuss what I was learning throughout the research. The names of individuals, churches, and organizations in this book have been changed, but still they will find themselves in this book. When they do, I hope that they find themselves represented with grace and truth. Getting this right affects us all. I am grateful beyond words for the trust and hope they gave to make this book what it is.

---

[9]Kirin Narayan offers a helpful exploration of this topic, concluding, "By situating ourselves as subjects simultaneously touched by life experience and swayed by professional concerns, we can acknowledge the hybrid and positioned nature of our identities" (Narayan, "How Native," 682).

APPENDIX B

Questions for Reflection and Discussion

PART 1: IS PERSEVERANCE POSSIBLE?

1. When have you experienced a moment of conviction or racial brokenness like that between Mark and Hannah? How would you describe your role in the situation? What words or emotions stand out in your memory of that incident?

2. What hesitancies do you feel as you begin a book with *race* and *Christians* in the title? What led you to pick up this book? What unanswered questions are you carrying with you into this reading experience?

3. Did anything surprise you in the statistics about White Christians' engagement with racial justice?

4. How were Christians and racial justice talked about in the communities that you have been a part of growing up and now?

PART 2: DARE WE HOPE?

1. How would you fill in this sentence: "In regard to racial justice, I used to hope _____. Now I hope _____." Try filling it in with goals and then again with adverbs to describe your ways of hoping. How has your hope been shaped (in helpful or unhelpful ways) by your social experiences?

2. Where have you witnessed the effects of delusional hope, including optimistic or conventional hope? Where do you see people being trained in these forms of hope?

3. Have you witnessed or been a part of well-intended groups that see themselves as bringers of hope? How would you describe the experiences and reasoning that undergirded that group's hopes? What can you learn from that experience?

4. How did these chapters challenge your understanding of hope?

PART 3: COLLISIONS

1. What details stand out to you in the account of Allan at the gas station between neighborhoods? What decisions did each person in the story make, and how were they also each shaped by people and circumstances outside their control? Why is it important to notice both agency and nonagency in our life stories?

2. What stories from your own life come to your mind when you fill in the sentence "I would not be committed to racial justice in the way that I am today if not for . . . ?" Consider journaling about the people and events that have shaped your own race-related perspectives.

3. Describe a time when you experienced one of the four types of collisions in these chapters: colliding with ranking, the invisibility of Whiteness, injustice, or culpability. How did that experience cause you to reshape your social imagination?

4. What difference does it make to diagnose the problem of racism as a tear in a social fabric versus a problem in the ways individuals interact with each other? What solutions to racism might people prescribe based on one or the other diagnosis?

APPENDIX B: QUESTIONS FOR REFLECTION AND DISCUSSION

PART 4: ASKING A LOT OF WHY

1. What is a topic that you have learned about through a combination of unintended collisions plus asking why questions? How did those two types of learning intertwine?

2. Which of the three areas of why questions—structures, culture, or morality—are you most curious to learn more about? How might you take a next step toward learning?

3. What details stood out to you in the story of Lynn? Are there times in your own life when you have you felt like "tapping out" from pursuing racial justice?

4. Have you observed people growing disinterested in addressing racism due to the pitfalls described in chapter nine: (1) gaps between knowledge and embodiment, (2) uncertainty around complexity, (3) loneliness, and (4) fear of guilt and shame? Are there other pitfalls you would add to that list?

PART 5: RESPONDING TO GRACE

1. Consider the different answers people might give to the question "What do we do with harm?" In the account of Hannah and Mark, what results might each of those possible responses have produced?

2. When have you extended grace to someone? When have you received grace? How did people respond, and was it the kind of response described in these chapters? How might those memories help you begin imagining a better future?

3. Consider types of exchanges you have with people around you. In which relationships do you tend toward precisely equalizing your exchanges, and in which do you oscillate between indebtedness one to the other? How have you seen these differing forms of exchange supporting or inhibiting ongoing relationships?

4. Chapter eleven begins with several examples of ways grace can be applied to racism in controversial or harmful ways. Have you seen people use grace (or false imitations of grace) in harmful ways? Why is it important to define grace carefully?

5. Are there ideas in the book so far that you disagree with? What are some ways that you can productively deal with disagreements that arise in conversations about racism?

6. Which of the four aspects of grace—acknowledging prior indebtedness; given, not demanded; traceable ultimately to God; and anticipating response—is most difficult for you to understand, accept, or practice? Why?

PART 6: ABIDING HOPE

1. What stood out to you in the account of Carl and Adele? How did their perspectives and activities change during their time living in the township, and what seemed to influence those changes?

2. If you have spent time in faith communities, how was hope talked about there? How has your spiritual or religious journey shaped the ways you think about and live out your hope?

3. When have you found hope in a seemingly hopeless situation? How do words from these chapters such as *interrupting*, *radical*, *struggling*, or *lamenting* relate to the ways you found to hope?

4. In what ways is mutuality a part of your relationships among people of differing racial, ethnic, socioeconomic, and other social groups? As you look at your relationships with people across history and the planet, in what ways have you been positioned to give, receive, and share with people you have never met?

5. What factors led Anna, Noah, Ezra, and Ed to develop their friendship? How does their friendship affect their wider

APPENDIX B: QUESTIONS FOR REFLECTION AND DISCUSSION

community? What steps would you like to take to deepen your relationships with people working together for justice?

6. Which of the four practices of a struggling hope (lamenting, mending, risking, and leaning into joy) do you see happening in your own life and in the communities you're a part of? Which would you like to grow in? What next step can you take to grow in that area?

Index

agency, 83-84, 137
agnosticism. *See* churches: attrition or deconversion from
anger, 136, 289
anthropology, 7-8, 12-13, 75, 177-78
antiracism. *See* diversity, equity, and inclusion; racial justice
antistructuralism. *See* racism: individualistic responses to
apartheid. *See* South Africa
apologies, 184, 201-2
approximating experiences, 107-8
Asian Americans, 23, 59, 77, 81, 259, 286
asking why
    agency in, 123
    as lifelong habit, 125, 129
    for people of color, 131-33
    relationship with collisions, 137-39
    structural learning, 126
    theological learning, 127-28
assimilation, 6, 12, 58, 229, 246
Barclay, John, 173, 180
Begay, Renee Kylestewa, 228-31
belonging, 152, 247, 261
Black churches. *See* churches: Black
Black Lives Matter movement, 38
blackface, 3-4
Brown, Michael, 42
Brueggemann, Walter, 55-56, 175
cancel culture, 202
Charles, Mark, 157, 201
Chicago World's Columbian Exposition, 101-3
Christianity
    forgiveness and grace in, 261
    history of, 27-28, 187-88
    interest in race, 7
    and justifications for racism, 79

churches
    attrition or deconversion from, 30-31, 113, 142
    Black, 130, 221, 223, 281-82
    as covenant community, 260-64
    multiethnic, 36, 247-48, 269-70
collisions, 70-71
    agency in, 83-84, 137
    characteristics of, 83-86
    with culpability, 111-15
    definition of, 70-71
    dislocation, 100
    frequency of, 82-83
    with hierarchy/ranking, 89-93
    with injustice, 105-10
    with invisibility, 97-101, 108
    among people of color, 80-82
    relationship with asking why, 137-39
    results of, 115-16
colonialism. *See* racism
communities. *See* churches; relationships: interracial
contact theory, 111
covenant communities, 202
Covid-19, 41
culpability. *See* guilt
cultural appropriation, 149
cultural learning, 126-27
    See also asking why
De La Torre, Miguel, 63-64
debt, 173-76
    See also gift exchanges; grace
disillusionment, 159, 227
    See also hope: hopelessness; microdiscouragements

diversity, equity, and inclusion (DEI), 133-36, 139-40, 149
    contradictions in, 147-50
Divided by Faith (Michael Emerson and Christian Smith), 110
double consciousness, 80
Du Bois, W. E. B., 80, 94, 137
embodiment, 144-47
emotional responses, 114-16
epistemology of ignorance, 82-83, 114
ethnography. *See* research methodology
failure, 143
    See also disillusionment
Floyd, George, 41-42, 57, 106, 135, 202
forgiveness, 179-81, 201-2
    See also grace
gaze, 3, 101, 103-4
    reversed, 104
gentrification, 231-32
gift exchanges, 172-175, 177-79
    See also debt; grace
good way. *See* relating in a good way
grace
    in church community, 261, 263
    definition of, 166-68, 172
    directionality of, 186-87
    false uses of, 185-88, 201
    as foundation of relationships, 232
    freedom of, 167, 175-77, 179-80, 183-84, 194-96
    frequency of, 167, 169-71
    responses to, 180-81, 201-4
    theology of, 168, 171-72, 175-77, 180-81, 197-200
    and trust, 263-65
    See also debt; forgiveness; trust
Graham, Billy, 57
guilt, 16
    responses to, 164-65, 167
    White guilt complex, 153
    See also grace; pitfalls to perseverance
habitus, 145-46
Han, Hahrie, 171
hooks, bell, 1, 100
hope
    conventional, 56-60
    definition of, 44
    delusional, 53, 60-65
    differences in, 44-45, 210
    effects on health, 45
    foundation in grace, 210, 220-21
    and grace, 164-66, 168, 171

hopelessness, 63-66 (*see also* perseverance)
    in interrupting goodness, 218-21
    learned through suffering, 223-24, 252-53, 266-68
    resilience of, 209-10, 213, 217
    smallness of, 225
    in story of Jesus, 218-21
    struggling in, 265-68
    for systemic change, 239-41
    theology of, 222
    weaponization of, 64
    what to hope for, 230-31
    White-supremacist, 61-64
    See also disillusionment; incrementalism; optimism
identity formation, 129-31, 246
imagination. *See* social imaginaries
imago Dei, 128
incrementalism, 57
Indigenous people, 6, 200, 228-30, 268-69
interracial families, 65, 97, 106, 232, 272-75
intersectionality, 133
joy, 265-68
    Black joy, 269-70
    false joy, 266
    as resistance, 267-68
King, Martin Luther, Jr., 25, 30, 32, 62-63
Ladson-Billings, Gloria, 252-54
lament, 115, 143, 266-68
learning. *See* asking why
loneliness, 150-52
Madison, Wisconsin, 4, 11-13, 288-90
    See also University of Wisconsin–Madison
Margolis, Michele, 129-30
methodology. *See* research methodology
microaggressions, 155-56
microdiscouragements, 159
missionaries, 39, 52
model minorities, 77
mutuality. *See* relating in a good way: as mutuality
normativity, 99-100, 116
Obama, Barack, 63
optimism, 53-56
perseverance, 138, 141, 143-44, 155, 159
    and hope 209, 213, 217
pitfalls to perseverance
    fear of guilt and shame, 152-59
    gaps between knowledge and embodiment, 144-47
    loneliness, 150-52
    uncertainty around complexity, 146-50

INDEX

political affiliations, 129-30
prefigurative politics, 248
pride, 154
race
    hierarchy, 89-91, 96-97, 104, 116
    invisibility of Whiteness, 97-99
    selective race cognizance, 99
racial battle fatigue, 156
racial justice
    definitions of, 10, 230
    goals of, 230
    as long-term posture, 253-54
    as mending social fabric, 257-59
    See also diversity, equity, and inclusion (DEI); racism
racialization, 91
racism
    colorblindness in, 96-97
    cultural racism, 96
    historical development of, 77-79
    individualistic responses to, 109-11
    legal establishment of, 78
    persistence of, 4, 18
    systemic nature of, 17, 239-41, 257-59
Rah, Soong-Chan, 157, 201
relating in a good way, 230-31, 250
    as addressing systems, 238-41
    as everyday love, 242-43, 248
    as mutuality, 235-38
relationships
    characterized by grace, 188, 202-3
    as incomplete solution to racism, 110, 238-39
    interracial, 65, 163-66, 169-70
    See also relating in a good way
religious identity. *See* identify formation
relocation, 100, 150-52, 158
re-membering, 268
reparation. *See* restitution
repentance. *See* apologies; forgiveness; grace
research methodology, 8-14, 245, 285-92
    insider ethnography, 291-92
    objectivity in, 292
    participant observation, 8, 12-13, 287-88
    qualitative versus quantitative, 285-86
    research assistant role, 13, 287
    research locations, 288, 290-91
restitution, 173-74, 180-81, 187, 200-201

risk taking
    as posture of struggling hope, 265
    in racial justice work, 260-65, 203
    and trust building, 263-65
shalom, 128
shame, 155
    See also guilt
Sisyphus, as metaphor for struggling hope, 253
slavery, 78, 252
social imaginaries, 158-59
    hope and, 159, 210, 221, 281
    prophetic imagination and, 222
    reality clashes with, 70-72, 74
    social imagination, 75
    See also collisions; White imaginary
South Africa, 12, 48-50, 52, 210-13, 216-18
status threat, 58
Tisby, Jemar, 79
trauma, 157, 184, 194, 249-50
    participation-induced traumatic stress (PITS), 157
Trump, Donald, 28
trust, 216, 261-65
unilinear evolutionism, 90-91, 94-95
unity, 197, 282
    across differences as witness, 282
University of Wisconsin–Madison, 4, 8, 13, 274, 276-78
Vaulx, Princess (research assistant), 13, 287
Volf, Miroslav, 168, 175-76, 181, 222
White imaginary, 77-80, 123, 125
    directionality of knowledge, 101
    fantasy of White innocence, 111-13
    invisibility of Whiteness, 97-99
    See also collisions
White people
    ability to walk away, 140
    fear of conflict, 54
    need for approval, 203
    seeking approval from people of color, 262-63
    ways of hoping, 53-57, 60-61
White savior, 148
White supremacy, definition of, 61
White tears, 5, 114-15
Whiteness, 79
    See also White imaginary
Wilkerson, Isabel, 60